The French Revolution 1787–1804

The French Revolution 1787–1804

Second edition

P.M. Jones

Longman
is an imprint of

Harlow, England • London • New York • Boston • San Francisco • Toronto
Sydney • Tokyo • Singapore • Hong Kong • Seoul • Taipei • New Delhi
Cape Town • Madrid • Mexico City • Amsterdam • Munich • Paris • Milan

PEARSON EDUCATION LIMITED

Edinburgh Gate
Harlow CM20 2JE
United Kingdom
Tel: +44 (0)1279 623623
Fax: +44 (0)1279 431059
Website: www.pearsoned.co.uk

First edition published in Great Britain in 2003
© Pearson Education Limited 2010

The right of P.M. Jones to be identified as author of this work has been asserted
by him in accordance with the Copyright, Designs and Patents Act 1988.

Pearson Education is not responsible for the content of third party internet sites.

ISBN: 978-1-4082-0438-2

British Library Cataloguing in Publication Data
A CIP catalogue record for this book can be obtained from the British Library

Library of Congress Cataloging in Publication Data

Jones, Peter, 1949–
   The French Revolution, 1787–1804 / P. M. Jones. – 2nd ed.
      p. cm. – (Seminar studies in history)
   Includes bibliographical references and index.
   ISBN 978-1-4082-0438-2 (pbk.)
1. France–History–Revolution, 1789–1779.   I. Title.
   DC148. J574 2010
   994.04–dc22
                                                2010007216

10   9   8   7   6   5   4   3   2
14   13   12

Set by 35 in 10/13.5pt Berkeley Book
Printed and bound in Malaysia (CTP-VVP)

Introduction to the Series

History is a narrative constructed by historians from traces left by the past. Historical enquiry is often driven by contemporary issues and, in consequence, historical narratives are constantly reconsidered, reconstructed and reshaped. The fact that different historians have different perspectives on issues means that there is also often controversy and no universally agreed version of past events. *Seminar Studies in History* was designed to bridge the gap between current research and debate, and the broad, popular general surveys that often date rapidly.

The volumes in the series are written by historians who are not only familiar with the latest research and current debates concerning their topic, but who have themselves contributed to our understanding of the subject. The books are intended to provide the reader with a clear introduction to a major topic in history. They provide both a narrative of events and a critical analysis of contemporary interpretations. They include the kinds of tools generally omitted from specialist monographs: a chronology of events, a glossary of terms and brief biographies of 'who's who'. They also include bibliographical essays in order to guide students to the literature on various aspects of the subject. Students and teachers alike will find that the selection of documents will stimulate discussion and offer insight into the raw materials used by historians in their attempt to understand the past.

Clive Emsley and Gordon Martel
Series Editors

Contents

Acknowledgements

We are grateful to the following for permission to reproduce copyright material:

The Bridgeman Art Library for Plates 1, 2, 5, 7 and 8; Sue Tungate/ The Birmingham Assay Office Collections for Plate 3; Alamy Images for Plate 4; Bibliothèque nationale de France, Paris for Plate 6.

Indiana University Press for Map 3, adapted from Gaspar, D. B. and Geggus, D. P. (eds), *A Turbulent Time: the French Revolution and the Greater Caribbean* (1997, reprinted with permission of Indiana University Press); Cornell University Press for Map 4, adapted from Jainchill, A., *Reimagining Politics After the Terror: the Republican Origins of French Liberalism* (2008).

Elsevier Ltd for Document 1, from Baker, K. M. (ed.), *The French Revolution and the Creation of Modern Political Culture. Volume 1: The Political Culture of the Old Regime* (Pergamon Press, 1987); John Wiley & Sons, Inc. for Document 7, from Kaplow, J., *France on the Eve of Revolution: a Book of Readings* (1971), translated by Susan Kaplow; Pearson Education Ltd for Documents 14, 15 and 16, from Wright, D. G., *Revolution and Terror in France, 1789–1794* (1990); Pearson Education, Inc. for Document 21, from Stewart, John Hall, *A Documentary Survey of the French Revolution*, 1st edn © 1951. Electronically reproduced by courtesy of Pearson Education, Inc., Upper Saddle River, New Jersey.

The author would like to thank Professor Howard G. Brown of State University of New York at Binghamton for supplying the original text for Document 23.

In some cases we have been unable to trace the owners of copyright material, and we would appreciate any information that would enable us to do so.

Chronology

1763

10 February Peace of Paris ending the Seven Years War.

December Fiscal crisis, Laverdy is appointed Controller General.

1766 Lorraine is ceded to France.

1774

10 May Death of Louis XV.

24 August Turgot is appointed Controller General.

1775

11 June Coronation of Louis XVI, grandson of Louis XV.

1776

12 May Turgot is dismissed.

1777

29 June Necker is appointed Director General of Finance.

1778

February France enters an alliance with the American colonists.

10 July France declares war on Britain.

1781

January Publication of Necker's *Compte rendu au roi*.

19 May Necker is dismissed.

1782

July   A third *vingtième* applicable to the years 1783–86 is introduced.

1783

3 September   Peace is agreed between France, the American colonists, Spain and Britain.

2 November   Calonne is appointed Controller General.

1785

10 November   France signs a treaty of alliance with Holland.

1786

20 August   Calonne submits to the king a package of sweeping reform measures.

26 August   A trade treaty ('the Eden Treaty') is signed between France and Britain.

1787

13 February   Death of Vergennes.

22 February   Opening session of the Assembly of Notables.

8 April   Calonne is dismissed.

1 May   Loménie de Brienne is appointed *chef du Conseil royal des finances* (subsequently Principal Minister).

25 May   Dissolution of the Assembly of Notables.

June/July   Provincial Assemblies reform goes ahead, as does grain trade deregulation, and the conversion of the *corvée* into a monetary tax.

6 August   King enforces registration of the land tax and stamp duty reforms by means of a *lit de justice*.

15 August   Parlement of Paris is exiled to Troyes.

September/October   Foreign policy crisis triggered by the civil war in the United Provinces; Prussia sends in troops in support of the Orangeists.

28 September   Return of the Parlement of Paris from Troyes.

19–20 November   King agrees to call an Estates General by 1792. Enforced registration of a 420 million *livres* loan. The Duke of Orleans is exiled and two *parlementaires* are arrested.

1788

3 May   The Parlement of Paris publishes a statement regarding the 'fundamental laws' of the kingdom.

8 May	Lamoignon, the Keeper of the Seals, issues the 'May Edicts'.
7 June	'Day of the Tiles' in Grenoble.
5 July	Loménie de Brienne agrees to call an Estates General for the following year.
16 August	Admission of partial bankruptcy.
25 August	Loménie de Brienne is dismissed. Lamoignon, the Keeper of the Seals, also retires a few days later.
26 August	Necker is appointed Director General of Finance and agrees to a meeting of the Estates General in January (subsequently delayed until May) 1789.
25 September	Restored to office, the Parlement of Paris declares in favour of the 1614 model for the Estates General.
6 November	A second Assembly of Notables deliberates inconclusively for five weeks.
12 December	Memorandum of the Princes of the Blood.
27 December	Procedures for the convocation of the Estates General are agreed.

1789

February/March	Rural unrest in Franche-Comté, Dauphiné and Provence.
March/April	The drawing up of *cahiers de doléances*.
5 May	Opening session of the Estates General.
4 June	Death of the heir apparent.
17 June	Third Estate rename themselves the 'National Assembly'.
20 June	Tennis Court Oath is sworn.
23 June	In a *séance royale*, Louis tries to wrest the initiative from the Third Estate.
11 July	Necker is dismissed.
12–17 July	Paris rises in revolt; the Bastille fortress is taken by force.
16 July	Necker is recalled.
22 July	Murders of Bertier, intendant of Paris, and Foulon, mayor.
late July/August	Great Fear; insurrections in many provinces.
4–11 August	Decrees abolishing the feudal regime.
10 August	Decree instituting the National Guard.
27 August	Promulgation of the Declaration of the Rights of Man and Citizen.
11 September	National Assembly votes for a 'suspensive' rather than an 'absolute' royal veto over legislation.
5–6 October	March to Versailles; return of royal family to Paris.
2 November	National Assembly votes to nationalise the property of the Church.

1790

February/March	Elections take place to create the new municipalities.
4 February	Rapturous support for Louis XVI when he visits the National Assembly.
26 February	Decree reorganising France into departments.
13 April	National Assembly declines to make Catholicism the religion of state.
22 May	National Assembly repudiates wars of conquest.
19 June	Decree abolishing hereditary nobility and titles.
12 July	Civil Constitution of the Clergy is voted.
14 July	Fête de la Fédération; celebration of the first anniversary of the revolution.
4 September	Resignation of Necker.
16–24 August	Decree reorganising the judiciary.
October/November	Start of disturbances among slaves and free blacks in Saint-Domingue.
27 November	Decree imposing an oath on the clergy.

1791

January	New tax system takes effect.
10 March	Pope condemns the Civil Constitution of the Clergy; links with the Holy See are severed.
2 April	Death of Mirabeau.
18 April	Royal family is stopped from leaving Paris for Saint-Cloud.
May	French forces occupy Avignon and the Comtat Venaissin.
15 May	Reubell's motion to grant some civil and political rights in the colonies.
20–21 June	Royal flight from Paris.
16–17 July	Petitioning and a 'massacre' in the Champ de Mars.
22 August	Slave revolt in Saint-Domingue.
27 August	Declaration of Pillnitz is issued.
14 September	Louis XVI accepts the new constitution; annexation of Avignon and the Comtat Venaissin.
1 October	First session of the Legislative Assembly.
9 November	Measures against *émigrés* (vetoed by the king).
29 November	Measures against non-oath-swearing priests (vetoed by the king).
December	Arguments for war begin to be debated in the Jacobin Club.

1792

1 January	Legislative Assembly decrees the beginning of the 'era of liberty'.
18 January	Comte de Provence is deprived of his rights to regency.

January/February	Sugar and coffee disturbances in Paris.
9 February	First measure to seize *émigré* property.
4 April	Decree granting full rights to free blacks.
20 April	War is declared on Austria.
May	Reports of military setbacks reach Paris.
27 May	Deportation of non-oath-swearing priests is voted (vetoed by the king).
20 June	Armed demonstration in the Tuileries Palace by the Paris Sections.
28 June	Manoeuvres by General Lafayette against Parisian 'agitators'.
11 July	Legislative Assembly declares 'the fatherland in danger'.
25 July	Publication of the Brunswick Manifesto.
10 August	Insurrection in Paris; deposition of Louis XVI.
2–6 September	Massacres in the prisons of Paris.
20 September	Victory over the Prussians and the *émigrés* at the battle of Valmy.
21 September	National Convention votes to abolish the monarchy and to declare France a republic.
6 November	French victory against the Austrians at the battle of Jemappes.
11 December	Start of the trial of the king.

1793

21 January	Execution of Louis XVI.
1 February	France declares war on Britain and Holland.
24 February	Decree to recruit an additional 300,000 troops.
7 March	France declares war on Spain.
9 March	Despatch of *représentants en mission* to the departments.
10–11 March	Start of the uprising of the Vendée.
18 March	French suffer a reverse at the battle of Neerwinden.
4 April	Defection of General Dumouriez to the Austrians.
6 April	Establishment of the Committee of Public Safety.
31 May–2 June	Insurrection in Paris; expulsion of Girondin deputies from the Convention.
June/July/August	'Federalist' revolts in the departments.
24 June	Constitution of 1793 is approved.
27 August	Toulon is surrendered to the British fleet of Admiral Hood.
5–6 September	Pressure is exerted on the Convention by the *sans-culottes* in order to secure implementation of the 'popular programme'.
17 September	Law of Suspects is passed.
29 September	Law of the General Maximum is passed.

10 October	Decree of 'Revolutionary Government'; the Constitution of 1793 is put into abeyance until peacetime conditions prevail.
16 October	Execution of Marie-Antoinette.
30 October	Closure of women's political clubs.
31 October	Execution of 20 leading Girondin deputies.
10 November	Dechristianisation in Paris; cathedral of Notre Dame becomes a Temple of Reason.
4 December	Passing of the Law of 14 Frimaire II formalising 'Revolutionary Government'.
5 December	First issue of *Le Vieux Cordelier* appears; start of the Indulgents Campaign.

1794

4 February	Abolition of slavery in the French Caribbean colonies.
13–24 March	Arrest and execution of the Hébertists.
5 April	Execution of Danton, Desmoulins, Delacroix, Philippeaux and the *pourris*.
7 May	Decree establishing the Cult of the Supreme Being.
8 June	Festival of the Supreme Being is held in Paris.
10 June	Law of 22 Prairial II increases the conviction rate of the Revolutionary Tribunal.
26 June	French victory against the Austrians and the Dutch at the battle of Fleurus.
27 July	*Coup* of 9 Thermidor; overthrow of Robespierre and his allies.
August/September	Relaxation of the Terror.
12 November	Closure of the Paris Jacobin Club.
8 December	The 75 deputies who had protested at the expulsion of the Girondins return to their seats in the Convention.
24 December	Repeal of the Law of the General Maximum.

1795

21 February	Formal separation of Church and State.
April/May	Start of the 'White' Terror against revolutionary personnel in southern France.
5 April	Signing of the peace treaty of Basle with Prussia.
23 May	Exclusion of women from the assemblies of the Paris Sections.
8 June	Death of the son of Louis XVI (styled 'Louis XVII' by the *émigrés*).
24 June	Publication of the Declaration from Verona.
27 June	*Emigré* forces land at Quiberon Bay in southern Brittany with the assistance of British warships.

22 August	Constitution of 1795 is approved.
October	Elections in progress to replace the National Convention.
3 November	The Executive Directory takes office.
16 November	Opening of the Pantheon Club.

1796

19 February	Production of *assignats* ceases.
26 February	The Executive Directory orders the closure of the Pantheon Club and all neo-Jacobin societies.
2 March	Bonaparte is appointed general-in-chief of the Army of Italy.
30 March	Gracchus Babeuf's 'Conspiracy of the Equals' takes shape.
April/May	French forces win a succession of battles against the Piedmontese and the Austrians in Italy.
10 May	Babeuf is arrested.
16 October	General Bonaparte sets up the Cispadane Republic (subsequently merged into the Cisalpine Republic).
December	General Hoche's naval expedition to Ireland ends in failure.

1797

March/April	Significant royalist gains in the 'Year Five' elections to the legislative Councils.
18 April	Peace negotiations with Austria begin at Leoben.
27 May	Execution of Babeuf and his comrade Darthé.
9 July	General Bonaparte sets up the Cisalpine Republic.
24 August	Repeal of the laws of 1792 and 1793 against non-oath-swearing clergy.
4 September	*Coup* of 18 Fructidor V; two Directors are removed; elections in 49 departments are annulled and 177 deputies are purged from the Councils.
8 September	Merlin de Douai and François de Neufchâteau replace Carnot and Barthélemy as Directors.
30 September	Partial bankruptcy; two-thirds of the national debt is repudiated.
15 October	France signs the Treaty of Campo Formio with Austria.
12 November	Centralised tax-collecting institutions are established in each department.

1798

15 February	Proclamation of the Roman Republic.
March/April	The neo-Jacobins make gains in the elections to the legislative Councils.

11 May   Coup of 22 Floréal VI; the election results of neo-Jacobins and other 'firm republicans' are set aside.

19 May   General Bonaparte sets off on Egypt expedition.

1 August   French expeditionary fleet is destroyed in Aboukir Bay by Rear-Admiral Nelson (battle of the Nile).

August   Second unsuccessful attempt by French forces to invade Ireland.

5 September   Loi Jourdan; general conscription is introduced.

1799

12 March   France declares war on Austria (War of the Second Coalition).

April   Legislative elections turn to the advantage of the neo-Jacobins.

9 May   Sieyès is elected to the Directory in the place of Reubell.

June/September   War crisis; France loses nearly all of her conquests in Italy and Germany.

18 June   Coup of 30 Prairial VII; the Councils force through a purge of the Executive Directory.

5–20 August   Royalist uprising in the south west.

25–30 September   Military situation is stabilised by the French victory over the Austrians and Russians at the second battle of Zurich.

9 October   General Bonaparte returns to France.

9–10 November   Coup of 18–19 Brumaire VIII; Executive Directory is overthrown and replaced by a 'Consulate'.

1800

17 February   Law providing for the administrative reorganisation of France; establishment of the prefects.

2 March   Partial amnesty for émigrés.

14 June   General Bonaparte defeats the Austrians at the battle of Marengo.

3 December   General Moreau defeats the Austrians at the battle of Hohenlinden.

24 December   Opera House (machine infernale) plot; Bonaparte narrowly escapes with his life.

1801

8 February   Peace signed with the Austrians at Lunéville.

18 February   Law establishing special tribunals to try cases of brigandage without juries or appeal.

14 July   The Concordat with Pope Pius VII is signed.

23 July   Discussions on the Civil Code begin.

1802

25 March	Peace treaty with Britain is signed at Amiens.
May	Establishment of the Legion of Honour.
2 August	Proclamation of the Life Consulate.

1803

18 May	Resumption of war with Britain.

1804

1 January	Independence of Haiti (formerly Saint-Domingue) is proclaimed.
9 March	Arrest of the royalist plotter, Cadoudal.
15 March	Promulgation of the Civil Code.
21 March	Execution of the Duc d'Enghien.
2 December	Coronation of Napoleon Bonaparte as Emperor of the French.

Who's Who

Barnave, Antoine: Barrister from Grenoble who played a prominent role in the Dauphiné revolt; a leading member of the patriot party from 1789–91; increasingly moderate in outlook thereafter, his moderate royalist sympathies would result in imprisonment and execution in November 1793.

Barras, Paul, Vicomte de: A disreputable army officer who was drawn into revolutionary politics for the pickings it offered; elected to the Convention, he was responsible for brutal repression in Marseilles and Toulon in the autumn of 1793; involved in the conspiracy against Robespierre in July 1794; returned to the Council of Five Hundred in October 1795; served as a Director from 1795–99; forced out of politics after Brumaire.

Bertin, Henri Léonard Jean-Baptiste: Secretary of State for Agriculture, 1763–80.

Billaud-Varenne, Jacques Nicolas: A schoolmaster turned lawyer, he first attracted attention as a radical member of the Cordelier and Jacobin Clubs; elected to the Convention in 1792 and to the Committee of Public Safety in September 1793, he acted as a spokesman for the extreme left; survived Thermidor, but was deported as a terrorist and never returned to France.

Brienne, Etienne Charles de Loménie de: Archbishop of Toulouse and Principal Minister, 1787–88.

Buzot, François: From a legal background, he came to notice as a patriot deputy in the National Assembly; elected to the Convention, his hostility to the Paris Commune and the Sections launched him into a short-lived career as a Girondin and a Federalist; escaped arrest only by means of suicide.

Cadoudal, Georges: One of the men who led the royalist rebels of the Vendée in 1793; subsequently involved in the *chouan* insurgency and the Quiberon Bay landings of June 1795; emigrated to Britain following the pacification of the west; participated in the 'second *chouannerie*' of

1799–1800; involved in the Opera House plot against Bonaparte of December 1800; returned to Paris for another covert operation against the First Consul in August 1803; betrayed and taken prisoner, he was executed on 25 June 1804.

Calonne, Charles Alexandre de: Controller General, 1783–87.

Castries, Charles Gabriel de la Croix, Marquis de: Minister for the Navy, 1780–87.

Collot d'Herbois, Jean Marie: Settled in Paris following a theatrical career in the provinces; involved in the uprising of 10 August 1792; elected to the Convention and recruited to the Committee of Public Safety following pressure from the Sections in September 1793; responsible for the savage repression in Lyons; conspired against Robespierre on 26–27 July 1794; deported as a terrorist in April 1795.

Couthon, Georges: A lawyer from Clermont-Ferrand who became a close ally of Robespierre in the Convention; despite disablement which confined him to a wheelchair, he undertook a number of missions; elected to the Committee of Public Safety in May 1793; fell victim to the Thermidor *coup* which resulted in his execution on 28 July 1794.

Danton, Georges: A lawyer by training who came to prominence as a Cordelier Club militant; deeply implicated in the uprising of 10 August 1792 from which he emerged to become Minister of Justice; a Montagnard deputy from 1792 until his execution in April 1794.

Desmoulins, Camille: Radical journalist, pamphleteer and Cordeliers Club militant, 1789–92; Montagnard deputy from 1792 until his execution in April 1794.

Dumouriez, Charles François du Périer: A professional soldier whose career blossomed into politics after 1789; briefly a government minister in the spring of 1792 before taking command of the Army of the North; victor at Valmy and Jemappes; loser at Neerwinden (18 March 1793); emigrated in April 1793 after a fruitless bid to lead his forces against Paris.

Fouché, Joseph: A member of the Oratorian teaching order in Nantes before the revolution; elected to the Convention in 1792; carried out a number of important missions, notably one that initiated the wave of dechristianisation in the departments; recalled to Paris in order to answer for his activities in April 1794; conspired against Robespierre, but survived the reaction after Thermidor; despatched as ambassador to the Cisalpine Republic in September 1798; returned to Paris in 1799 and was made Minister of Police following the Brumaire *coup*.

Frederick William II: King of Prussia; ruled 1786–97.

Hébert, Jacques René: An artisan by background, he found his metier as the publisher of the scurrilous journal *Le Père Duchesne*; militant of the Cordelier Club in 1792; to the forefront of several insurrections, or near-insurrections; a dechristianiser, he was targeted by the Indulgents in late 1793 and early 1794; executed March 1794.

La Révellière-Lépeaux, Louis Marie: A patriot of 1789 vintage who made his name in the Jacobin Club of Angers; his national career as a deputy in the Convention was marred by association with the Gironde, and he only came to prominence after Thermidor; elected to the Council of Elders in October 1795, and to the Directory the following month; an architect of the Fructidor purge and pillar of the regime, he remained in office until June 1799; played no part in the public life of the Consulate; declined to take the oath of allegiance to the Emperor.

Lafayette, Marie Joseph Paul Roch Yves Gilbert Motier, Marquis de: Wealthy nobleman with liberal leanings who had fought in the War of American Independence; member of the Assembly of Notables in 1787; appointed commander of the National Guard of Paris in July 1789; appointed to an army command early in 1792; tried unsuccessfully to persuade the Legislative Assembly to act against the Jacobin Club in July 1792; defected to the Austrians in August 1792.

Lamoignon, Chrétien François de, Marquis de Bâville: Keeper of the Seals, 1787–88.

Leopold II: Archduke of Austria and Habsburg Emperor; ruled 1790–92.

Loménie de Brienne: *see* Brienne.

Louis XIV: King of France; ruled 1661–1715.

Louis XV: King of France; ruled 1715–74.

Louis XVI: King of France; ruled 1774–92 (deposed).

'Louis XVII': Unproclaimed accession, 1793–died 1795.

Louis XVIII: Self-proclaimed accession 1795; ruled as King of France 1814–23.

Marat, Jean-Paul: A physician by training, he edited the uncompromisingly violent and democratic journal *L'Ami du Peuple*; implicated in the September Massacres, he was nonetheless elected to the Convention; assassinated in July 1793.

Maupeou, René Nicolas Charles Augustin de: Chancellor, 1768–90.

Merlin de Douai, Philippe Antoine: A deputy to the Estates General, National Assembly and then the Convention whose legal expertise brought him to public notice; chief architect of the legislation on the abolition of feudalism in 1790; completed a number of missions during the Terror; helped to negotiate the Treaty of Basle with Prussia in April 1795; elected to the Council of Elders in October 1795; served several stints as a minister; became a Director in September 1797, after the Fructidor *coup*; resigned just before Brumaire and retired from public life.

Mirosmesnil, Armand Thomas Hue de: Keeper of the Seals, 1774–87.

Moreau, Jean Victor: Participated in the Breton pre-revolution as a law student in 1788; joined the colours in 1791; promoted briefly to command the Army of the North in October 1794; in charge of the Army of the Rhine and the Moselle in 1796–97; victor at Hohenlinden in December 1800; returned to Paris, but became estranged from Bonaparte; accused of links with the *émigrés* and Pichegru and arrested; in self-imposed exile from 1804 to 1813.

Necker, Jacques: Finance Minister, 1776–81; 1788–89; 1789–90.

Pichegru, Charles: Of humble background, he made his way in the army; promoted to a command position in the Army of the Rhine in October 1793; converted to royalism in 1795; elected to the Council of Five Hundred, but the chance of a political career was blocked by the Fructidor *coup*; threatened with deportation, he fled abroad and thereafter worked with the *émigrés* for a Bourbon restoration; arrested in Paris on 28 February 1804, he was found dead in his prison cell on 5 April 1804.

Reubell, Jean-François: A lawyer from Alsace who served in most of the revolutionary Assemblies; a Director from the inception of the regime until May 1799; retired from public life after Brumaire.

Robespierre, Maximilien: A provincial lawyer who came to attention for his unswervingly democratic opinions in the National Assembly; Montagnard deputy in the Convention from 1792; powerful member of the Committee of Public Safety who was overthrown in a *coup* on 27 July 1794; executed the following day.

Roux, Jacques: A priest and militant member of the Cordelier Club; spokesman of the *enragés*; imprisoned in September 1793 and committed suicide.

Saint-Just, Antoine, Marquis de: An austere comrade-in-arms of Robespierre; elected to the Convention where he made his maiden speech on the subject of the trial of the king in November 1792; member of the Committee of Public Safety from May 1793; carried out several missions as a political commissar attached to the armies; defended Robespierre unflinchingly during the Thermidor crisis and was duly executed on 28 July 1794.

Ségur, Philippe Henri, Marquis de: Secretary for War, 1780–87.

Terray, Jean Marie, abbé: Controller General, 1769–74.

Thibaudeau, Antoine: An obscure member of the Convention who rose to prominence after Thermidor when he spurred on the tide of political reaction; elected to the Council of Five Hundred in October 1795; accepted the Brumaire *coup*; briefly prefect of the Gironde in 1800; appointed to the Council of State September 1800 where he was involved in drafting the Civil Code.

Turgot, Anne Robert Jacques: Controller General, 1774–76.

Turreau, Louis-Marie: A career soldier before the revolution; appointed to the rank of general in September 1793; remembered chiefly for his brutal pacification of the Vendée.

Vadier, Marc Guillaume Alexis: Despite a parliamentary career between 1789 and 1791, only came to prominence following his election to the Convention; aligned himself firmly against the Gironde; key member of the Committee of General Security from September 1793; an extreme anticlerical, he joined the plot against Robespierre but was denounced in turn for his role in the Terror; sentenced to deportation in April 1795, but went into hiding; survived to become a neo-Jacobin stalwart under the Directory.

Vergennes, Charles Gravier, Comte de: Foreign Secretary, 1774–87.

Voltaire, François Marie Arouet de: Author and *philosophe*.

Glossary

agents nationaux: Chief executive officers of the Districts and the municipalities during the Terror.

aides: Indirect taxes on articles of consumption.

arrêt: A ruling.

Assembly of Notables: A gathering of eminent individuals called into being by the monarch; convened in February 1787, and again in November 1788.

assignats: Interest-bearing bonds exchangeable for nationalised Church lands; would eventually become a paper currency.

bailliage: A judicial and administrative subdivision.

biens nationaux: Property of the Church and of *émigrés* seized and sold off by the nation

bourg: A large village; often possessing a market.

Brumaire: Shorthand for the *coup* of 1799 that brought Napoleon Bonaparte to power.

Brunswick Manifesto: The threatening declaration of 25 July 1792 issued by the commander-in-chief of the Austrian and Prussian invading forces.

capitation: A universal and graduated poll tax first introduced in 1695.

chambres des comptes: 'Sovereign' courts entrusted with the task of scrutinising the returns of royal accountants.

champart: A seigneurial harvest due.

chevaliers du poignard: Young noblemen who occupied the Tuileries Palace in February 1791 in a gesture of support for Louis XVI.

chouans: Royalist insurgents; chiefly to be found in Brittany between 1793 and 1802.

Compte rendu au roi: Necker's controversial budgetary statement; published in 1781.

conciliar monarchy: A system of rule according to which the monarch is dependent upon the advice of the royal council in which the aristocracy have a preponderant voice.

contribution foncière: The new net land tax introduced in place of the *taille* and the *vingtièmes* in 1791.

contribution patriotique: A one-off tax introduced in 1789 to stem the deficit.

Contrôle Général [des Finances]: A rambling Ministry with multiple administrative responsibilities. Headquarters of the Controller General.

corps: An order, estate, or body of individuals with a collective character.

corvée [royale]: Labour service performed by commoners for road maintenance; converted into a monetary tax in 1787.

cours des aides: 'Sovereign' courts heading the fiscal judiciary; equipped with auditing powers.

'dead hand': [of the Church] Inalienable property owned by monasteries, hospitals, etc.

dechristianisation: The policy of closing down churches, defrocking priests and imposing the worship of secular abstractions such as 'reason' and the 'supreme being'.

déclassé: An individual occupying a position lower than that accorded by his status.

don gratuit: A subsidy offered by the Assembly of the Clergy in lieu of direct taxation.

Federalism: The resistance of dissident republicans in the spring and summer of 1793.

fédérés: Militants and enthusiasts who were despatched to Paris for the Fête de la Fédération of July 1790, and again in 1792 when they were deeply implicated in the overthrow of Louis XVI.

Feuillants: Constitutional monarchists who quit the Jacobin Club in July 1791 and founded their own political club in the monastery of the Strict Bernardines (*feuillants*).

First Estate: The functional category to which all clergy belonged.

fouage: Hearth tax.

gabelle: Salt tax.

Grève [Place de]: The square in front of the Paris *Hôtel de Ville* where executions traditionally took place.

Indulgents: Deputies who, late in 1793, called for a relaxation of the Terror.

Intendant [de province]: Royal executive agent in charge of a province before 1789.

jour: An area measurement (0.4 hectare) in use in Lorraine.

lit de justice: [literally, 'bed of justice'] An enforced registration of laws by a Parlement in the presence of the monarch.

livre: [*tournois*] The money of France until finally displaced by the *franc* in the later 1790s.

masses de granit: The social sub-stratum of 'notables' upon which Napoleon Bonaparte endeavoured to secure his regime.

Maximum: State-imposed price controls, first introduced in May 1793 and generalised in September of that year.

Metropolitan: Archbishop in charge of an ecclesiastical province.

Monarchiens: Deputies located on the moderate wing of the patriot party in the National Assembly, who favoured a two-chamber legislature and an 'absolute' veto for the monarch.

Montagnards: Deputies in the National Convention who challenged the Girondins and took power during the Terror.

national guard: Civic militia originating in Paris in July 1789 and subsequently established in towns and villages throughout the country.

octrois: Municipal tolls levied on goods entering towns.

ordonnances: Edicts.

parlementaires: Magistrates of the Parlements.

Parlements: Appeal courts with important administrative powers in addition. There were 13 of these 'sovereign' courts at the end of the *ancien régime*.

pays d'états: Regions governed by Provincial Estates.

pourris: A group of deputies and their racketeer backers who peddled influence and blackmailed bankers and trading companies in the summer and autumn of 1793.

prévôté: [provostship] A unit of seigneurial jurisdiction.

procureur général: Attorney-general.

séance royale: A royal session before the Parlement of Paris, or the Estates General.

Second Estate: The legal category to which all nobles belonged.

Sections: [of Paris] Local subdivisions of the municipal government of Paris created in May 1790.

sénéchaussée: A judicial and administrative subdivision.

sindic: Delegated person.

sous: [or *sols*] Twentieths of a *livre*.

subvention territoriale: A universal land tax proposed by Controller General Calonne.

taille: The principal direct tax; confined overwhelmingly to commoners.

Thermidor: Shorthand for the *coup* against Robespierre in 1794 that resulted in the ending of the Terror.

Third Estate [Tiers Etat]: The legal or functional category to which all non-clerics and non-nobles belonged.

tithe: A payment made by owners of land towards the upkeep of the clergy.

tribunal de cassation: Supreme court set up in 1791.

venality: The practice of selling offices, or titles, for money.

Vendée: The department that became the epicentre of the royalist rebellion of the west.

vingtièmes: (twentieths) Proportional taxes applicable to all sources of income and paid by privileged and unprivileged alike; first introduced in 1750. They were of limited duration, but up to three twentieths might be in force at any one time.

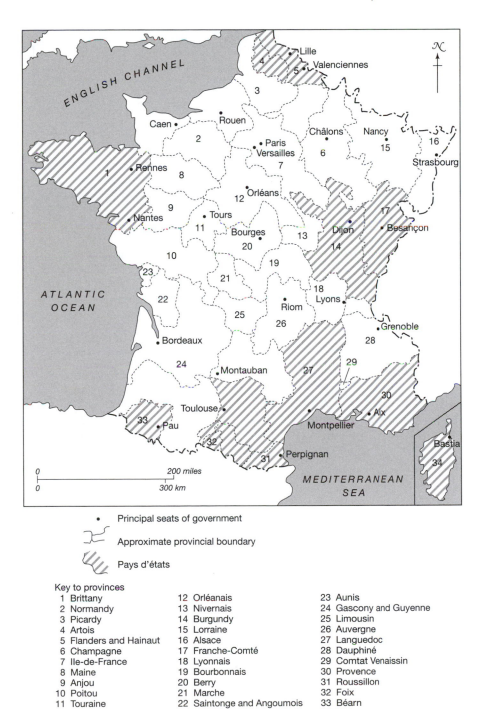

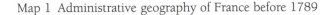

Map 1 Administrative geography of France before 1789

Principal seats of government

Approximate provincial boundary

Pays d'états

Key to provinces

1 Brittany	12 Orléanais	23 Aunis
2 Normandy	13 Nivernais	24 Gascony and Guyenne
3 Picardy	14 Burgundy	25 Limousin
4 Artois	15 Lorraine	26 Auvergne
5 Flanders and Hainaut	16 Alsace	27 Languedoc
6 Champagne	17 Franche-Comté	28 Dauphiné
7 Ile-de-France	18 Lyonnais	29 Comtat Venaissin
8 Maine	19 Bourbonnais	30 Provence
9 Anjou	20 Berry	31 Roussillon
10 Poitou	21 Marche	32 Foix
11 Touraine	22 Saintonge and Angoumois	33 Béarn
		34 Corse

Map 2 Administrative geography of France after 1789

Source: Adapted from Woloch, I., *The New Regime: Transformations of the French Civic Order, 1789–1820* (W.W. Norton and Company, 1994)

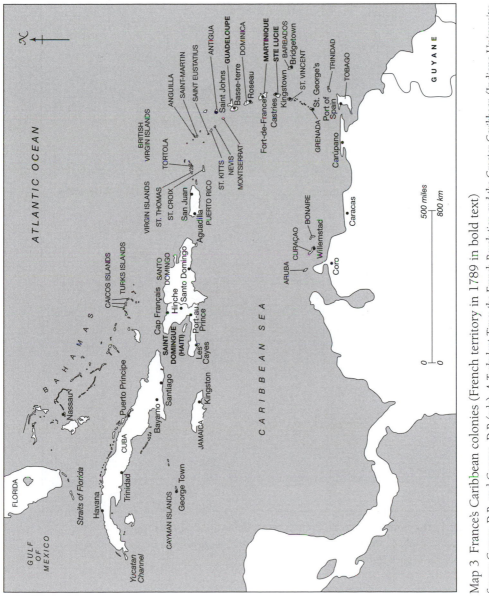

Map 3 France's Caribbean colonies (French territory in 1789 in bold text)

Source: Gaspar, D.B. and Geggus, D.P. (eds), *A Turbulent Time: the French Revolution and the Greater Caribbean* (Indiana University Press, 1997)

Map 4 The Grande Nation (French republic and the sister republics)
Source: Jainchill, A., *Reimagining Politics after the Terror: the Republican Origins of French Liberalism* (Cornell University Press, 2008)

PART 1

1

The Setting

France in the eighteenth century was a powerful country – a fact that the descent into turmoil and revolution after 1787 should not be allowed to obscure. By comparison with her continental neighbours, she achieved territorial unity early on and in an irrevocable fashion. Even at the start of the century, the 'hexagon' figured unmistakably on the map of Europe: once the absorption of Lorraine had been completed in 1766, the frontiers of the Bourbon kingdom would come to resemble closely those of the present-day Fifth Republic. France was a large, compact and well-populated state, then. With perhaps 21.5 million inhabitants in 1700 and over 29 million by the century's end, she bestrode the Continent. England and Prussia (12 million and 6 million respectively in 1800) were minnows by comparison. Only the Habsburg Empire (about 20 million) and the untapped and largely unmeasured resources of the Russian Empire appeared to offer some counterweight. A fifth of all Europeans were born French (compared with a little over one-tenth today). Historians in search of explanations for the train of events beginning in 1787 tend to dwell upon the ramshackle features of the Bourbon state, but not so contemporaries. By the standards of the second half of the eighteenth century, France was a prosperous, well-administered country whose rulers possessed an enviable (if still inadequate) capacity to extract tax revenue from their subjects.

Bourbon rule was based on compromise and consent – at least until the summer of 1787. Although styled 'absolute monarchs', Louis XV and Louis XVI were nothing of the sort in practice. They ruled – or rather their agents governed – by means of an elaborate exercise in negotiation. Yet the theory of Bourbon rule remained completely innocent of this day-to-day reality. At his coronation in 1775, Louis XVI, like Louis XV before him, swore an oath not to his subjects but to God. The fundamental laws of the kingdom admitted no distinction between the body of the nation and the person of the monarch, and woe betide anyone who pretended otherwise [**Doc. 1**]. Only in 1791 would Louis XVI accept the theory of contractual monarchy in the

Bourbons: The first Bourbon king was Henry IV, who acceded to the throne in 1589, following the extinction of the Valois line. The last would be Louis-Philippe I, who abdicated in 1848.

shape of his oath of allegiance to the constitution drawn up by the National Assembly.

So, with whom did the monarch and his agents in the provinces negotiate, before 1787? *Ancien-régime* France was a corporate society which was enclosed within a firm framework of hierarchy. This is another way of saying that mere individuals did not count for very much unless grouped together into recognised 'orders' or 'estates' of the realm. It was with such groupings that the king and his officials negotiated. Individuals might lay claim to corporate status by virtue of a common possession (noble blood, for example); or by affinity (membership of the same professional body); or else by virtue of a common geographical origin. For instance, all Bretons, whether highborn or lowborn, believed that they were set apart from other French men and women – and with good reason, as we shall see. Yet all of these relationships presupposed an unceasing round of negotiation, and it was thanks to the skills of successive monarchs and their servitors in this area that the *ancien régime* survived for as long as it did.

In common with most large European states of the period, France's population was divided into three supposedly functional categories: clerics who prayed, nobles who fought and commoners who laboured. Known as the First, Second and Third Estates respectively, each grouping was buttressed with rights and responsibilities. In the case of the clergy and the nobility, the jurisdictional immunities which they enjoyed far outweighed any duties attaching to their status by the end of the *ancien régime*, whereas the Third Estate was chiefly defined not by rights, but by the responsibilities its members were required to shoulder. Indeed, the clergy and the nobility would come to be referred to as the 'privileged orders' when the battle to reform the structures of absolute monarchy began in earnest in 1787. Nobody knows for sure how many nobles there were on the eve of the revolution. Estimates range from 120,000 to 400,000, although the lower figure – corresponding to roughly 25,000 families – seems likely to be the most accurate. The clergy, by contrast, are easier to count and cannot have numbered more than about 125,000 individuals (59,500 priests and curates; 60,000 monks and nuns; 5,000 non-beneficed persons). By process of simple deduction, therefore, the Third Estate must have totalled around 27,475,000 or 98 per cent of the population. The *abbé* Sieyès's pamphlet *What is the Third Estate?* [**Doc. 4**], which would be published at the start of 1789, just as preparations for the meeting of the Estates General were getting under way, scarcely fell short of the mark, therefore.

However, a three-part classification that lumped together the vast majority of French men and women, whether rich or poor, town or country dwellers, in the latter category had little utility in practice. Only during the crisis of transition from absolute to contractual monarchy (see Chapter 2) was

ancien régime: Literally, 'former regime'. The term was invented soon after the start of the revolution. It is used to describe the structure of government and society under the Bourbon monarchs.

explicit reference made to the 'society of orders'. The corporate texture of the *ancien régime* found expression in far more meaningful ways. Although she was united in the physical sense, pre-revolutionary France was honey-combed with overlapping jurisdictions and privileges which conferred advantages on one group of individuals, or group of territories, at the expense of another. Voltaire once quipped that a traveller would change law codes more often than he changed his post-horses. An exaggeration no doubt, but the fact remains that the *ancien régime* had evolved on the principle of 'particularism' – that is to say, respect for diversity and vested interests. Reformers had long spoken of the need for a single hierarchy of courts, uniform machinery of local government, an integrated and universal tax regime, a common system of weights and measures, the eradication of road and river tolls and so forth. Yet none of these things existed prior to 1787. Litigants had to cope with a bewildering jumble of courts: some seigneurial, some royal, with others belonging to the admiralty, the forest authority, the salt administration, and even the Church. Merchants bent on moving goods around the country encountered toll gates every step of the way: more than 2,000 customs posts still impeded inland traffic at the end of the *ancien régime*. Consumers paid more or less for salt depending on where they lived; even farmers could be restricted by regulations as to the crops they might grow. The cultivation of the tobacco plant, for instance, was confined to certain 'privileged' provinces within the realm.

The price charged for salt varied because the kingdom was divided into different tax zones. In no other domain, in fact, is the diversity and particularism that lay at the heart of the *ancien régime* more apparent. Individuals classed as clergymen or as nobles paid little direct taxation. Their contributions to the common good were made in other ways. Yet beneath this comparatively straightforward – if increasingly contested – attribution of roles and responsibilities, we find a picture of great incoherence. The privilege of exemption from tax was attached to persons, but it was also attached to territories. No inhabitant of Brittany – irrespective of status – paid tax on salt (the *gabelle*) and the inhabitants of Poitou, Flanders, the Artois and several other territories were similarly exempt. By contrast, an inhabitant of the provinces of Maine, Normandy or Picardy (see Map 1) might well be required to pay up to ten times the market rate for this indispensable commodity. In an age when governments relied increasingly on revenue generated by indirect taxation (duties charged on items of everyday use or consumption), such discrepancies would not pass unnoticed. Yet the mechanisms which had evolved for the assessment and collection of taxes on incomes and property were scarcely uniform across the country either. Only members of the Third Estate were liable to the *taille* – the main direct tax on which the monarchy had relied for centuries. But in the south, where land surfaces as well as households carried the label 'noble' or 'commoner', members of the Second Estate could find themselves paying the *taille* if they owned any of the latter. As for the Church, it managed to avoid almost entirely any form of income tax on its considerable assets in land and buildings.

Needless to say, different territories also paid direct tax at different rates, and some were exempted altogether. Inhabitants of Paris, Rouen, Bordeaux and several other privileged towns enjoyed a block immunity from the *taille*, a situation that also prevailed across Brittany, Flanders and Artois. All three provinces numbered among the *pays d'états* – regions making up a large quarter of the kingdom in which local assemblies or Estates (*états*) still met at the end of the *ancien régime*. Most were to be found at the extremities of the country – a fact that provides an important clue as to the nature and extent of royal authority in the eighteenth century. As the power of the Valois and the Bourbon monarchs expanded, territories were added to the core kingdom on a pledge that their distinctive characteristics as once-independent duchies and fiefdoms would be respected. Thus Brittany retained its hearth tax (*fouage*) in place of the *taille* and remained outside the scope of the salt tax, while Provence (acquired in 1481) was assured that its antique 'constitution' would not be set aside. Such assurances, offered in abundance by Louis XVI's predecessors, represented so many barriers to the exercise of absolute monarchy. The larger of the *pays d'états* (Brittany, Burgundy, Languedoc), indeed, had even retained their powerful organs of regional government. In matters of taxation, as in so much else, the king and his ministers were forced to negotiate with these bodies and to offer compromises in order to get their business through. The corporate status of the **Gallican Church** likewise prompted the monarch to adopt a posture of compromise. Until the very end of the *ancien régime*, the clergy were able to insist that any pecuniary assistance they might provide towards the running costs of the state be treated as a 'voluntary grant' (*don gratuit*).

Gallican Church: The Catholic Church as controlled after 1682 by the monarchs of France rather than the Holy See.

So many misunderstandings cling to the image of absolute monarchy that it is necessary to dwell upon these restraints. However, it is important also to keep matters in proportion: Bourbon France was admired by contemporary commentators precisely for the progress that she had made in overcoming provincial particularism and the studied resistance of private interest groups. No other continental European state had yet escaped the thrall of medieval or Renaissance monarchy, and all were envious of the success of their larger and stronger neighbour. The sour reactions of some English travellers who tempered their wonderment at the Palace of Versailles with references to the arbitrary power of absolute monarchy were definitely a minority view. Yet the fact remains that French governments experienced increasing difficulty in tapping into the fiscal capacity of a country whose wealth and population were expanding significantly in the second half of the eighteenth century.

Moreover, their anxiety was heightened by the knowledge that the costs involved in sustaining Great Power status were starting to spiral out of control. France had been defeated in the Seven Years War (1756–63), both on land and at sea, and paid a heavy price in terms of the loss of overseas territories. True, she remained the most powerful state on the Continent, even after the conclusion of the Peace of Paris, but for how much longer, the pundits would ask.

Immediately after the Seven Years War, governments all over Europe turned to reform. Whether those reform initiatives took the shape of measures to rationalise the machinery of state, to liberalise trade, to curtail immunities, to release unproductive assets from the 'dead hand' of the Church, to bring new land into cultivation or to improve fiscal record-keeping, the spoken or unspoken assumption was nearly always the need to augment the flow of tax revenue. The pressure to compete on the international stage was irresistible. France went to war again in 1778 – as an ally of the American colonists in their struggle for independence from Britain. The aim was to obtain revenge for the humiliations of the Seven Years War, and to convert the young American republic into a profitable trading partner. However, the only certain outcome of the conflict was a sharp escalation in the frictions generated by the drive to modernise absolute monarchy. Jacques Necker, the banker, whose rise and fall was encompassed by the American War, knew better than anyone the price of international rivalry. 'Many states have turned into vast military barracks', he wrote in 1784, 'and the steady augmentation in disciplined armies has led to a proportional rise in taxes' (Kwass, 1994: 376).

The dilemma facing servants of the Crown in what would prove to be the last decades of the *ancien régime* can thus be summarised in the following manner. Should His Most Christian Majesty abdicate the role of arbiter of Europe? This was an unthinkable proposition, therefore the state would have to change, but in what direction? Doing nothing was not an option since the future was mortgaged by virtue of the need to repay war debt; besides, the tax 'take' from the country at large was almost certainly declining as a percentage of national wealth as the eighteenth century advanced. Contrary to the belief of contemporaries and some historians, France cannot be regarded as an overtaxed state, but rather one in which taxes were malassessed and maldistributed. So what were the options? A streamlined – that is to say, authentic – absolute monarchy was probably the outcome favoured by Louis XVI who, unlike his grandfather, took an intelligent, if fluctuating, interest in matters of government. It was certainly the solution preferred by ministers such as Terray, Maupeou, Calonne, Vergennes, Lamoignon and Barentin. Another alternative, which would not have displeased the grandees of the Court and influential figures in the Parlements and the Provincial Estates, was a return to the organic roots of kingly power: a kind of aristocratic or conciliar monarchy from which all traces of absolutism were expunged. Even though it is difficult to imagine how a dispersal of authority to tax-exempt elites would have served to strengthen the fiscal sinews of state, such a course of action had powerful advocates (Miromesnil, Castries, Ségur) within the royal councils of the 1780s. A third scenario would be to move towards contractual – that is to say, liberal – constitutional monarchy on the plausible hypothesis that some form of partnership with affluent, educated and politically docile commoners would bring fresh ideas and hitherto untapped resources to the business of government. We may guess that Turgot and Necker entertained hopes that the Bourbon monarchy might develop in this direction, but the only minister actually to try to achieve this outcome would be Loménie de Brienne.

Whereas the Parlement of Rouen had been ritually humiliated when, in 1766, it dared to assert the existence of a body called the 'nation' that was separate from that of the monarch [**Doc. 1**], there are good grounds for supposing that the absolute monarchy was indeed moving in this direction by the 1780s. Louis XVI may not yet have been prepared to swear an oath to his people, but the pretence that politics was the 'secret du roi' (the private preserve of the king) had become unsustainable. There were two reasons for this development which, although closely connected, are best examined separately. Enlightened thinking was making inroads and equipping the most literate and articulate social groups with arguments – and a language – with which to berate the government and, by extension, the monarchy. No doubt a 'public opinion' of some sort had long existed, but hitherto it had taken its cue from the Court. Now political events became the topic of conversation. Chancellor Maupeou's decision in a rare display of force to have done with one source of opposition to the Crown and in 1771 to truncate the Parlements caused many to reassess the relationships on which the absolute monarchy had been built. Participation in the American War after 1778 produced a similar intellectual ferment. In 1786, the minister plenipotentiary to the Court of Versailles reported that France's intervention on the side of the colonists had nurtured a spirit 'of discussion of public matters which did not exist before' (Browning ed., 1909: 147). No less significant was the fact that Louis XVI's ministers now felt it necessary to justify their policies and, if possible, to secure public support for them by actively canvassing public opinion.

The second reason for the shift is to do with the nature of government itself. Some historians prefer to stress its medieval or Renaissance features and the continuing centrality of the Court (Campbell, 1988). Every minister, we are told, was first and foremost a courtier. Others, by contrast, are more impressed by its modernity, in terms of both institutions and ways of thinking. Most would agree on two things, however. The neat picture drawn by Alexis de

Tocqueville (1969, Headlam edn: 41–69) which has the monarchy progressively depriving corporate bodies of their rights and privileges in the onward march towards centralisation does not do justice to the complexity of the *ancien régime*. Moreover, it seems to be accepted by historians that the evolution of the institutions of government towards modernity did accelerate after 1750, or thereabouts. Indeed, it has been claimed that 'French politics broke out of the absolutist mould' (Baker ed., 1987: xvi) at about this date. But this is to go too far and too fast, if only for the reason already mentioned. A more streamlined version of absolute monarchy remained a realistic option even as late as 1787. The important point to grasp is that no one – and least of all the personnel of government – was content with the status quo after 1760. It should not cause surprise, therefore, to discover that the main consumers and promoters of Enlightenment ideas were government ministers and their advisors. Nearly all of the great reform projects of the age (grain trade liberalisation; agricultural enclosure; the secularisation of the monasteries; the commutation of feudal obligations; religious toleration; internal customs abolition; the universal land tax, etc.) were gestated in the offices of the Contrôle Général. This sprawling administration was the closest the Bourbons ever came to devoloping a civil service.

A more efficient and far-reaching tax system, if nothing else, presupposed a significant growth in the bureaucratic weaponry of government. An example is the anxiety of ministers to place the new across-the-board taxes (the *capitation* and the *vingtièmes*) in the hands of professional administrators who could be controlled from the centre. Such taxes were the key to financial recovery after the strains of the Seven Years War because they applied to all and sundry (with the exception of the clergy). Yet everyone knew that self-assessment would soon erode their yield. Aware of what was at stake, Jacques Necker, who headed the Contrôle Général as the Director General of Finance between 1777 and 1781, fought long and hard to ensure that his officials would not be hampered in their work of verification. When his conciliatory offer to allow local landowners to become involved in the activities of the inspectors was spurned by the Parlement of Paris, he went ahead with the reform nonetheless.

Such reforms, pursued admittedly in a somewhat staccato fashion throughout the 1770s and early 1780s, helped to foster a new, utilitarian ethic within government. The old lubricants of politics – nepotism, cronyism, clientism, pluralism and even venality of office – started to look increasingly out of place. Some historians have employed the phrase 'administrative monarchy' in order to capture this transition (Jones, 1995: 46). The label lays stress on the growth of forms of interventionism with wider objectives than the mere collection of tax. Administrative monarchy was not hostile to power sharing, but the elites whose energies it wished to harness were not necessarily those ensconced in the corporate bodies of the realm. Whether this ethic of administrative monarchy would have turned Louis XVI into a constitutional ruler in the fullness of time is an interesting question, but one which was overtaken by events before it could be answered.

Taxation was a problem that would not go away. In 1764 – that is to say, just after the Seven Years War – roughly half of the French government's revenue had to be earmarked in order to meet interest payments on the debt. Or, to put it another way, the accumulated capital value of the state debt was equivalent to about six and a half years of income. By 1788 – the last year of the *ancien régime* – loan servicing charges were still eating away up to 50 per cent of a (much larger) revenue flow, but the accumulated debt had risen to 5,000 million *livres*, or the equivalent of eight years of income. With figures such as these, no one in possession of the facts could doubt that France suffered from structural weaknesses in her public finances and, increasingly, public anxieties as to her long-term creditworthiness. But advice, if not help, came readily to hand. Before 1750, barely one or two works each year had been published on the themes of finance and political economy. In the decade that witnessed the conclusion of the Seven Years War, 61 books and pamphlets appeared, whereas the 1780s unleashed a flood of printed material on taxation and allied topics. Between 1780 and 1789, 243 works appeared (Félix, 1999: 20). Much of this advice was unpalatable and it is here that we touch upon the central paradox of Bourbon rule. Far from having been erected on the ruins of particularism and 'privilege', absolute monarchy coexisted with these older forms of power sharing. It even drew strength from them.

'Privilege' (literally, private law) was intrinsic to the *ancien régime*. The term can be expanded to cover rights of immunity, exemption, independent jurisdiction and self-government, as well as the more familiar concept of non-liability to direct taxation. The eighteenth-century mind often conceived of these rights as 'liberties', and when that word was used in negotiations with the Crown it usually signalled a defence of privilege. But this was not necessarily a 'selfish' defence: individuals and corporate bodies genuinely believed that, if their 'freedoms' were taken away, the country would fall victim to tyranny and despotism. Perhaps it was not such an unreasonable assumption in view of the absence of any other form of representation. However, there are grounds for supposing that the personnel of absolute monarchy shared this view also, which enormously complicated their task. A senior servant of the monarchy, such as a provincial intendant, might enjoy personal privilege (as a near-tax-exempt noble); might embody an obliga-tion to defend corporate privilege (by virtue of his family connections, his profession, or his geographical roots); and yet still be required to police and, wherever possible, to curtail the ramifications of privilege as a direct employee of the Crown.

Viewed from Versailles or Paris, privilege was both a hindrance and a help. It hindered the programme of national recovery inasmuch as the reforms mooted in the 1760s and 1770s nearly always involved a challenge to corporate rights and immunities. Most obviously, the tax privileges enjoyed by the clergy and the nobility, together with certain provinces, sheltered some of the most affluent groups in society from the spiralling cost of the burdens of state. It could also be a help, though. For all the modernising ambitions residing at the heart of government, the absolute monarchy could scarcely manage without privilege. There were three reasons for this. Corporate bodies supplied a fairly efficient system of local government which the monarchy was either unable or unwilling to provide from its own resources. Moreover, such bodies collected revenue for the government, and did so in a manner that was generally thought to be more equitable and enlightened than that employed by the monarchy's own direct tax collectors. Third, and most important of all, the existence of corporate bodies helped to sustain the creditworthiness of the state. As royal finances became ever more precarious, loan monies were raised increasingly on the strength of institutions such as the Provincial Estates or the **Hôtel de Ville** of Paris.

To have dispensed with privilege in a clean-sweep reform would have been a huge gamble, then. Hence the cautious – not to say, contradictory – spectacle of ministers of the Crown chipping away at immunities for fiscal reasons, while consolidating and even extending other forms of privilege, such as office-holding – also for pecuniary reasons. With uniformity on the agenda, and equality waiting in the wings, such a policy was inherently difficult to manage, of course. There would come a time when the monarchy risked losing control. The exasperation of elites when faced with a revenue-hungry government is not difficult to understand. Nobody likes to pay additional tax, particularly when the reasons for the increase are left unclear. In the eighteenth century, kings were still expected to finance the business of government very largely from their own pockets: taxes could be raised for special needs as long as they were of fixed duration and yield. Yet the *capitation,* first introduced in 1695, had become a permanent, near-universal tax, and by the 1770s it looked as though the *vingtièmes* were heading in the same direction. However, there was also a principle at stake, for the three-tier division of *ancien régime* society into 'estates' turned ultimately on the question of exemptions. Direct taxation was demeaning and to be liable to it was an unmistakable sign of baseness. Bringing the clergy and the nobility – not to mention sundry other groups – into the tax net might make perfect economic sense, but the social implications were enormous.

Nevertheless, the Bourbon monarchy clearly did enjoy some success in taxing elites during the course of the eighteenth century. No doubt, this was the chief reason why it was so admired by neighbouring rulers who entertained

Hôtel de Ville: Literally, 'town hall'. Seat of the Paris city government, which helped the Crown to raise money via bonds issued on the security of its revenues.

similar ambitions. Historians differ on how much success was achieved, though. Indeed, some question whether 'privilege' really lay at the root of the tax problem (Norberg, 1994: 253–98). The comments of contemporaries suggest that reform in this area still had a long way to go. Turgot, the future Controller General, remarked in 1767 that the *capitation* paid by the nobility was exceedingly modest (Hincker, 1971: 27), and in 1787 the Duke of Orleans admitted that his standard practice had been to strike deals with the intendants, enabling him to pay in tax 'more or less what I please' (Jones, 1995: 64). Members of the Second Estate may not have contributed very much then, but, equally, it is certain that they had never paid more than at the end of the *ancien régime*. Bertin's proposal of 1763 for a general land tax (*subvention territoriale*) therefore prompted an outcry and was swiftly aborted. However, Chancellor Maupeou's blow against the Parlements in 1771 opened a window of opportunity for the *abbé* Terray – the man who was now in charge of the finances. In 1771, he succeeded in making the first *vingtième* a permanent tax and the second was prolonged until 1781. A third *vingtième*, dating back to the latter part of the Seven Years War, would also be reintroduced in 1782.

The American colonists' slogan 'no taxation without representation' applied to France as well, and the body that considered itself to be the guardian of the corporate structures of the kingdom was the Parlement of Paris. It informed Louis XVI that all of his subjects were linked together in a great chain of being 'divided into as many different *corps* as there are different estates in the realm' [**Doc. 2**]. Yet despite its name, the Parlement of Paris was not a quasi-representative assembly but a court of law which judged on appeal cases emanating from subordinate courts in a jurisdiction covering roughly one-third of the kingdom. Jurisdiction in the remaining two-thirds was parcelled out between 12 other Parlements. This is to understate its role, however. The Parlement of Paris also possessed regulatory powers, a recording power and a power of 'remonstrance'. Unless and until royal edicts and declarations had been transcribed into the registers of the Parlement, they lacked the force of law in the territory over which it exercised jurisdiction. Moreover, the 'sovereign courts', as they were evocatively known, were entitled to formulate criticisms ('remonstrances') of the laws submitted to them for registration. This could amount to a power of veto on the royal will, although in most cases doubts and misgivings were smoothed away by negotiation. In cases of utter stalemate, however, the king could resort to a constitutional device known as a Bed of Justice (*lit de justice*) by which he commanded registration by virtue of his physical presence before the Parlement.

On his accession in 1774, Louis XVI reversed the policy pursued by his grandfather and by Maupeou, and reinstated the Parlements to their ancient powers and prerogatives. It was a popular, if unfortunate, move in view of subsequent events. Historians tend to judge the Parlements harshly, arguing in effect that they were chiefly responsible for the breakdown of the *ancien régime*. In a tenacious defence of privilege – not least their own – they lost sight of the larger constellation of problems confronting the monarchy. Yet this was not how public opinion viewed their stance. Parlementaire resistance to the royal will enjoyed huge support among the educated classes and it was sustained almost to the end. We are bound to ask why, and the answer is unequivocal. The Parlement of Paris, in common with the other sovereign courts, was able to pose successfully as the champion of the law at a time when the absolute monarchy appeared completely reckless as to the knock-on consequences of its reform agenda. By the 1780s, the issue had become one of consent to taxation, and to accede to the monarchy's demands without any checks and balances looked to many observers like a short route to despotism. Necker was no longer in power by this time (he fell in 1781, following the publication of the *Compte rendu au roi*). His Provincial Assemblies initiative, which might have provided a solution to the conundrum of 'no taxation without representation', was on hold and the partisans of streamlined absolute monarchy had the upper hand once more.

The extent to which these debates reverberated in the country at large prior to 1787 is difficult to estimate. In a town like Dijon, probably two-fifths of householders were privileged office-holders of some description and therefore personally involved in the weighty constitutional questions of the day. But Dijon was the seat of a Parlement; most towns – indeed, most large towns – were not. Located hundreds of miles away from the nerve centres of power, cities such as Nantes, Bordeaux, Marseilles and Lyons had rather different preoccupations. The merchant elites of Bordeaux, for instance, were far more concerned about the state of the economy than the state of politics in the council chambers of Versailles. Commenting somewhat gleefully on the setbacks to have hit this port city since the conclusion of the American War, the British ambassador reported in 1784 a spate of bankruptcies, and not a single American vessel seen in the harbour since the previous year (Browning ed., 1909: 15). But should we link the mounting political difficulties of the 1780s with a larger crisis of the urban and rural economy? If only by reason of her large and expanding population, France was a rich land by eighteenth-century standards. Economic historians agree that the country enjoyed a long period of growth until the late 1770s. Thereafter a recession set in, to be followed by a much sharper downturn between 1786 and 1789.

Yet this growth was shallow-rooted and patchy. The onset of revolution would rapidly knock it off course. Overseas and particularly colonial trade boomed, notwithstanding periodic bouts of global conflict between European states. However, there were few signs that the commercial wealth of the port cities was providing a stimulus to the vast hinterland of rural France. The agricultural economy continued to develop largely in accordance with its own rhythms of change. In a large and climatically diverse country, harvest shortfall continued to be a depressingly commonplace occurrence. There were six interregional dearths in the eighteenth century – seven if we count the famine linked to the currency collapse in 1794–95. Each produced ripples in the industrial sector. High bread prices rapidly depressed demand for manufactured goods, as the royal intendants frequently observed. However, we cannot say for certain that the troubled economic climate after 1776 or thereabouts played a role in the growth of tension between the absolute monarchy and its critics. The *ancien régime* did not die of a weak, or poorly integrated, economy. Only during what proved to be the last act of the drama – in 1788–89 – is it reasonable to argue that a decade of mounting economic difficulties began to weigh in the political balance. But, by this time, elite resistance to the designs of the monarchy had begun to draw support from the lower classes of both town and country.

Even as late as 1788, very few – if any – French men and women would have been aware that a 'revolution' was in the offing. In fact, it seems unlikely that the majority would have been equipped with a political vocabulary enabling them to think in these terms. Historians believe they know better, of course. But hindsight knowledge of what would come next is not as much of a help as it might seem. Despite its impressive longevity, the *ancien régime* stands condemned because ultimately it failed. For historians inspired by a Marxist analytical approach, the socio-political order which Louis XV bequeathed to his grandson could not long survive for the reason that it was unable to contain and to express the powerful economic forces that were reshaping the kingdom from the bottom upwards. A great deal of research undertaken by Georges Lefebvre (1947) and Albert Soboul (1974) during the middle decades of the twentieth century documents this divergence. Though highly effective in explaining the socio-economic fissures that would open up when the crisis began in earnest, their findings cannot shed much light on the process by which the monarchy was weakened by the actions of its own elites.

Perceptive contemporaries had been remarking on the build-up of tensions within the regime since the 1760s, if not earlier; yet crises had come and gone at intervals without major institutional and societal upset. Why, we might reasonably ask, did the absolute monarchy manage to ride out the perils of the year 1763, only to succumb to those of 1788? After seven years of warfare conducted on a global scale, France undoubtedly faced a substantial debt mountain by 1763 and a dramatically widening budget deficit. Yet the 'political' ingredient that might have endowed this fiscal crisis with explosive repercussions was lacking. Not so in 1787–88, as we shall see. It is therefore necessary to supplement the traditional explanation of the outbreak of the revolution, which is rooted in a systemic crisis of the *ancien régime*, with the more recent reassessments undertaken by Keith Baker (ed., 1990), François Furet (1981) and others. This research enables us to understand rather better the role played by public opinion in the life cycle of absolute monarchy. Crucially, it demonstrates how 'opinion' could be transformed into an ideology of resistance as ministers outlined yet another round of reforms to cope with an all-too-familiar and predictable fiscal and budgetary crisis.

PART 2

2

Reform or Revolution, 1787–89?

The last crisis experienced by the *ancien régime* was essentially man-made, then. Indeed, it was triggered in large measure by the needs and actions of the monarchy. If the Bourbons had avoided foreign policy entanglements which required heavy war expenditures, it is possible that the budgetary problem could have been managed within existing structures. But it was not to be, and Alexis de Tocqueville's dictum which holds that the most dangerous moment for an authoritarian government occurs when it embarks on reform was framed precisely to accommodate the situation in which France now found herself (1969, Headlam edn: 182). Yet no one *knew* that the country's governing system was in its death throes at the start of 1787. A few commentators reached for the word 'revolution' in order to describe what was happening as early as the autumn of that year, but they used the term imprecisely and with little sense of what it might mean. In his travel journal, Arthur Young recorded much dinner-table wisdom, including the opinion expressed on 17 October that France stood on the threshold 'of some great revolution in the government' (Young, Betham-Edwards edn, 1900: 97). But 'revolution' – in this context – can be taken as the superlative of 'reform'. Even as late as the spring of 1789, the majority of thinking men and women had little inkling of what lay in store. This chapter lays out the sequence of events that led from reform to revolution. It explains why reform from above failed to win sufficient support in the country at large, and how this failure helped to unleash forces that would cause the *ancien régime* to fall to pieces within a short span of time.

GRIPPING THE NETTLE OF REFORM

After two decades of stop–go reform, it is plain that, by 1783, Louis XVI's most senior officials were keenly aware of the gravity of the situation facing the country. The window of opportunity to carry out meaningful reform would not remain open much longer – if only because the third *vingtième* tax was scheduled to expire in 1787, the year in which the contract for the collection of indirect taxes also fell due for renewal. Even the most devoted servants of the Crown were coming to the realisation that only by reining in foreign policy commitments and abolishing tax exemptions could the power of absolute monarchy be preserved. Calonne, the Controller General, numbered among them. It is true that he continued to spend on a lavish scale in order to sustain the confidence of creditors, but he could not have been unaware of the difficulties that lay ahead. After a period of calm, relations between ministers and the Parlement of Paris were becoming strained again too – another reason for action sooner rather than later. Calonne's diminishing freedom of manoeuvre can be traced in the reports despatched from the British embassy in Paris. Daniel Hailes, the chargé d'affaires, noted in August 1785 that recent attempts to secure a loan of 125 million *livres* had proved 'very unsuccessful'. Another, floated in December to the tune of 80 million *livres*, incurred similar difficulties – particularly after registration was refused by the Parlement. 'M. de Calonne must have now nearly exhausted all his resources', reported Hailes, 'and it seems next to impossible that he should remain in office. The expenses of Government have exceeded its income near 160 millions of *livres* this year' (Browning ed., 1909: 44, 86). Nevertheless, Calonne tried, in April 1786, to raise 30 million *livres* via a lottery and a further 24 million on the strength of the credit rating of the Paris Hôtel de Ville.

1786 was the last year in which the *ancien régime* exhibited an outward appearance of normality, in fact. Yet Calonne knew that both his own position and that of the monarchy had become precarious, and in August he obtained the king's assent to a thoroughgoing financial recovery programme. Its key was the proposal for a universal land tax. The new levy would apply to all owners of land, irrespective of rank; it would not be susceptible to reduction via negotiation; and it would replace the two remaining *vingtième* taxes. This was the proposal, packaged with a number of other reforms, which was placed before a specially convened Assembly of Notables in February 1787. The Notables were a hand-picked body of dignitaries whose endorsement of the reforms would, it was hoped, discourage any obstructionism on the part of the Parlement of Paris. Unfortunately, they were not very well picked (too few members of the Third Estate), nor were they particularly compliant. Commentators likened their summoning to the convocation of a 'national assembly' (Jones, 1995: 116), which was not at all the intention of the ministry. This misapprehension reveals the extent to which the government was beginning to lose control of public opinion.

In the event, a whole programme of reform proposals, albeit somewhat hastily assembled, was submitted to the Notables for their consideration.

Nearly everything it contained (the deregulation of the corn trade; commutation of the *corvée* into a monetary tax; the reform of local government; reform of the *taille* tax; redemption of the clerical debt, etc.) had been talked about endlessly for several decades. Nevertheless, Calonne made no bones about the need for swift and far-reaching action, disclosing publicly for the first time that government spending outstripped tax receipts by a wide margin. The deficit, he suggested, was attributable to the American War and, more particularly, to Necker's financial mismanagement of France's intervention in that conflict. In fact, it went back much further – to the Seven Years War. For a minister with powerful enemies at Court, it was scarcely a statesmanlike move to antagonise in this way Necker's numerous friends within the Assembly. Nevertheless, the Notables were not incapable of responding to the urgency of the situation. They endorsed the proposals regarding the grain trade, the *corvée* and even the *taille*, and raised no serious objection to the scheme for a more uniform system of local government. On the other hand, they declared themselves not qualified to approve any new financial impositions. Both the land tax and the proposal for a duty to be charged on stamped documents were open-ended, they noted, and therefore gave rise to the usual 'constitutional' objections. As for the suggestion as to how the Church might clear accumulated debts, it amounted to an attack on property. Calonne tried to outflank the body that he had so recently called into existence, claiming that it was only interested in defending the edifice of corporate privilege. But government ministers who were widely suspected of 'despotic' tendencies could no longer expect to win the battle for public opinion, and with the king's support ebbing as well, he was dismissed and exiled to his estates.

RESISTANCE TO THE ROYAL WILL

By April 1787, therefore, the ploy to substitute the sanction of an Assembly of Notables for that of the Parlement of Paris had succeeded only in increasing the number of voices calling for restraints to be placed on the powers of absolute monarchy. But Loménie de Brienne, the prelate-administrator who replaced Calonne a month or so later, did try to find a middle way between the proponents of the streamlined state and those who discerned in the Notables an opportunity to wreak an aristocratic revenge on the monarchy for ever having pioneered the theory of absolutism in the first place. Loménie de Brienne had no better idea than Calonne of how to overcome the fiscal problem in the short term; however, he had a medium-term strategy. The local government reform initiative would be used to bring regional elites into a new partnership so as to widen the basis of consent to taxation. Chosen on the basis of a tax-paying franchise and unencumbered by distinctions of 'estate', well-to-do landowners would occupy seats in a tiered structure of municipal, district and provincial assemblies. Over time – Brienne reckoned on five years – such a structure would surely evolve a 'national' assembly of deputies recruited on the basis of their wealth and public spiritedness.

But such a vision belonged to the future, and to a future that even the small circle of enlightened advisors clustered around the Controller General could scarcely anticipate. Loménie de Brienne's most immediate problem remained the Assembly of Notables and, secondarily, the Parlement of Paris. Having succeeded only in embittering the political atmosphere, the king sent the Notables home towards the end of May. This turned the spotlight onto the Parlement and simplified the battle lines in the sense that a confrontation between the monarchy and the powerful body of Parisian magistrates could not now be averted. Ministers resolved on a softly-softly approach initially, although Lamoignon, the new Keeper of the Seals and a firm adherent of absolute monarchy, expressed his misgivings. As a result, the Parlement was induced to accept the proposals regarding the grain trade and the *corvée*. More surprisingly, the magistrates also endorsed the local government reform. However, on the land tax and the stamp duty they were obdurate. Only an Estates General could sanction new taxes, they declared, thereby echoing a call first uttered in the Assembly of Notables. Brienne thus had little choice but to proceed to a *lit de justice* and enforced registration of the key financial reforms on 6 August 1787. When the magistrates persisted in their resistance, the whole body was sent into exile.

Exile to some dismal provincial town (Troyes in this case) far removed from the pleasures of the capital was a method of cooling heads that the monarchy had employed before. Most dispassionate observers drew the conclusion that the advantage now lay with the government. The new provincial, district and municipal assemblies were coming into being amid widespread satisfaction, and the Parlements risked being left behind by events. Hailes, writing from the British embassy, thought them at their 'last gasp' (Browning ed., 1909: 232) unless the call for that long-forgotten institution – the **Estates General** – could be rooted in the public imagination. In a polemical foretaste of what was to come, the *abbé* Morellet informed Lord Shelburne that the magistrates were defending nothing more than their privileges: 'You should know, milord, that there is not a single counsellor in the Parlements of the realm who pays his *vingtième* or *vingtièmes*, nor a tenant farmer of these messieurs who pays his *taille* on the same footing as his neighbours' (Fitzmaurice ed., 1898: 248).

What would change these perceptions of relative strength, however, was a foreign policy crisis in the Netherlands. For a year and more, the Dutch

Estates General: The body of representatives of the three orders of the state; convened by the monarch at intervals since 1302.

provinces had been moving in the direction of a civil war as a 'patriot party' of lesser bourgeois and artisans exerted pressure on the Stattholder William V and the ruling oligarchy. The Patriots enjoyed the support of France, whereas the House of Orange had ties both to Great Britain and to Prussia. Having secured promises of assistance from Britain, Prussia decided to intervene decisively in the Dutch crisis. On 13 September 1787, troops were sent over the border to aid the Orangeists. The Patriots, or republicans, now looked to France for assistance, but the conclusion of a full-blown alliance between Britain and Prussia early in October brought home to the Bourbons that they were no longer in a position to back up their clients with force. The pledges previously given to the Dutch republicans were repudiated.

A more dramatic, and humiliating, demonstration of the connection between taxation and the ability to wage war could scarcely have been conceived. Some form of accommodation with the Paris Parlement, if only short-term, would have to be reached. In return for their recall, the magistrates agreed to endorse the reinstatement or extension of the *vingtièmes* taxes for a further five years – this despite the fact that they had earlier declared themselves incompetent to approve any new taxes whatsoever. But Brienne's needs were more pressing, and this enabled the magistrates to wring from the government a major political concession. As the price of its consent to a 420 million *livres* loan spread over five years, the Parlement secured an undertaking from the monarchy to call an Estates General by 1792. Presumably, the Principal Minister calculated that he would have his new system of assemblies up and running by this time, in any case. As for Lamoignon, the other strong figure in the government, he intervened to make sure that it was understood that a future Estates General would serve merely as an adjunct to the king's existing councils. It would not possess any legislative or executive initiative. Dismayed, the magistrates prepared to resist once more, whereupon the king forced through the registration of the loan by means of a *lit de justice* on 19 November 1787. When his cousin, the Duke of Orleans, protested, he was ordered to his estates and two outspoken magistrates were arrested.

The year ended in suspicion, recrimination and stalemate, then. The Parlement of Paris, together with its lesser brethren in the provinces, stood accused of wishing to turn the monarchy into an 'aristocracy of magistrates', probably unfairly, whereas ministers fumed at the waste of another year in procrastination and palliatives that failed to address the key issue. Investors in government funds, meanwhile, had begun to weigh up the risks of a declaration of bankruptcy, but there was no unrest in the country at large and the harvest had been plentiful.

The year 1788 would witness a deterioration on all of these fronts, however. The denouement was set in motion by Lamoignon, the Keeper of the

Seals, who has been described as 'the last true servant of the old monarchy' (Hardman, 1993: 136). In April, it became known that the head of the judiciary was secretly planning to destroy the constitutional powers of the Parlements once and for all, and to curtail severely their judicial responsibilities. This was a gamble of the highest order, since measures of such severity risked giving substance to the allegations of 'ministerial despotism' and provoking a general rallying of all the discontented against the government. Daniel Hailes, the perspicacious envoy in the British embassy, even alerted his superiors to the possibility that the populace might become involved in the conflict, resulting in 'the total subversion of the monarchy' (Browning ed., 1910: 33). For a comment made on 17 April, this was prophesy indeed. The blow fell in the shape of a *lit de justice* on 8 May, which compulsorily registered Lamoignon's Six Edicts dismantling the authority of the Parlements. Henceforward, the formality of registering royal edicts would be transferred to a special 'plenary court' whose composition was tailored to ensure that it would remain a docile tool of government.

All 13 Parlements protested [**Doc. 3**], and by July 1788 9 had been ordered into exile. That of Rouen railed against 'these rash innovators [who] have dared to advance the fatal project of bringing everything into a system of *unity* . . .' (Stone, 1994: 189). This is the familiar language of corporate, *ancien-régime* France and it reminds us that, even at the moment of their greatest trial, the magistrates scarcely had the 'rights' of a proto-liberal 'nation' uppermost in their minds. But all would change with the news from Grenoble in the Dauphiné. On 7 June, as troops sought to enforce the exiling of the Parlement, they were assailed by riotous citizens who hurled bricks and tiles from the rooftops. This 'Day of the Tiles' (Plate 1), followed as it was by the meeting at Vizille near Grenoble (21–22 July), would transform the character of the resistance movement. The magistrates and those of their supporters who reconvened in the chateau of Vizille announced their intention to campaign not merely for the particular rights attaching to the inhabitants of the Dauphiné, but for those of 'all Frenchmen' (Jones, 1995: 152). Popular demonstrations against the king's representatives (the intendants and military commanders) occurred in Pau and Rennes as well, but it was the Dauphiné example that became the pacemaker for constitutional change. Nevertheless, it should not be supposed that the whole of the country was up in arms. Provincial France, while inwardly digesting the lesson of judicial disobedience, remained calm for the most part.

Loménie de Brienne, if not Lamoignon, was not unduly alarmed by these developments. More than 20 of his provincial assemblies were now on an active footing, and the talk of a 'nation' embracing all Frenchmen was perhaps more of a help than a hindrance to his plans. Detached observers agreed: 'This nation is rising from the dust', the American ambassador,

Thomas Jefferson, reported to William Stephens Smith. 'They have obtained, as you know, provincial assemblies in which there will be a more perfect representation of the people than in our state assemblies' (Boyd ed., 1956: vol. 13, 458). However, the Dauphiné model envisaged that the 'nation' would regroup within a framework of revived **Provincial Estates** rather than provincial assemblies. And there remained the ticklish question of the Estates General, of course. Brienne's response was to lift the censorship and to invite suggestions as to how this body might be converted into 'a truly national assembly both in terms of its composition and its effects' (Brette, 1894: vol. 1, 19–22). Why then did the ministry succumb, thereby negating the gains made since the spring? The plain answer, and there can be no other, is that the monarchy was finally overtaken by its debts. All governments relied on short-term credit in order to carry on day-to-day business – that is to say, on the willingness of bankers to accept promissory notes drawn against future income in return for cash advances. That willingness ebbed away in the first week of August 1788, even though Brienne signalled that he was ready to abandon the 'plenary court' and to bring forward the meeting of the Estates General to 1 May 1789. On 16 August, he was forced to announce a delay in payments to creditors and part reimbursement in Treasury bills rather than cash. Confidence collapsed.

Provincial Estates: Regional representative bodies with the power to redistribute royal taxation.

THE NATION AWAKES

Brienne left the ministry in a matter of days, notwithstanding the efforts of the queen to protect her favourite. He was replaced by the Swiss banker Jacques Necker, whom public opinion judged to be the only person capable of rescuing the country from what amounted to an admission of state bankruptcy. Since the king agreed with Necker that it would be necessary to recall the Parlement of Paris from its second experience of provincial exile, Lamoignon's days were numbered too. Sure enough, the triumphant magistrates demanded a complete return to the old status quo and on 23 September 1788 a royal declaration revoked the Six Edicts. Financial confidence was already returning when, on the following day, the magistrates were escorted by a joyful Parisian crowd to their courthouse like conquering heroes. After the excitement and tumult of the past month, their pronouncement that the forthcoming Estates General ought to be convened in accordance with the practices followed in 1614 (when it had last met) seemed like a detail [**Doc. 5**].

Signs that the ripples from this long-running and high-profile dispute between the government and the sovereign courts had spread beyond the confines of polite society were not wanting by the autumn of 1788. The departure of both Brienne and Lamoignon was accompanied by extensive rioting in the central districts of Paris. Not unconnected was the fact that the price of bread rose sharply in the capital towards the end of the summer once it became apparent that the harvest had not been plentiful. Anticipating trouble, Necker advised that free trade in corn, enacted only a year earlier, be suspended. By November, the first reports of food riots in the provinces started to come in. By November also, the implications of the Parlement's determination to follow the precedent and protocol of 1614 began to strike home. Since the Estates General would be a gathering of orders, it followed that each order would meet and vote separately. This meant that the commoner deputies would be unable to make their numerical presence felt; indeed they would find themselves in a permanent minority. One of Brienne's last acts before retiring had been to solicit opinions on the course that the monarchy should follow in the months to come; in effect, therefore, to remove the last remaining restraints on open political discussion. Press freedom would now be used to devastating effect against the Parlement of Paris and its provincial siblings. They were accused – rightly or wrongly – of having mounted a selfish defence of their own privileges from the very beginning. Proof, if proof were needed, could be found in the magistrates' efforts to stay in control of events by recommending that the procedures adopted on the occasion of the meeting of the Estates General of 1614 be followed.

Pamphlets, political squibs and satires had long been an accompaniment to the public life of the monarchy. They were easily produced on small, hand-operated printing presses that could be found in nearly all provincial towns. Anonymity, if required, could be guaranteed, and street vendors would see to the business of circulation. That autumn, the trickle of such material became a flood. In Paris, about 150 political pamphlets and manifestos were produced in the six weeks following the reinstatement of the Parlement. By mid-November, they were appearing at a rate of three or four a day, and by mid-December, ten to twelve a day (Garrett, 1959: 126). Between 12 and 27 December, over 200 pamphlets were offered for sale or posted up at street corners. And at the turn of the year *abbé* Sieyès's devastating critique of the privileged orders entitled *What is the Third Estate?* [**Doc. 4**] came out. In a dramatic escalation of the political temperature, he encouraged his readers to believe that they already possessed everything required for incipient nationhood. If it is true that ordinary French men and women did not have much of a political vocabulary before 1789, the means of acquiring one now lay close to hand. 'Who read what?' is not a question that can be easily answered, of course, and without a doubt the inhabitants of Paris and Versailles were more advanced than the rest of the population. Nevertheless, outside observers were in agreement that an elemental shift in the focus of public opinion was under way. The Spanish ambassador reported on 10 November 1788 that 'The passion for the Parlements is diminishing. A third party is rising up with nothing but the word *liberty* on its lips, which it shouts to the point of speechlessness' (Mousset, 1924: 41).

With all around in movement, it seems strange that Necker, the Director General of Finance, should studiously confine himself to budgetary matters and resolutely decline to use his powers of initiative. But all government reform agendas were on hold until such time as the Estates General was able to assume the burdens of office. As for the word 'revolution', it had been spoken at intervals, but chiefly in the now redundant context of the monarchy's conflict with the Parlements. Further ingredients would need to be added – fear, famine and the numbing cold of the winter of 1788–89 – before 'revolution' could be construed to mean the threat of a collapse of the state rather than simply an alteration to its fabric. Yet the notion that 'reform' had been placed on hold was pure fiction in practice. The ministry might have wished to wait upon the Estates General but no one else chose to do so, whether in Paris or in the provincial capitals of the kingdom. Pamphleteers filled the vacuum with an increasingly well-articulated programme for change which identified both short- and medium-term objectives.

The most pressing need had to be a revision of the protocols governing the convocation of the Estates General. Time had moved on since 1614; the wealthy elite of the Third Estate were now more numerous and socially adept and it made no sense to restrict the contribution they might make to the regeneration of the kingdom purely on the grounds of respect for precedent. The representation of the Third Estate should be doubled so that it at least matched that of the other two orders, and the deputies of all three orders or estates should be required to work together in a common assembly. This was alarming talk to magistrates, to much of the aristocracy and the upper clergy (also nobles by birth), and to anyone else who still considered the corporate heritage of the monarchy to be sacrosanct. More alarming still was the tendency of pamphleteers to take their cue from Sieyès and argue as though the Third Estate alone constituted the source of the common good [**Doc. 4**].

Necker bestirred himself sufficiently in order to call into being a second Assembly of Notables on 6 November. However, five out of its six working committees declared against the pretensions of the Third Estate. Even though the opening of the Estates General had been put back to April of the following year, the time needed in order to carry through the preparations was beginning to look tight. There could be no substitute for executive action and finally, after a marathon session of the royal council, the king took the weighty decision to allow the Third Estate the same number of representatives as the clergy and the nobility combined. Although greeted as a great victory for the nation-in-the-making when made public on 27 December 1788, the

'Result of the King's Council' had nothing to say about the issue of voting (by order or by head), however. On the other hand, Louis XVI used the opportunity to assert his sincere wish to rule henceforward as a constitutional monarch.

COUNTDOWN TO A REVOLUTION

At this point the time-bomb of revolution can be said to have started ticking, if only because the initiative began to pass from powerful men in Versailles and Paris to individuals unknown, or barely known, on the streets of the great cities and in the small towns and villages of the provinces. Three factors can be identified, all acting upon one another. Rural France had been a silent spectator to the political manoeuvring and jousting of the previous two years, but this was now coming to an end. From November onwards the agrarian distress caused by harvest failure was exacerbated by the severest winter conditions that anyone could remember. Country dwellers in eastern France led the way and on 5 January 1789 the local newspaper for the Franche-Comté confirmed that 'agitation has spread from the towns to the countryside' (Jones, 1988: 61). At this stage the ferment was mostly confined to threats directed against the owners of monastic storehouses and the collectors of feudal dues, but in February and March it spread to the rural populations of the Dauphiné and Provence and took on a more purposeful appearance. By April, reports were describing the mobilisations in the southeast as both organised and explicitly anti-seigneurial in character.

The second factor in play can be described as the mobilisation of minds consequent upon the publication, in late January, of detailed electoral regulations for the forthcoming Estates General. All three orders were to choose deputies and to draw up lists of grievances (*cahiers de doléances*) for presentation to the monarch. Since the Third Estate alone constituted a constituency of between 4 and 5 million adult males, this was a massive and complex undertaking. In small towns and villages there can be no doubt that the consultation process conjured up thoughts that would have been literally unthinkable only a few months earlier [**Doc. 9**].

The third factor in the equation which looked as though it might trigger something more radical than an orderly rectification of fiscal abuses once the Estates General had settled down to business was the ongoing pamphlet campaign. As early as December, the **Princes of the Blood** had taken fright and signed an appeal to the king warning that the state was in mortal danger – all, that is, save for the Duke of Orleans and the Comte de Provence [**Doc. 6**]. The Princes were concerned lest a struggle over tax exemptions should

cahiers de doléances: Grievance lists drawn up by all three orders for submission to the king on the occasion of the Estates General.

Princes of the Blood: Male blood relatives of the monarch who were not members of the royal family, but entitled to attend royal councils.

become the pretext for a more general interrogation of the legitimacy of a society based on ranks or orders. It is true that spokesmen for the Third Estate were starting to envisage that the Estates General might acquire legislative powers, enabling it to enact a bill of rights and a modern constitution. The utility of social distinctions had even been opened to question, as had the feudal regime and the corporate status of the clergy.

The opinions of historians differ as to just how much was at stake when the Estates General finally opened in Versailles on 5 May 1789. Had a metropolitan caucus of nobles persuaded their order to make prudential sacrifices? It seems unlikely. Once again, Thomas Jefferson is our surest guide. On 13 March, he felt able to assert that 'equal taxation is agreed to by everybody' and went on to predict that the majority of noble deputies would accept voting by head. However, on 9 May, he reported that 'the Noblesse on coming together shew that they are not as much reformed in their principles as we had hoped they would be. In fact there is a real danger of their totally refusing to vote by persons.' He went on, in a subsequent letter, to clarify the nature of the impediment: 'The great mass of deputies of that order which come from the country shew that the habits of tyranny over the people are deeply rooted in them' (Boyd ed., 1958: vol. 14, 652; 1958: vol. 15, 110). In other words, the elections had exposed the fault-line between enlightened opinion in the capital and the mood of the Second Estate in the kingdom as a whole [**Docs. 7 and 8**]. In a sense, though, the divisions within the nobility (or, for that matter, the clergy) were not the most telling factor. What soured the Estates General almost from the start was the protracted political stalemate running from early May until the middle of June. The refusal of clerical and noble deputies to countenance common voting with the Third Estate prevented a meeting of minds from taking place, while the ministry itself proved to be internally divided and therefore incapable of responding to the gravity of the situation by taking the lead.

With the benefit of hindsight, it is possible to identify three steps that, once taken, led unmistakably in the direction of a full-scale revolution. On 17 June 1789, an impatient chamber of Third Estate deputies – or Commoners, as they now preferred to call themselves – decided to adopt the title 'National Assembly'. This amounted to an acceptance of Sieyès's logic that sovereignty resided in the majority of the nation. As a corollary, they then 'decreed' (as befitted a sovereign body) that the collection of existing taxes should be brought to a halt if, for any reason, they were to be dissolved. Thus, a group of deputies who had come to Versailles with no real intention of challenging the prerogatives of the Crown seized control of the most important sinew of government.

Louis XVI's response to this defiant and illegal act reflected both his vacillating character and the deep divisions among ministers. It brought forward the second step in the direction of revolution. Assailed on all sides with conflicting advice (and mourning the death of the dauphin, his eldest son), Louis agreed that firm action was required. But what kind of action? The Parlement of Paris urged that the so-called National Assembly be disbanded, by force if necessary, and a powerful faction of courtiers and ministers headed by the Comte d'Artois (youngest brother of the king) and Barentin (the Keeper of the Seals) appears to have shared this view, too. In fact, Louis adopted the less brusque middle course of calling all of the deputies together and telling them what he would, and would not, accept.

In the Royal Session of 23 June 1789, the Bourbon monarchy stood at the crossroads. Had the king made the gentler, more accommodating statement proposed by Necker, it is possible that the final crisis might have been averted. But this assumes that the Commoner deputies – notwithstanding the famous Tennis Court Oath sworn three days earlier – did not really possess the courage of their convictions. In the event though, Louis delivered the judgement scripted by the hardliners. Although some fiscal and budgetary concessions were offered, he declared that the 'decrees' issued by the National Assembly on 17 June were unacceptable to him and therefore null and void. As for the ancient distinctions between the orders, they were to remain. Since Versailles had been packed with troops for the occasion, the 'body language' of the Royal Session was scarcely conciliatory, either, and indeed Necker took care to absent himself. On being ordered to return to their separate chamber by the master of ceremonies, the Commoner deputies hesitated; but then their resolve was stiffened by an intervention from within their ranks by a *déclassé* nobleman, the Comte de Mirabeau. He retorted: 'We shall not leave; return to those who have sent you and tell them that we shall not stir from our places save at the point of the bayonet' (Goodwin, 1959: 70).

The third and final step towards revolution followed swiftly on the heels of this riposte. Louis's conservative advisors – and particularly his sibling, the Comte d'Artois – argued for the military solution, but Necker was still a part of the ministry and the noisy demonstrations in his support urged caution. Moreover, the pressure (or menace) directed towards those who were now routinely dubbed 'the privileged classes' was beginning to have an effect. Already large numbers of deputies drawn from the lower clergy had defected to the National Assembly and liberal-minded nobles were beginning to follow suit, encouraged by royal assurances that the distinction of orders was not in jeopardy. By 27 June, the intransigents among the clergy and the nobility had dwindled to 371, whereas the representatives of the 'nation' numbered 830.

At this point, the king simply ordered the diehards to fuse with the Third Estate. Arthur Young, who was in Paris when the news came through, noted in his journal: 'The whole business now seems over, and the revolution complete' (Young, Betham-Edwards edn, 1900: 182). Historians have found it difficult to fathom this decision on the part of the monarch. Most likely, it was taken under duress – under the threat or rumour of an invasion of the Palace of Versailles by an expeditionary force of Parisians. But it was also a decision that bought time – time to bring up more troops and to position them in and around the capital. When Louis XVI was finally prevailed upon to dismiss Necker on 11 July, he must have had some inkling of what was likely to happen. Hopefully, the troops would contain any violent reaction. They did not, and the taking of the Bastille was the outcome. This was the step that finally acknowledged the failure of attempts at reform from above and tipped France into revolution.

3

Renewal, 1789–91

The king had been out hunting as usual when the first reports of events in Paris reached him. 'So, this is a revolt?' he is said to have remarked, only to be corrected: 'No Sire, this is a revolution' (Cobb and Jones, 1988: 61). There can be no doubt that the news that a lightly armed crowd of Parisians had contrived to seize control of the principal royal fortress in the capital had an electrifying effect. The intention of the new conservative ministry headed by the Baron de Breteuil had been to use the troops to secure Paris. There is little evidence that an offensive operation to dissolve the National Assembly sitting in Versailles had also been in preparation (Price, 1990: 318). But, of course, this is not how matters appeared in retrospect. The Comte d'Artois and a number of courtier families immediately packed their bags and left Versailles (see Chapter 6).

The Parisians could scarcely believe their success. Long before the account of the events of 14 July had penetrated to the extremities of the kingdom, they were at work knocking down the Bastille. The building contractor Pierre-François Palloy took charge of the operation and quickly seized on its marketing potential. The lugubrious myth of the Bastille as a lock-up for state prisoners was suitably embroidered with the 'discovery' of dungeons. Visitors were escorted around the sights and invited to make contributions to assist the families of the 83 Parisians killed during the assault. Blocks of stone toppled from the battlements were carved into effigies of the Bastille and sent to the rest of France as patriotic souvenirs (Plate 2).

Two mutually reinforcing impulses now began to drive events: a desire both to dismantle and to rebuild. This chapter will explore each in turn, and it will emphasise the negotiated character of the regime that came into being. Amidst the euphoria of nationhood rediscovered, it was only natural that French men and women should imagine that their collective energies would wipe away the past and put something different and superior in its place virtually overnight. But this was not to be. Even if France's newly minted legislators had possessed a blueprint for renewal, which seems most unlikely, the business of expunging the *ancien régime*, converting Bourbon absolutism into constitutional monarchy and building consensus would prove harder than anyone could have imagined in the summer of 1789.

ENDING THE *ANCIEN RÉGIME*

The uprising in Paris produced a ripple effect across the whole of the kingdom. Even in localities where there were no disturbances or violence, the servants of the monarchy (intendants, sub-delegates, military commanders, etc.) either abandoned their posts or remained studiously inactive in an effort to determine which way the political wind was blowing. But in many towns and rural areas violence did form a part of the reaction to the news. The self-appointed oligarchies ruling the cities usually made haste to attach to themselves 'committees' consisting of individuals who enjoyed a greater measure of public confidence. Even so, it was not always possible to contain the anger and unrest. Arthur Young arrived at the gates of Strasbourg on 20 July just as an insurrection looked about to begin. The populace, he noted, 'show signs of an intended revolt. They have broken the windows of some magistrates that are no favourites; and a great mob of them is at this moment assembled demanding clamorously to have meat at 5s[ous] a pound' (Young, Betham-Edwards edn, 1900: 206). His remark serves to remind us that the dearth consequent upon the harvest shortfall of 1788 reached a distressing climax in the northerly half of the kingdom during the second and third weeks of July. In fact, he claimed elsewhere in his travel journal that 'the *deficit* would not have produced the revolution but in concurrence with the price of bread' (Lough, 1987: 293). This is a debatable point, but it can be taken as certain that the scale and the scope of the rural uprisings did not stem solely from the ripple effects caused by the news of the taking of the Bastille.

As we have seen, the mobilisations of country dwellers did not wait upon 14 July. Refusals to pay taxes, attacks on grain convoys, episodes of popular price fixing in the market places (*taxation populaire*), food rioting and even punitive expeditions to chateaux had all been widely reported throughout the spring. Once the news from Paris arrived, law and order broke down almost completely and whole new theatres of insurgency (Normandy, Alsace, the Maconnais) appeared. Moreover the *jacqueries*, as they were known, became increasingly anti-seigneurial in character. Lay and ecclesiastical overlords who removed a part of the harvest by virtue of their right to collect feudal dues or the tithe were obvious targets during periods of seasonal scarcity. But reports, albeit garbled, of Necker's departure, of the Paris insurrection,

taxation populaire: The fixing of the prices of food commodities by means of crowd pressure.

and of courtiers fleeing from the Palace of Versailles under cover of darkness, triggered a dramatic shift in popular perceptions of the aristocracy. A surge of fear and anxiety coursed through the countryside, motivated, it appears, by the suspicion that departing aristocrats had hired bands of 'brigands' to lay waste the crops in a spiteful act of political revenge. Few, if any, such bands were ever positively identified, but the merging of at least five regionally distinct 'fears' into one overarching Great Fear (20 July–6 August 1789) had a huge impact on events. Existing theatres of insurrectionary activity acquired fresh energy, whilst in others, such as the Dauphiné, insurgency flared up anew.

The biggest impact was in Paris, or rather Versailles, though. To the deputies of the erstwhile Estates General, the dramatic and bloody scenes that had punctuated the week commencing with the news of the dismissal of Necker came as a sudden and not entirely welcome surprise. They had been settling down in a fairly unhurried fashion to debate the political future of the country, and to that end had resolved on 9 July to rename themselves the 'National Constituent Assembly'. Nobody at that time supposed that the drawing up of a constitution would take more than a few weeks, and no one – again at that time – had a clear set of ideas as to what other changes it would be necessary to make, save perhaps in the fiscal domain. This was the context in which the first reports of agrarian insurrection began to filter through to the deputies, mainly by way of letters from constituents. As the volume of such correspondence grew, so did the level of alarm in the Assembly, with the result that the paramount need to pacify the countryside rose swiftly to the top of the agenda. The result was the evening session of 4 August during which the National Assembly voted to dismantle the *ancien régime.* The next day, deputies from the province of Anjou sat down to draft an account of the session from which they had just emerged. They related how the Vicomte de Noailles had argued that the only sure means of restoring law and order was to offer country dwellers concrete reforms. He had then put the motion that all feudal rights and obligations be abolished. Once this had been accepted, a spate of other, more or less disinterested, motions had been put, resulting in a massive and collective act of repudiation of the past.

Whatever the mix of motivations in the minds of the deputies, there can be no doubt that the 'night of 4 August' tore the old order to shreds. Sacrificed on the altar to national renewal were all forms of provincial and municipal privilege, all remaining relics of serfdom, all feudal jurisdictions and courts, all harvest dues and quit rents, exclusive hunting reserves, the sale of public offices, ecclesiastical pluralism, the tithe, and much else besides. On the days following the deputies contemplated what they had done with 'stupefaction', according to the Spanish ambassador, and not a little 'consternation and regret' (Mousset, 1924: 67). More prosaically, Jefferson reported to John Jay: 'They last night mowed down a whole legion of abuses', adding, 'this will stop the burning of chateaux and tranquilize the country more than all the addresses they could send them' (Boyd, 1958: vol. 15; 334). Although there was some backsliding (on the subject of feudal dues and the tithe notably), the deputies were prepared to live with what they had done, and the bonfire of privilege lit that night did achieve the desired effect in the sense that lawlessness in the countryside gradually subsided. It also gave them the courage and the confidence to hack away at those other pillars of corporate France: the Parlements, the Provincial Estates and the Gallican Church. On 3 November, the Parlement of Paris and its 12 siblings were 'buried alive' – to use the Comte de Mirabeau's striking phrase. That is to say, they were put on permanent summer vacation until such time as a new system of courts could be brought into being.

Not surprisingly, the Parlements were deeply offended at their sudden ejection from political life and imminent extinction. Several questioned publicly the authority of 'the deputies of the *bailliages*' as the Parlement of Toulouse scornfully referred to the National Assembly. During the Terror they would pay with their lives for that remark; but by that time about 40 per cent of magistrates (*parlementaires*) had chosen the path of emigration (Stone, 1986: 252). The other big losers as the new regime began to take on shape were the Provincial Estates, whose claim in 1787 and 1788 that they constituted a bulwark against the depredations of absolute monarchy had mostly been exposed as a sham. In Brittany, Burgundy and even Languedoc, the defence of provincial 'liberties' had amounted in practice to the defence of the privileges of the nobility and the Church. Provincial Estates, the deputies decided, belonged to the old order of things and could not be fitted into the new. The same applied to the tax and audit courts (Cours des Aides, Chambres des Comptes), which also claimed sovereign status on a par with the Parlements. Despite much grumbling and even obstructionism – the Chambre des Comptes of Lorraine is a case in point – they were disbanded. With the nation now claiming sovereignty, there could be no role for such 'intermediate' bodies.

The decision on 5 November 1789 to abolish the distinction of 'orders' or 'estates' flowed naturally from this conception, of course. But opinions were divided as to whether the regenerated nation could allow a category of citizens in possession of the honorific title of 'noble' to subsist in its midst. Whatever constitutional theory now postulated, the 1,315 deputies comprising the National Assembly continued to think of themselves as commoners and nobles (and clerics), as we shall see. Nevertheless, on 19 June 1790, they voted to do away with honorific privilege in a decree abolishing hereditable nobility, together with all the titles and symbols attaching to it.

Pierre-François Lepoutre, one of the few Third Estate deputies from a farming background, described the decree with relish in a letter to his wife as 'the final humiliating blow to the nobility' (Jessenne and Le May eds, 1998: 278). Charles-Elie de Ferrières, the one-time noble deputy representing the *sénéchaussée* of Saumur, was more matter-of-fact: he counselled his wife to stop writing to him as 'Monsieur le Marquis', and to have the family coat of arms obliterated with whitewash (Carré ed., 1932: 212). Whitewash could always be removed later on if necessary.

BUILDING THE NATION

The work of clearing away the rubble of the *ancien régime* and of building afresh were overlapping tasks. Although the majority of the deputies shared certain fixed ideas (devolution of power, employment on merit alone, public accountability, equalisation of fiscal responsibilities, etc.), they did not plan what they were going to do between 1789 and 1791. After all, none of them had arrived in Versailles with a mission to legislate, and no one had expected to be in office for more than a few months at the most. After July 1789, most historians would agree, they fell under the influence of events like any other group of politicians. It was the largely unscheduled events of the night of 4 August that propelled them into a frenzy of renewal. Yet even the dawning realisation that the kingdom would now require a complete institutional overhaul could not be neatly translated into a plan of action. For all its anomalies, the *ancien régime* worked. Until 1787, ordinary people paid their taxes on time, had little difficulty in securing basic judicial redress, and made few complaints about the quality of the spiritual care available to them. Simply to destroy without a thought for the continuities of daily life was not an option, no matter how appealing such an approach seemed in abstract, ideological terms. For two years, therefore, France resembled a vast building site, with old structures left temporarily in place even as the foundations of new ones were being dug alongside them. Tax revenue was still needed by the revolutionary state, and the people still needed to have access to courts. Not until 1791 did it prove feasible to replace the old system of direct taxes; and seigneurial courts – nominally abolished on 4 August 1789 – would continue to function until the end of 1790.

Renewal was taking place simultaneously with demolition and on a broad front, then. But in the interests of clarity it is worth separating the legislative achievements of these years and looking at each in turn. Fiscal reform preoccupied the deputies right through the decade. Indeed, it was not until 1807 and the Imperial government's decision to initiate a new, thorough and comprehensive land survey that the most anomalous features of the *ancien régime* tax system would start to be rectified. Nevertheless, the financial situation of the monarchy towards the end of the summer of 1789 was every bit as precarious as it had been when Brienne left office and, on 2 November, the deputies voted to take possession of the property of the Gallican Church. In return, the state would assume responsibility for the funding of public worship (essentially, the salaries of the clergy) and for poor relief. Since the sale of lands and buildings owned by the Church would take a little while to organise, the National Assembly created a paper currency known as the *assignat*. These notes were to be withdrawn from circulation progressively as the cash proceeds of the sales were received by the Treasury, thereby limiting their inflationary impact on the economy. At least, this was the theory, and for a time the expedient of the *assignat* did create a financial breathing space, enabling both commitments to creditors and the costs incurred in rebuilding the country to be met. However, by the end of 1795, the *assignat* had become almost worthless, and state bankruptcy was looming once more.

As a buttress to this measure, the deputies took two further steps: they introduced a special one-off income tax, known evocatively as the *contribution patriotique* and payable over three years, and they satisfied the heartfelt wish of the nation that all should pay tax on the same footing with a backdated levy on the 'privileged' (i.e. those hitherto largely exempt from paying direct tax) to cover the last six months of 1789. The question of indirect taxes was more difficult to resolve, for the reason that the monarchy had come to rely heavily on them, yet they were abolishing themselves willy-nilly. Many of the tollgates erected around Paris had been destroyed in the disturbances preceding the taking of the Bastille. As for the *gabelle*, or salt tax, its iniquities have already been mentioned, but the deputies were initially reluctant to forgo this source of revenue, notwithstanding violence against customs officials and widespread smuggling. Only the realisation that resistance to collection would continue indefinitely prompted abolition in March 1790. It was the same story with the drinks taxes (*aides*) and municipal tolls (*octrois*). Both were only finally dispensed with in the spring of 1791, by which time the new land tax (*contribution foncière*) had replaced the *taille* and the *vingtièmes*. In so far as tax is concerned, one of the central aims of the reformers since the 1760s had therefore been realised by 1791: everyone now contributed to the running costs of the state. But it was a hollow satisfaction for individual commoners who had widely assumed that they would be paying less because the 'ex-privileged' were now paying more. Also, the long-standing problem of regional differences in tax 'load' had still to be sorted out.

The urgency of a territorial and administrative reorganisation of the kingdom could have escaped no one after 4 August. The privileges attaching to provinces had been repudiated, the municipal government of towns and cities was in turmoil and Brienne's plans for tiered regional assemblies were in a state of suspended animation. Until the new regime had some solid local government institutions of its own, the chances of restoring law and order must have seemed remote. On 7 September, Sieyès suggested the setting up of a Constitution Committee, and in November it duly proposed that the kingdom be divided into about 80 roughly equal subdivisions to be known as 'departments' (see Map 2). In view of the manifest reluctance in some parts of the country to espouse the new gospel of national 'togetherness', it was thought best to avoid the administrative vocabulary of 'provinces', 'estates' and 'assemblies'. And besides, power devolution rather than Bourbon centralism was the new watchword. The provinces were dismembered, therefore: Brittany was split into five departments, Normandy into six, Languedoc into seven, and so on. Each department was subdivided, in turn, into districts, cantons and a base unit that would become known as the 'commune'. By mid-January 1790, a definitive list of 83 departments was ready to receive the Royal Assent – just as soon as names could be found for them. In addition, the new post-1789 administrative map would demarcate 547 districts, 4,872 cantons and about 44,000 communes (Margadant, 1992: 359; 361 note 91).

The second phase of this remarkable operation overlapped the first and consisted of attaching administrative bodies to the newly created territorial entities. Everyone agreed that it was necessary to begin at the base, partly because the lower units of jurisdiction would play a role in generating recruits for the higher echelons, and partly for the reason that the regime urgently needed a buttress of law and order that only local institutions created by consent could provide. In December, the deputies resolved that each 'town, *bourg*, parish or community' (Jones, 1995: 195) should enjoy the right to manage its own affairs through the institution of a municipality whose members would be elected. The elective principle enshrined the early revolutionaries' commitment to merit, transparency and accountability, and it would be applied systematically. Once the municipalities were securely in place, in February and March 1790, the voters would be called upon to nominate the personnel forming the administrative bodies of the districts and the departments. By the end of the year, they had been called out on numerous occasions, in fact, and a *de facto* electorate comprising around 4 million adult males had come into being. Voting fatigue would be one of the first signs that this unwieldy local government structure owed more to idealism than a firm grasp of administrative realities. Nevertheless, there can be no doubting the enthusiasm with which the local government reforms were received – initially. By the end of the first full year of revolution, scarcely any reminders of the civil administration of absolute monarchy remained. By the standards of *ancien-régime* Europe, change was taking place at a break-neck speed. The fixed points in the lives of generations of French men and women were being overturned or uprooted – literally, in some cases. On 10 July 1790, the newly elected council of the Yonne department authorised a contractor to remove and dispose of the wooden post which for centuries had marked the border between the provinces of Burgundy and the Ile-de-France.

Whereas the pedigree of some aspects of the local government renewal can be traced back to Brienne's assemblies initiative of 1787–88, the judicial reforms of the National Assembly undoubtedly marked a sharp break with the past. They were constructed around three principles: the notion that justice was a public rather than a private expression of authority, with the nation as its source; the notion that judicial redress should be cost-free to users; and the notion of public accountability embodied in the decision to subject judges to a process of election. At the base an entirely new institution – the Justice of the Peace – would take over the role performed by seigneurial courts. In the Charente-Inférieure department, therefore, roughly 500 seigneurial jurisdictions were replaced by 53 elected Justices of the Peace once the system was up and running towards the end of 1790 (Crubaugh, 2001: 7; 139). Whereas the judicial services provided by lords tended to be slow, expensive and incurred suspicions of partiality, the Justice of the Peace and his assistants judged speedily and with minimal formality. The institution was one of the success stories of the revolution and despite an attempt to curtail it by Bonaparte it survived until modern times. First-instance justice was dispensed at the level of the canton, a subdivision which otherwise played only a small part in the new administrative landscape. More serious cases were to be sent before higher courts and, again, the deputies resolved to build upon the foundations of their newly created units of civil administration. Each district subdivision became the site of a civil court, and each department a criminal court. Needless to say, there was no room for the Parlements in this new scheme, and little room, either, for the multitude of more specialised courts and jurisdictions that had characterised the *ancien régime*. Appeals would be heard by a single high court (*tribunal de cassation*), but it did not come into being until 1791.

At least reform of the judiciary had been foreshadowed in the *cahiers de doléances*. Yet no one could have foretold the fate in store for the Gallican Church on the basis of opinions circulating in the early months of 1789. A wider measure of religious toleration was on the table for discussion, to be sure, for in 1788 the monarchy had actually taken a big step in this direction in respect of Calvinists. But the restructuring of the Church began almost incidentally as a by-product of decisions made on the night of 4 August and subsequent days. However, once the 'in principle' decision had been taken to treat the Church as a bloated corporation whose wealth was not entitled to the protection normally afforded to private property, the deputies set to work with a will. Enlightenment convictions and prejudices which had been held in rein by a spirit of pragmatism, now began to come out into the open. Having created a common template for civil and judicial administration, the National Assembly could see no reason why the spiritual infrastructure of the emergent nation should not be pulled into line also. Bishoprics were reduced in number from 136 to 83 (one per department) and plans were made to streamline the parish structure – a contentious move that would soon provoke opposition. In keeping with the utilitarian spirit of the age, monastic orders and cathedral chapters were abolished outright, forcing a flood of ordained men and women to go in search of more productive occupations. Those clergy who retained their posts found themselves salaried employees of the state and, as such, liable to much tighter discipline. Pluralism and non-residency had been outlawed, and parish priests now had secular responsibilities thrust upon them. A decree of 23 February 1790 required them to read out the laws from the pulpit, and to explain their meaning to worshippers.

The deputies of the lower, parish-based, clergy had been among the first to break the deadlock in the Estates General, of course, but even they were beginning to grow nervous as the scope of the National Assembly's reforming ambition for the Church became apparent. The move to destroy the corporate existence of the Gallican Church was understandable, even laudable to many, but where would the reform impulse lead next? Towards a *de facto* situation where adherents of all religions, and indeed those adhering to none, were tolerated on an equal footing? The pointed refusal of the Assembly, in April 1790, to endorse a motion calling for Catholicism to be declared the sole religion of state was none too reassuring in this respect. Nor was the determination of the majority of deputies to apply the electoral principle to the priesthood as though ecclesiastical appointments were no different from any other type of office-holding. Priests, whether bishops or country parsons, would be chosen by the voters – just like mayors, municipal officers and judges. The spiritual confirmation and canonical institution of bishops – powers vested in the heirs of Saint-Peter – were repudiated, in common with all other manifestations of jurisdictional supremacy asserted by the Holy See. Having been elected by their fellow citizens, bishops would be consecrated by their metropolitans. All of these far-reaching changes were packaged together in a legislative text known as the Civil Constitution of the Clergy [**Doc. 11**]. The National Assembly approved the draft on 12 July 1790 and it was sanctioned by the king, with misgivings, a few days later. Such was the brimming confidence of the deputies that no one imagined that the clergy might demur, or the pope prove reluctant and withhold his consent.

EXPANDING HORIZONS

With the anniversary of the fall of the Bastille approaching, town and country dwellers alike prepared to celebrate a festival of thanksgiving for the achievements of the past year. Observers commented on the mood of pride and optimism that had taken possession of Parisians. On a stroll through the Champ de Mars, Pierre-François Lepoutre noticed smartly attired women as well as men pushing wheelbarrows of earth in an effort to get the arena ready in time for the Festival of Federation (Plate 3). There can be no doubt that at this juncture – 14 July 1790 – men and women of all backgrounds were willing the revolution to succeed. In the tiny hamlet of Rennemoulin on the outskirts of Versailles, the entire population assembled at the appointed hour, but only the men stepped forward to swear the oath of allegiance, as was customary. However, the womenfolk of the village then insisted that the whole ceremony be staged afresh 11 days later so that they, too, could affirm publicly their commitment to the new regime. The king showed less grace, by contrast. In the vast and rain-soaked concourse of the Champ de Mars, he lounged in his armchair throughout the protracted ceremony and observers noticed signs of reticence when his turn came to swear.

Hundreds of miles to the south-east, the people of Allan had also been willing the revolution on. But as in many other small localities far removed from the new sources of political power, the speed and the magnitude of the changes taking place in the summer of 1789 required a real effort of mental adjustment. For centuries the village had formed part of the 'nation' of Provence and, in consequence, the residents had looked to Aix, the provincial capital, for leadership. Now the momentum for constitutional change was coming from a different quarter. Yet it was not until the late autumn that it fully dawned on the village elders that they were caught up in a truly elemental process of regeneration which was likely to bypass time-honoured calls for the reinstatement of the Provincial Estates of Provence (in abeyance since 1639). The turning point came in December when they were invited to send a delegation of national guardsmen to an encampment, or federation, at Montélimar. In a collective act of solidarity intended to transcend all sectional allegiances, they swore an oath of fidelity to the law and to a nation of undifferentiated French men and women. Within a matter of months, the mental adjustment had been effected. In March, the village council waved goodbye to provincial privilege forever and voted to enter a new territorial entity 'known by the name of the department of the Drôme' (Jones, 2003: 106).

There was to be no turning back for rural, provincial France. No doubt it was the perceived sense of sacrifice that explains the energy which the inhabitants of Allan summoned up for their celebration of the completion of the first year of revolution. Dawn on 14 July 1790 broke to the drumbeat of the national guard. After Mass and with flags deployed, the population went in procession to the seigneurial rabbit warren. With the village clock striking noon, the administering of the oath began. The choice of the warren for the climax to the day's events was no accident, for during the Great Fear Allan had enacted its own Bastille-taking with an invasion of its feudal chateau. A long-running dispute over grazing had gone to court and judgement against the seigneur's agent was expected in the summer of 1789. To the backdrop of the news of events in Paris, the villagers stopped bringing their dough to the seigneurial bread oven and put the payment of harvest dues and the tithe on hold. In September, with an almost palpable sense of satisfaction, the village council acknowledged the legislation now being promulgated by the National Assembly and recorded that it alone was vested with the power of police, not the seigneur.

Anti-seigneurialism would prove a potent political fixative. During the phase of renewal it both cemented loyalty to the new regime and provided an incitement to country dwellers to remain actively involved in the work of reconstruction. When it was discovered that the promises made by the deputies on the night of 4 August were not going to be honoured in full, ordinary men and women likewise discovered that they had within their grasp a hitherto undreamt-of capacity to manoeuvre and exert pressure. Elective municipalities possessed formidable powers to hold the agents of seigneurs to account, national guard detachments could be mobilised to ensure compliance, or else to intimidate. And, if all else failed, there always remained the option of insurrection. In fact, localised peasant insurrectionism punctuated the early years of the revolution. Often enough, it was driven by the realisation that many feudal dues would continue in force, since it transpired that they could only be extinguished by payment of compensation. Not until the summer of 1792 would the legislature finally acknowledge the futility of expecting peasants to buy their way out of the seigneurial regime. In the meantime, the issue helped to maintain an impressive degree of support for the revolution in the countryside – even if that support was often manifested in turbulent and disquieting ways. In June 1790, Pierre-François Lepoutre urged his wife to speak to the seigneur's agent so that the gibbet could be taken down 'in order to avoid the possibility that the populace would come and demolish it' (Jessenne and Le May eds, 1998: 278).

TOWARDS A POLITICAL SETTLEMENT

Even though French men and women wanted desperately to associate Louis XVI with their reforming efforts, his goodwill towards the revolution could never be taken for granted. Louis's visit to the capital three days after the assault on the Bastille was received by Parisians in stony silence; and in the aftermath of the **October Days** they would insist that he, the royal family and the National Assembly take up residence in Paris rather than Versailles. Louis and his queen came to regard this enforced residence in the capital as tantamount to imprisonment, and for good reason. Yet the king's speech before the Assembly on 4 February 1790, in which he promised his full co-operation, had the deputies in semi-religious transports of devotion. Pierre-François Lepoutre hailed the experience as 'one of the finest days of my life' (Jessenne and Le May eds, 1998: 187), and sent a copy of the speech to his wife so that it could be read out to the farm servants.

October Days: Events surrounding the march to Versailles by the women of Paris on 5 October 1789, and the return of the royal family to the capital the following day.

The distribution of political power within the regime that was now taking shape represented something of a problem, therefore. Patriarchal leadership by a good king who had forsworn the practices of absolutism implied a subordinate role for the Assembly; on the other hand, a monarch whose bona fides remained suspect and who appeared beholden to the Court suggested the need for a strong and vigilant parliamentary body. This is what the debates of September 1789 on the subject of the veto and a two-chamber legislature were all about. In the aftermath of the blood spilt on 14 July and subsequent days, a group of deputies who became known as the *Monarchiens* had learned to fear popular violence more than they feared the prospect of a riposte to the revolution launched by the Court. However, they were opposed by tougher-minded individuals whose political outlook was most effectively expressed by the barrister-deputy from Grenoble, Antoine Barnave. These deputies continued to distrust the monarch and when it came to a vote, the majority in the Assembly backed their judgement. The proposal to build into the constitution a power of absolute veto that would have enabled Louis to block legislation indefinitely was lost, as was the proposal to establish an hereditary second chamber which would play a moderating role on the model of the English House of Lords.

It is true that appalling acts of violence, including public beheadings and impalings, had soiled the uprising against absolute monarchy, prompting some historians to argue that 'terror' was intrinsic to the revolutionary experience from the very start (see Part Three). It is also true that the political education of the masses was proceeding at a pace that many of those who had been involved in the guerrilla struggle against absolute monarchy now found disturbing. The American businessman Gouverneur Morris captured in his diary the fumbling progress of ordinary people as they grappled with new concepts and the language in which they were enshrined. Whilst walking the streets of Paris on 5 October, he overheard a soap-box orator declaiming against bread shortages with the words: 'The king has only had this suspensive veto for three days and already aristocrats have bought up the suspensions and sent corn out of the kingdom' (Morris, 1939: vol. 1: 244).

Informal bodies such as the 'electors' of Paris and the militias (national guards) that had sprung up all over the kingdom in response to the law and order emergency of July–August 1789 were also starting to show worrying signs of becoming a source of unrest and agitation.

However, the deputies' own legislative pronouncements were steadily tracing out the social frontiers of the revolution that was now under way. The principle of accountability raised the question: 'Accountable to whom?' To the disembodied nation first glimpsed in the spring and summer of 1789, no doubt. Yet reforms that prescribed the election of village mayors, parish priests and Justices of the Peace demanded a more practical answer to the question. Having completed its move from Versailles to Paris, the National Assembly began to debate these matters towards the end of October. In an all-male legislature no one paused to consider seriously the right of women to the vote. At this stage in the revolution, the most that women could hope for was some easing of paternal authority within the family (see Part Three). Rather, the issue became one of defining the limits of 'citizenship', a male noun. According to the Declaration of Rights voted on 27 August 1789 as a preliminary statement of the constitution to come: 'Men are born, and always continue, free, and equal in respect of their rights' [**Doc. 10**]. But this levelling doctrine proved something of an embarrassment when the time came to construct viable institutions of government. Instead, the deputies invented a gradated form of citizenship, based on the size of individual tax contributions. Those in the lowest tier (described as 'passive citizens') could not vote at all, whereas those in the upper tier ('active citizens') were entitled to participate in electoral assemblies and, provided they paid enough tax, to stand as candidates as well. Approximately 39 per cent of adult males over the age of 25 were disqualified from the vote as a result (Gueniffey, 1993: 77, 97). The sovereign nation of political rhetoric was already looking somewhat reduced by the end of the first full year of revolution, then. However, it is worth remembering that scarcely 17 per cent of Englishmen possessed the vote at this time.

The artificial distinction drawn between 'political rights' and 'civil rights' attracted considerable criticism at street level. For the freeing up of expression had triggered explosive growth in the publishing industry. The number of print shops operating in Paris quadrupled (from 47 to 223) between 1789 and 1799, and it is likely that more than 600 newspaper titles appeared in the provinces during the same period (Hesse, 1991: 167). Most were ephemeral creations, of course, but there can be no doubt that the size of the reading public was increasing by leaps and bounds. Organs such as Camille Desmoulins's *Révolutions de France et de Brabant* or Marat's *L'Ami du Peuple* maintained a constant, and critical, commentary on the doings of the deputies.

The desire to participate also found expression in the creation of political clubs. Initially, these meeting places were confined to parliamentarians and the bourgeois elite of the great cities, but they, too, expanded down the social scale and into smaller centres of population. The Cordeliers Club began life as an assembly of electors in the Cordeliers district of Paris, and it would become the training ground of many future radicals (Danton, Desmoulins, Santerre, Chaumette, etc.). By 1791, it was allowing 'passive citizens' and even women [**Doc. 13**] into its meetings. However, the most successful forum for the new political sociability was the Society of the Friends of the Constitution, otherwise known as the Jacobin Club. The origins of this body can be found in the informal gatherings of Breton commoner deputies during the opening weeks of the Estates General. It would be dominated by parliamentarians and tended, nearly always, to reflect official, patriotic opinion in successive revolutionary legislatures. Unlike the other Paris clubs, though, the Jacobins replicated themselves across the length and breadth of the country. By 1794, the Jacobin network embraced around 5,500 clubs, all working in close collaboration with the established authorities (Boutier, Boutry and Bonin eds, 1992: 9).

Historians tend to refer to those deputies undeterred in their mission by the spasms of violent and vengeful activity of July and October as the 'patriot party'. But the label is misplaced, for the revolution never at any point generated parties in the modern sense. In any case, the political dynamic of the National Assembly remained fluid for many months. In all probability, most deputies continued to think of themselves in *ancien-régime* terms – as members of 'estates'. That said, though, observers who were actually present at the sessions, such as Lepoutre, did recognise the existence of political affiliations linked, usually, to prominent personalities (Lafayette, Barnave); and they increasingly referred to a group known as the 'blacks' ('les noirs'). In fact, it was the continuing strength of conservative opinion, even after the debates on the veto and the second chamber, which prompted their opponents to organise more effectively. The Jacobin Club, properly speaking, came into being in January 1790 and over the next 12 months or so, the 'patriots' not only became more coherent as a body seeking to control the business of the Assembly, they began to subdivide into moderates and radicals as well. If ever there was a precise moment that 'fixed' the spectrum of opinion, it was probably the vote to abolish noble status and titles on 19 June. Nobles all over the country took stock, pondering whether they had a role to play in the new regime.

Yet all but the extreme right (the 'blacks') and the trickle of ex-Second Estate deputies who now started to absent themselves from the Assembly, remained committed in theory to reaching a political settlement that would endow France with a constitution. Crowd violence in Paris had subsided,

Martial Law: Decree of 21 October 1789 empowering the municipality of Paris to use force against crowds which refused to disperse.

helped no doubt by the much-delayed arrival of the new harvest, and by the **Martial Law** decree (21 October 1789). However, nagging fears about the goodwill of the monarch persisted. Louis retained control of his ministers and, of course, he could delay the implementation of laws by using his suspensive veto. Yet matters were not quite so simple in practice. Ministers tended to defer to the authority of the committees of the Assembly; as for the veto, it had limited value if use was going to incite a popular uprising. Of all the legislation that Louis XVI was persuaded to sanction during the first year of revolution, it is likely that the Civil Constitution of the Clergy gave him greatest pause for thought. When, on 27 November 1790, the National Assembly resolved to enforce compliance by means of an oath which all serving priests would be asked to swear (see Chapter 4), Louis was distraught. A pious man left rudderless by the failure of the Holy See to make known its verdict on the revamping of the Gallican Church, he sanctioned the measure (on 26 December) only to regret his action for the remainder of his life. The decision to try to extricate the royal family from the revolution was probably reached at about this time. However, the gap that was now opening in the project to give France a written constitution only became fully and painfully apparent in April of the following year.

At the start of Holy Week 1791, Louis ordered his carriage to be brought to the Tuileries so that he could go to Saint-Cloud – a palace just outside Paris – and receive the sacraments from a clergyman who had not sworn the oath of allegiance to the as yet unfinished constitution. An unruly crowd prevented him from going, although Lafayette, the commander of the Paris National Guard, offered to force a passage. Apart from revealing the equivocal attitude of the monarch for all to see, the Saint-Cloud affair served notice on Barnave and the other 'patriot' deputies that the settlement towards which they had been working might very well collapse under its own weight. A constitution without a monarch as its chief fixture and adornment was not to be contemplated. Yet some sections of radical opinion in the capital appeared to be pushing in this direction. Moreover, they could expect to get some support from the intransigent deputies of the extreme right, who scarcely bothered to conceal their hope that the experiment in constitutional monarchy would not prove successful. By the spring of 1791, the political horizon no longer seemed as trouble-free as it had appeared 12 months earlier, therefore. Parisians no longer worshipped the very ground on which Lafayette stood, for a national guard made up mainly of 'active citizens' was losing the close link with ordinary people that had attended its creation. And in the country at large, the oath legislation was driving a wedge into the very heart of the nation. Barnave and his political allies took note and redoubled their efforts to complete the constitution.

4

The Failure of Consensus, 1791–92

fter two years of continuous effort, the deputies were weary and ready to go home. Pierre-François Lepoutre had not once been back to his farm near Lille since arriving in Versailles to attend the Estates General in the spring of 1789. Its management was entirely in the hands of his wife, whom he had only seen twice during that period, although they exchanged letters every five or six days. Like everyone else, he wanted to bring the revolution to a satisfactory conclusion. Why, then, does the story not end on 14 September 1791, when Louis XVI, King of the French, swore a solemn oath to uphold the constitution? On receiving the news of his acceptance, Madame Lepoutre wept tears of joy and relief, describing the event as 'a knock-out blow for aristocrats' (Jessenne and Le May eds, 1998: 523). Festivities took place in the village in common with localities all over France (Plate 4). The revolution did not end in September 1791 for the simple reason that the consensus enshrined in the constitution so laboriously negotiated by the National Assembly was more apparent than real. As we shall see, a significant number of those enjoying privileges under the *ancien régime* had opted out by this date, the revolutionaries themselves had fallen into disarray, and the king's own acceptance of the transition from absolute to constitutional monarchy was patently insincere.

THE FLIGHT AND ITS AFTERMATH

The departure of the royal family from the Palace of the Tuileries in the centre of Paris during the night of 20–21 June 1791 caught everyone unawares, except for those closely involved in the preparations. This is surprising in view of the many months of planning that had taken place, the logistics of the operation, and the fact that the king kept changing his mind at the last moment. Louis left behind a *déclaration* or manifesto, written in his own hand, stating his objections to the revolution as it had unfolded since June 1789. Whilst not a plea for a return to the *ancien régime*, it reads nonetheless as a pretty uncompromising statement [**Doc. 12**]. It is uncertain whether the travelling party intended actually to cross the frontier into the Austrian Netherlands, because they were recognised and stopped in the little town of Varennes, some 35 miles short. The king would claim that he was heading for the royal citadel of Montmédy.

For the leading 'patriot' deputies in the Assembly, who were close to putting the finishing touches to the constitution, the flight was extremely bad news. However, their nerve held: the legislature took over the executive functions of government, placed the nation in a state of defensive readiness, and word was circulated that the king had been 'kidnapped'. This fiction proved very convenient when the king and the queen were found and brought back to Paris some four days later. Lepoutre was among the crowds of Parisians who watched their carriage go past. Not a word was uttered, not a hat removed. On his return, Louis was suspended from office rather than dethroned without further ado – a clear indication that the deputies under the leadership of Barnave were working for a negotiated solution to the crisis. Yet the calm deliberation of the Assembly contrasted starkly with the turmoil and apprehension in the clubs and in the radical press. Moreover, many aristocratic army officers serving on the frontiers had chosen this as the moment to became **émigrés**, as had the Comte de Provence, the king's younger brother and future Louis XVIII. Everyone was expecting a war of intervention, with Leopold II of Austria – the brother of Marie-Antoinette – at its head.

In fact, war was very unlikely at this stage, although few in France could have known this. Leopold was a reformer, not a crusader, and took the view that his brother-in-law should strike the best deal he could secure in the circumstances. This was also the view of Barnave, Adrien Duport, Alexandre de Lameth (the so-called Triumvirate) and their parliamentary allies; and on 15 July they induced the Assembly to exonerate Louis and to blame unidentified others for his 'abduction'. Desperate to achieve a political settlement, they had been negotiating secretly with the queen and had offered to revise the constitution in a sense more favourable to the monarch if she would prevail on her brother, the Emperor, to secure international recognition for the transformation of France since 1789. Barnave put the issue neatly in a rhetorical question to his fellow deputies: 'Are we going to finish the revolution, or are we going to begin it afresh?' (Jessenne and Le May eds, 1998: 491). The issue was not as clear-cut at street level, or in the villages, though. For all his hesitations, the monarch was viewed as the cornerstone of the new regime and confidence in him had plunged, leaving public opinion rudderless. In Paris, radical journalists proceeded to mount a

émigrés: Individuals opposed to the revolution who left France and joined the counter-revolution.

campaign against the *raison d'état* solution of reinstating Louis following acceptance of the constitution, although they scarcely had a better set of alternatives to offer. In Caen, a statue of the king was overturned by angry citizens.

Plainly, the flight of the king had aggravated tensions within the patriot camp that had been growing since the start of the year, but the situation was by no means irretrievable. Even in the cockpit of the revolution – Paris – the views of ordinary people were not yet sharply etched (Andress, 2000: 137, 166, 223). What changed the face of politics as far as firm supporters of the revolution were concerned was the so-called massacre perpetrated in the Champ de Mars on 17 July 1791. A noisy, if unfocused, barracking of the deputies had been in progress since the start of the month, but it gained in intensity as the news came through that the Assembly was preparing to rein-state Louis, as though his dereliction of duty had been a mere trifle. Hostile petitions and demonstrations were organised in which the Cordeliers Club played a major role; however, the protestors displayed little unity of purpose. Should the king's political fate be determined by popular referendum? Should a regency be declared under the Duke of Orleans – a republic even? In the event, it was the petition-signing ceremony organised by the Cordeliers for 17 July that caused the reinstatement crisis to detonate. Bloodshed that morning (the lynching and beheading of two men found hiding under the platform) provided the authorities with the pretext to intervene and the municipality ordered the proclamation of Martial Law. Under Lafayette's command and in the presence of the mayor of Paris, Jean-Sylvain Bailly, the national guard fired volleys of shots into the crowd of petitioners when they failed to disperse. Perhaps as many as 50 were killed.

If the spilling of blood in the Champ de Mars had not been premeditated, there can be little doubt that the majority of the deputies had willed the confrontation. A trial of strength was felt to be necessary in order to clear the air and prepare the way for an eleventh-hour revision of the constitution. In the aftermath, the infrastructure of a street-level republicanism that dared not speak its name was dismantled. Danton fled to England, Desmoulins, Santerre and other leading lights of the Cordeliers were arrested, and Marat temporarily disappeared following the seizure of the presses on which *L'Ami du peuple* was printed. Even the survival of the Jacobin Club was placed in jeopardy as a large number of its more moderate members – including Barnave – withdrew to another meeting place (the former monastery of the Feuillants).

Yet the crisis had gravely weakened the staunchest parliamentary friends of the revolution as well, for the blood shed by the national guard, supposedly a pillar of the new order, now became a festering source of division [Doc. 13]. On the other hand, it could be argued that a pre-emptive strike by the Great Powers had been averted and that the conditions now existed for an orderly revision of the constitution. Yet war had never been a serious prospect, and the rebalancing of the constitution never took place. Why not? Because the Feuillant moderates could not win a cross-party vote to achieve anything substantial. For this they needed the support of the alienated block of strongly royalist deputies, who no longer bothered to participate in the life of the Assembly. Indeed, the intransigents among them could see no advantage whatsoever in helping to turn the country into a conservative constitutional monarchy. What about Louis himself? In theory, he could have rejected the constitution when it was finally submitted to him on 13 September, but, had he done so, the only alternative would have been abdication.

MANAGING THE NEW REGIME

With the acceptance by Louis XVI of the constitution, the deputies' task came to an end. They spent the last few days of September settling outstanding business, which included a generous recompense to the owner of the covered tennis court in Versailles that had sheltered the Third Estate in its hour of need. They also passed an amnesty law applicable to all men and women who had been indicted for riot since May 1788. Then, on 30 September 1791, the president pronounced the words: 'The National Constituent Assembly declares that its mission is fulfilled and its sessions are over' (Jones, 1995: 237). The transition to constitutional monarchy was now complete, on paper at least. Since the deputies had voted a 'self-denying' decree, making it unlawful to prolong themselves in office, the new men who gathered for the opening session of the Legislative Assembly on 1 October were just that. Moreover, their powers would be circumscribed by a constitutional text that they were not allowed to alter. The revolution had gone on longer than anyone had expected, but it was now over. All that remained was the routine business of legislation; the managing of the new regime. Of course, this cosy allocation of roles and responsibilities rested on a fallacy, as all French men and women with a modicum of political awareness must have understood. The constitution had *not* been achieved consensually, and a great deal of unfinished business was waiting in the wings. Far from being 'over', the revolution was only just beginning or, as one of the king's advisors put it, 'the storms in store for us will be far greater than those we have experienced' (Bacourt ed., 1851: vol. 3, 194).

The individuals elected to seats in the Legislative Assembly may have been new to the hot-house world of Paris, but they were not political novices. Most had served an apprenticeship in local government, which was usually how they had come to the notice of the voters in the first place. Unsurprisingly, they were nearly all drawn from the ranks of the old Third Estate. Only about 5 per cent (26 clerics and 20 ex-nobles) hailed from the former privileged orders. By profession, the majority were small-town attorneys or barristers, although a sprinkling of bankers, merchants and military men had been chosen as well. In effect, they constituted the upper and most visible stratum of a 'revolutionary class-in-the-making' which had its roots in the well-to-do peasants and tenant farmers of country parishes, and in the notaries, ex-seigneurial officials and small-time professionals (doctors, barber-surgeons, land surveyors, teachers, millers, etc.) who congregated in every market town. They were politically opaque on arrival in Paris and mostly determined to remain so. Whereas 169 of the new deputies swiftly joined the Feuillant Club (to which the Triumvirate, as out-of-office politicians, had retreated) and 51 joined the Jacobins, the majority (547) tried to steer clear of the loose alignments spawned by the Flight and the Champ de Mars affair. Courtiers such as the Comte de Lamarck heaped scorn upon these hand-me-down revolutionaries: 'Nineteen-twentieths of the members of this legislature', he commented to the Austrian ambassador, 'are equipped with nothing but clogs and umbrellas' (Bacourt ed., 1851: vol. 3, 246).

The desire to make a name for themselves and the lack of seasoned leadership may help to explain why the deputies of the Legislative Assembly were so willing to throw political caution to the winds. In three main policy areas they sailed cheerfully into the eye of the storm, losing the 1791 Constitution on the way and risking the very survival of the revolution in the process. It is true that the split in the constitutional Church that the oath legislation of November 1790 had provoked would have required real statesmanship to mend. Yet there had been signs in the spring that the Triumvirate had recognised the need for a more conciliatory approach to 'non-jurors' – that is to say, clergymen who were refusing to swear the oath. However, the new deputies were vulnerable to pressure from their former colleagues in the Department and District administrations, and the message they received was stark. Only if the activities of the non-jurors were curbed could the Civil Constitution of the Clergy be made to work. Accordingly, a law of 29 November imposed a fresh (albeit purely political) oath, with sanctions for those who failed to comply. Non-jurors lost the right to hold their own services in church buildings and their pension entitlements. They were also liable to municipal surveillance, a procedure that could result in expulsion from their homes in extreme cases of religious infighting. The Assembly stopped short of ordering the imprisonment of non-jurors. Nevertheless, the king still used his suspensive veto to block the measure.

The mounting hostility to the refractory clergy was undoubtedly linked to the suspicion that dissident priests might very well become aiders and abetters of counter-revolution. In October and November, the deputies worked themselves into a fury on the subject of those French men and women who had fled the revolution. It is true that the news of the king's acceptance of the constitution had precipitated a fresh wave of departures, but it required a fertile imagination to suppose that *émigré* 'armies' represented a serious threat. Without Great Power support, the *émigrés* were powerless, and neither Leopold II of Austria nor Frederick William II of Prussia were at this stage prepared to commit troops to an intervention in France, notwithstanding the declaration at **Pillnitz** (27 August 1791). Still, the rhetoric of national solidarity in response to a perceived threat of invasion had a good deal of populist appeal and, on 31 October, the Assembly warned the Comte de Provence that he would lose his right of succession to the throne if he did not return to France within three months. A few days later, all *émigrés* were put on notice that they risked expropriation and denunciation as conspirators if they remained outside the country beyond the end of the year. Even firm patriots such as Nicolas Ruault, editor of *Le Moniteur* newspaper, thought these measures rather draconian, and, in any case, they were vetoed by the monarch.

Declaration of Pillnitz: The statement jointly issued on 27 August 1791 by the Habsburg Emperor and the King of Prussia urging the Powers to intervene in support of Louis XVI.

The third and most blatant sphere in which the deputies of the Legislative Assembly gambled with the nation's fortunes was that of foreign policy. Although the schism in the Church and the posturings of the *émigrés* were irritants, there was nothing inevitable about the recourse to armed conflict. Britain remained neutral, and the continental powers were far more preoccupied with events in eastern Europe (the fates of Turkey and Poland) than with the embarrassments of the King of France. As for the revolutionaries, they had proclaimed their pacific intentions and renounced the use of force for the purposes of conquest in May 1790. The new diplomacy of self-determination (the notion that the rights of peoples overrode those of states) was still in its infancy. It would be invoked in September 1791 as a partial justification for French annexation of the two papal enclaves of Avignon and the Comtat Venaissin, but the strident and bellicose ideology of nationalism still lay in the future.

What changed, then, during the winter of 1791–92? Most accounts emphasise the central role played by the deputies themselves in the decision-making process that led to war, and in this regard it is helpful to recall the circumstances that brought the Legislative Assembly into being. Because of the 'self-denying' decree, there could be no carrying over of accumulated parliamentary wisdom from one legislature to the next. All the deputies who had become household names while the new France was being forged were now out of office. The caucus built up by Barnave (latterly called the

Feuillants) were on the sidelines and scarcely able to control events; likewise, Lafayette and his allies. Even the democrats were in tactical disarray. The best-known parliamentary radicals – Maximilien Robespierre and Jérôme Pétion – had been saluted by the Paris crowd as they exited the National Assembly. But after 30 September, they too were confined to journalism and the oratorical platform provided by the Jacobin Club. They were replaced on the rostrum by new men, such as Jacques-Pierre Brissot, François Chabot and Pierre Vergniaud, who offered demagogic leadership and forthright policies that would give the Assembly the chance of escaping from the shadow of its illustrious predecessor.

According to Brissot and his allies (who would be known as the Girondins in the subsequent legislature), a policy of squaring up to the Emperor in the knowledge that it would unleash hostilities offered the prospect of settling the *émigré* issue once and for all. More important, though, were three concrete advantages that such a policy might very well deliver. First and foremost, the king would be forced to take sides, thereby resolving the ambiguity at the heart of the constitution. Second, a war of liberation would release the oppressed peoples of Europe from the twin yokes of feudalism and absolutism. Third, a war would reinvigorate an economy ailing from unemployment and the inflationary effects of overreliance on the *assignat*. All of these supposed advantages were predicated on the conviction that war would be fought on foreign territory and would result in a victory for the armies of revolutionary France, of course.

Others begged to differ. The Feuillants saw clearly that any descent into hostilities would destroy the constitution they had laboured long and hard to bring into being. Though he had precious little confidence in the men of 1789 (Barnave, the Lameth brothers, Lafayette, etc.), Robespierre came to agree with them. In a series of speeches between mid-December and the end of January, he subjected Brissot's blithe foreign policy assurances to relentless scrutiny. A war might very well resolve the king's divided loyalties, but who was to say that the revolution would be the gainer thereby? An imperfect constitution was better than no constitution at all. A war, he continued, would create opportunities for powerful generals to intervene (an oblique reference to Lafayette, who had resigned as commander of the Paris National Guard and taken up a military post on the eastern border). Finally, and in a memorable phrase, he pointed out that no one liked 'armed missionaries' (Hampson, 1974: 100) – a reproof to Brissot's confident prediction that French troops would be welcomed with open arms once they had crossed the Rhine. Reasonable and prophetic though these arguments were, Robespierre found himself in a minority even in the Jacobin Club. As for the deputies, they quickly rallied to a policy that provided an opportunity to leave their mark on history.

The harvest of 1791 had been poor, unlike that of 1790, and in Paris basic food prices began to rise again from the month of November onwards. However, it was the interruption in the supply of semi-luxuries (coffee, sugar) that triggered the first crowd disturbances. Ever since the summer, the plantations on the French Caribbean island of Saint-Domingue had been convulsed by a slave revolt. The consequence was a sharp increase in prices and, by mid-January 1791, repeated invasions of grocers' shops in order to commandeer the commodities in question and sell them off at a 'fair' price (*taxation populaire*). The rioting broke out again in February and observers noted particularly the leading role played by women drawn from the *faubourgs* of Saint-Antoine and Saint-Marcel, to the east and south-east of the city. The disturbances served notice on the deputies that the Paris 'crowd' was on an active footing once more, and could easily be politicised by problems of provisioning and food supply. In fact, ordinary Parisians by no means confined their activism to matters of daily susbsistence. In March, Pauline Léon, the daughter of a chocolate manufacturer, read out a petition before the Assembly, calling for the right of women to organise their own national guard units. The situation was becoming just as precarious in the country-side around the capital, and also in the south of the country. Large-scale peasant disturbances broke out in the Beauce that same month, resulting in the death of the mayor of Etampes at the hands of a rioting crowd when he refused to place controls on bread prices. In the south-west, the prime source of frustration was the failure to legislate a clean break with the seigneurial regime, as we have seen. Attacks on chateaux resumed, prompting Georges Couthon – an invalid radical lawyer, elected in September – to warn his fellow deputies that the revolution was running the risk of forfeiting the support of the rural masses.

But all eyes in the capital were fixed on the prospect of war. Even the disturbances occasioned by shortages and the declining value of the *assignat* died down as the event approached. For Robespierre and his tiny band of suspicious democrats (Couthon, Danton, Desmoulins, Billaud-Varenne, etc.) the dangers inherent in Brissot's reckless sabre-rattling were demonstrated by the fact that the king's ministers, and also the Court, had swung in favour of war. The Comte de Narbonne, a distinguished career soldier who had been appointed Minister of War in December 1791, probably hoped that a military promenade in the Rhineland would bring the generals to the fore. They could then use their power to enforce an alteration in the trajectory of the revolution in a manner more favourable to the monarch. The Court, by contrast, was desperate for a military intervention on almost any terms, even one led by the *émigrés*. Louis wrote personally to Frederick William II of Prussia to ask for help, and Marie-Antoinette urged her brother to intervene. Evidence of counter-revolutionary plotting inside the country was also

faubourgs: Working-class neighbourhoods on the periphery of the capital.

coming to light, with the southern uplands of the Massif Central and the west the main theatres of unrest at this stage. The deputies riposted, on 9 February, with the first move towards the seizure of *émigré* property. The sudden and unexpected death of the Habsburg Emperor on 1 March removed one of the final impediments to the outbreak of hostilities, particularly when the king dismissed his remaining Feuillant ministers and replaced them with a cabinet of allies of the Brissotins (Dumouriez, Clavière, Roland, Servan, etc.) instead. The new Minister of Foreign Affairs, Dumouriez, was a professional soldier with a taste for politics – exactly the breed which Robespierre so distrusted. On 20 April 1792, the Assembly voted overwhelmingly, and in the presence of Louis XVI, to declare war on Austria.

THE FALL OF THE MONARCHY

As Louis Becquey – one of the few deputies to vote against the motion for war – predicted would happen, the constitutional settlement reached only seven months earlier now began to unravel at alarming speed. Although Britain, Holland and Spain would not intervene in the conflict until the following year, France was diplomatically isolated. Prussia could not be detached from Austria, and Marie-Antoinette had ensured that Dumouriez's plans for a thrust into the Belgian provinces were well known in Vienna. As Robespierre had anticipated, France's state of military preparedness left much to be desired, and the country appeared to have been thrown on the mercy of ambitious generals.

What no one anticipated, however, was the extent to which war would alter the social contract on which the revolution had rested until this point. If the regenerated nation was about to ask ordinary French men to make a blood sacrifice, something would have to be offered in return. From the spring of 1792, fictions such as the active/passive distinction that were designed to keep the 'people' at arm's length began to look out of place. So, too, did the approach to government that concentrated on matters of 'high politics' to the exclusion of everyday concerns such as food shortages and hoarding, inflation, taxation and land hunger. Ordinary Parisians were already democratising the lower-level institutions of local government (the Sections; the national guard), and the crisis of the summer would demonstrate that they alone possessed the necessary energy to move the revolution forward. The task facing the Brissotins was how to adjust to these new realities, and how to keep up with events.

To judge from the letters of the printer-publisher Nicolas Ruault to his brother, the first reports of the military reverses around Lille and

Valenciennes began to filter back to the capital in the early days of May. As one of the institutions most closely identified with the *ancien régime*, the army had found it particularly difficult to adjust to the values of the revolution. There had been violent mutinies in several parts of the kingdom and, by the start of 1792, about a third of the officer corps had resigned. Many were nobles, of course, who had not merely resigned but emigrated. Ruault would pass on two more scraps of relevant information: the Flemings had not risen, as expected, to welcome the French forces, and Lafayette's army encamped at Metz had neither advanced nor retreated. Despite the accusations levelled at this general, he felt it necessary to add: 'I am far from believing [him] a traitor' (Ruault, 1976: 284). Nevertheless, the sight of aristocratic officers defecting en masse, and the realisation that French troop movements had been betrayed, caused accusations of treachery to fly in all directions. Whilst calling for volunteers to be rushed to the front, the deputies lashed out with punitive measures against non-oath-swearing priests and the royal bodyguard. In addition, they summoned 20,000 provincial national guardsmen – known as *fédérés* – to Paris in order to protect the Assembly, whether from the threat of a *coup* or the threat of an armed uprising of the Sections.

The 48 Sections were the municipal subdivisions of the capital that had replaced the 60 electoral districts whose existence had been formally recognised in 1790. Each possessed a deliberative body and organs of control and repression, and although the political complexion of the Sections tended to vary, some were becoming redoubtable vehicles for popular militancy. Ruault commented in February that the well-to-do were withdrawing from the assemblies of the Sections, leaving the field of action open to workmen and artisans. As a result, the socio-economic undertow of popular militancy began to come to the surface. There were calls for corn prices to be fixed (the Maximum) in both Paris and Lyons; and in May Jacques Roux, a future

enragés: The pejorative label attached to militants in the Sections who called for government action to legislate the 'popular programme'.

spokesman for the *enragés*, demanded that hoarding be punishable by death. It is true that Dr Guillotin's new beheading machine had been brought into service the previous month. Although the apparatus was impressive to look at, Palloy reported that Parisians found its action rather too quick compared with hanging by the neck.

With help apparently at hand, the king took the risk of withholding his consent to the deportation legislation directed against non-jurors and the proposal for a *fédéré* encampment. In fact, he dismissed most of his Brissotin ministers on 13 June – a move that finally persuaded Ruault to abandon all illusion and to conclude that a mixed constitution was unattainable. Lafayette's violent letter of denunciation aimed at the Jacobin Club shattered another illusion, and the scene was now set for the fall of the monarchy – unless the Austrians and the Prussians reached Paris first. A massive, broad-based demonstration organised by the militants of the eastern Sections on 20 June, and no doubt aided by the Brissotins who wanted to get themselves back into power, failed to sway Louis. He agreed to don the red bonnet of liberty that had become the fashion throughout the capital, but refused to withdraw his veto. Eventually, Pétion, the mayor, came to the rescue and ordered that the demonstrators be cleared from the Tuileries Palace. The clock of insurrection was ticking, though, and everyone looked to the deputies of the Legislative Assembly for a lead. Yet the deputies were paralysed by constitutional scruples and turned a deaf ear to the calls for the king to abdicate. To be sure, with the Court on one side and the Sections on the other, they had very little room in which to manoeuvre. Exasperated, Lafayette returned to Paris in the hope of galvanising the Assembly into taking action against the Jacobin Club and the street-level militants who had organised the *journée* of 20 June. But if many of the deputies and a large swathe of the national guard were alarmed at the direction of events, they were even more alarmed by the prospect of military dictatorship. He would return to his army and, a week after the fall of the house of Bourbon, defect to the Austrians.

journée: Literally, 'day'. The occasion of a popular demonstration or uprising.

The insurrection that finally produced the dethronement of Louis XVI could have happened at any point from late July onwards. The distinction between 'active' and 'passive' citizenship was collapsing, the *fédérés* were arriving in droves, irrespective of the royal veto, and individuals who are hard to identify were making plans for an uprising. The only uncertain factors lay at the higher organisational level: what roles, if any, would the Brissotin deputies play, radical figureheads such as Robespierre and Marat, and Pétion, the mayor of Paris? By the end of that month, nearly all of the Sections had expressed an opinion in favour of abdication, whether by legislative action or by physical force. An abortive call to arms occurred on the night of 26–27 July, and there was another false start on the night of 4–5 August. Threats issued by the commander-in-chief of the advancing Austro-Prussian forces (the so-called Brunswick Manifesto) served only to make matters worse, and, on 6 August, a meeting of *fédéré* and Sectional chiefs warned the Assembly of what lay in store if it did not act.

The deputies' reluctance even to bring proceedings against Lafayette proved to be the last straw. During the night of 9–10 August, alarm bells were rung all over Paris and delegates from the Sections converged on the Hôtel de Ville, where they ousted the legally constituted municipality [**Doc. 14**]. Mayor Pétion was confined to his room. This insurrectionary General Staff then directed the battalions of national guardsmen towards the Tuileries Palace, which was defended by Swiss troops, an assortment of nobles and a large body of national guardsmen drawn from the more affluent Sections of western Paris. The king and the queen sought safety in the chamber of the Legislative Assembly before the fighting started. By 11.30 on the morning of 10 August, it was all over. Several hundred assailants and defenders were killed in the exchanges of gunfire, and perhaps as many as 600 Swiss guardsmen were massacred subsequently.

The *journée* of 10 August 1792 amounted to a second revolution, as Ruault, writing to his brother, was at pains to emphasise. It marked the end of the experiment with constitutional monarchy; it marked the beginnings of partnership government between the bourgeois elite of the old Third Estate, who had inherited power in 1789, and the people; and, in the view of many historians, it signalled the onset of the Terror. It is true that, for the next six weeks, France scarcely had a properly constituted government. Politically bankrupt, the Legislative Assembly largely gave up any pretence of independence and awaited its replacement. Two days after his second flight from the Tuileries, Louis was placed in detention, together with his queen and their two surviving children. The ever-obliging handyman of the revolution, Palloy, was called in – first to put out the fires still raging in the palace, and then to fit up central heating in the gloomy Temple prison, so as to provide the royal family with a modicum of physical comfort. Louis's next move would be to the scaffold. In the capital, meanwhile, nearly everyone accepted the inevitability of the abolition of the monarchy and the proclamation of a republic, but Ruault spoke for many when he asked himself: 'Are we fit, are we worthy enough to be republicans?' (Ruault, 1976: 303). For most educated French men, the idea of a republic could scarcely be grasped outside the pages of classical authors.

Partnership with the people took two forms: the presence of the people's spokesmen in government and the issuing of long-overdue legislation that addressed the hopes and fears of ordinary town and country dwellers. In the aftermath of the uprising, the Insurrectionary Commune, as the municipal body representing the Sections was known, could see no reason why it should play second fiddle to an Assembly which had been elected indirectly and by 'active' citizens alone. For six long weeks, therefore, it held power alongside an interim executive body in which Danton, playing the role of Minister of Justice, was the moving force. Only when new deputies had been chosen on the basis of universal manhood suffrage would the municipal authorities of Paris return, reluctantly, to their normal role. Chastened by the experience of 10 August, the deputies dutifully passed ameliorative legislation under the watchful gaze of the Commune. Virtually all outstanding feudal dues were now abolished without compensation, and orders were given for the partition of common land and the sale of *émigré* property in small and more easily affordable parcels. The responsibility for the registration of births, deaths and marriages passed from the clergy to the municipalities and, on 20 September, a law was passed to facilitate divorce by mutual consent (Phillips, 1981: 11–12). There was also some easing on the contentious question of the food supply and price controls, although even the most radical deputies and their allies in the clubs were not prepared at this stage to give up the principle of liberty in the economic sphere.

In his letter of 28 August 1792, Ruault pondered the implications of the fact that the first guillotinings on a charge of 'royalism' pure and simple had just taken place. There can be little doubt that the revolution crossed a civil rights threshold during that summer. Words like 'suspect' and 'aristocrat', or indeed 'royalist', had acquired connotations of subversion that would have made very little sense back in 1789 or 1790. Guilt by association, or by social category, was starting to become acceptable. Hundreds of Swiss defenders had been killed *after* the fighting on 10 August – that is to say, in acts of reprisal and public vengeance. The same would happen again in Paris (and several provincial towns) in early September, as murder squads went around the prisons and systematically emptied them of their 'political' prisoners (nobles, non-oath-swearing priests, alleged counter-revolutionaries, etc.). European governments were appalled by these deeds; more so even than by the dethronement of King Louis. As for Ruault, he told his brother on 8 September that he had stepped in puddles of human blood in the courtyard of the former abbey of Saint-Germain.

CITIZENSHIP IN THE COLONIES

Bourbon France had colonies in both the Caribbean and the Indian Ocean. They were exploited using slave labour on plantations which produced tropical foodstuffs (sugar, coffee, spices) for European consumers, or supplies for passing vessels. In the case of the Caribbean possessions (principally Saint-Domingue, Guadeloupe, Martinique and French Guyane), the bulk of the workforce consisted of enslaved blacks, shipped from ports on the west coast of Africa, and their descendants. Saint-Domingue (the western third of the island of Hispaniola), which Spain had ceded to France in 1697, was the jewel in this colonial crown. In the second half of the eighteenth century, it was the source of half of the sugar and coffee traded in Europe and was the western world's most valuable piece of real estate. Although they were less lucrative possessions, France would cling to Guadeloupe and Martinique as well, giving up the whole of the Canadian province of Quebec at the conclusion of the Seven Years War in 1763, in order to bring to an end the British occupation of these islands.

Since Saint-Domingue would emerge from the revolutionary cycle as the independent black republic of Haiti, it is here that we need to concentrate our attention (see Map 3). This extraordinary development would come to pass in 1804 and it has been described as one of the events that has defined the modern world (Popkin, 2007: 1). By 1789, the fertile coastal plain and lower mountain slopes were covered with plantations which necessitated the importation of around 30,000 slaves each year in order to maintain and expand production. The total population of the colony by this date probably amounted to a little over half a million (523,000), of whom 89 per cent were slaves, about 6 per cent whites and 5 per cent mulattoes (*gens de couleur*). The mulattoes were an intermediate population between the free whites and the enslaved majority. Although of African descent for the most part, they were legally free, often educated and fluent in French. In fact, many had become land owners, and some owned slaves in their own right. Yet they suffered disabilities *vis-à-vis* the whites and were discriminated against even before revolution broke out in the metropole. The islands of Guadeloupe and Martinique were much smaller, but, with tiny white populations, their racial make-up was not dissimilar to that of Saint-Domingue. Guyane, by contrast, was thinly inhabited, yet still 80 per cent enslaved.

gens de couleur: Literally, 'people of colour'. The free blacks in France's Caribbean territories.

Contrary to what we might expect, Enlightenment authors did not pay much attention to the issue of colonial slavery. This, despite the fact they acknowledged the iniquities of serfdom as a form of human bondage in the old world, and were attempting actively to secure the recognition of civil rights on the continent of Europe. Hence the paradox: the institution of slavery and the slave-based economic system pioneered in the Caribbean were being consolidated at a time when freedom had become a watchword not only of *philosophes*, but of reform-minded government ministers as well. This paradox was not unique to France, of course. Britain and Spain and Portugal also possessed colonial empires which were substantially reliant on slave labour. However, in Britain domestic public opinion had been sensitised to the issue of slavery in the late 1770s, and, within a few years, campaigns to boycott the consumption of sugar were afoot. We find nothing of the sort in *ancien-régime* France. In fact, the Society of Friends of the Blacks, founded by the future revolutionary politician Jean-Pierre Brissot, did not come into being until the start of 1788 and was chiefly inspired by the activities of the British abolitionists.

philosophes: Literally, 'philosophers'. The term is used to describe free-thinking intellectuals and writers in the eighteenth century.

The debate about slavery only became a matter for practical politics in France as a consequence of the calling of the Estates-General. Nevertheless, it would raise fundamental questions about what citizenship meant under the new order. Reports of what was happening in the metropole tended to reach the Caribbean with a delay of some three months and the first issue to arise was one of representation. Should the colonies be represented by deputies of their own and, if so, who exactly was entitled to a political presence in Versailles (or Paris) – the whites only, or the scarcely less numerous *gens de couleur* as well? However, nearly simultaneous rumours had begun to circulate on the island of Martinique that outright abolition of slavery had been proclaimed by the King of France in the Estates General. This was not true, nor had the deputies who had refashioned themselves into a National Assembly any intention of taking this step. Article one of the Declaration of the Rights of Man and of Citizens proclaiming that 'Men are born, and always continue, free, and equal in respect of their rights,' was never intended to apply to the slave population, and the session of 4 August 1789 which dismantled so many features of the *ancien régime* had nothing to say about slavery either. However, a political consensus which seemed secure in Paris looked anything but that on the spot. The tiny white minorities subdivided into supporters and opponents of the changes being ushered in, whilst the mulattoes spotted an opportunity in the rhetoric of revolution to obtain citizenship for themselves, if not for the enslaved majority.

After all, the rhetoric of revolution applied universally, did it not? The subordinate groups in France's colonies were not alone in supposing that laws and manifestos should be taken at face value. After 4 August 1789, French peasants drew the conclusion that the feudal regime had been entirely abolished, and for entirely plausible reasons, too. The deputies of the National Assembly might be certain in their own minds about the limits attaching to their policies, but these still had to be interpreted by officials on the ground. When the tricolour cockade reached Guadeloupe by ship in September 1789, it was adopted with enthusiasm by the young. After some expressions of misgivings by the colonial authorities, the mulattoes were *not* prevented from wearing this emblem of liberty. However, the governor warned of severe penalties if the slave population were to do the same. It is fair to say that, in Paris, the important role which free people of colour played in the colonies was not well understood and, of course, the white planters had little interest in enlightening the parliamentarians. Those who were prepared to accept the revolution nonetheless argued that its legislation did not apply to the internal arrangements which had grown up in the colonies.

The confusion and heat generated whenever the National and Legislative Assemblies proceeded to debate colonial issues are scarcely to be wondered at, therefore. Throughout 1790, the campaign by the mulattoes to widen the definition of citizenship produced contradictory results in Paris and was followed by a brief uprising in Saint-Domingue at the end of the year. Then, in May 1791, a partial concession of civil and political rights to free blacks passed through the Assembly in the teeth of opposition from white colonists and their supporters. However, this rather mealy-mouthed acknowledge-ment that race was not, after all, a fundamental barrier to French citizenship did not hold for long. The Saint-Domingue planter lobby managed to obtain the repeal of the law in the dying days of the National Assembly

(24 September 1791). Only in April of the following year was this internecine struggle between the 'free' finally resolved with the granting of full rights to all *gens de couleur*. By this stage, though, the context had completely altered because an insurrection of the enslaved majority was under way in Saint-Domingue and the white planters had begun to ask the British for assistance. This massive slave revolt began in August 1791, was known about in the metropole by the start of November, and was producing shortages in the grocery shops of Paris early the following year, as we have seen. Although the insurgents were not initially fired with a vision of liberation, it was this long struggle which finally persuaded the revolutionaries to emancipate the majority black population on 4 February 1794, with immediate and unconditional effect. A product of the struggle with Britain and royalism in the Caribbean, the decree owed more to *realpolitik* than to the undiluted application of Enlightenment reason, and it was never applied to the colonies in the Indian Ocean.

5

War and Terror, 1792–94

The deputies of the Legislative Assembly concluded their business on 20 September 1792, all too aware that they had failed to steer the revolution into calmer waters. Having held power – ingloriously – for barely 12 months, most of them would be relegated to the footnotes of history. Instead, the revolution was heading into uncharted waters on which few vessels of state had sailed before. But at least there no longer existed any constitutional obstacle to prevent the most experienced and talented deputies and former deputies from assembling on the bridge. The National Convention, as the new legislature was called, would contain a large contingent of representatives (269) who had sat before, whether in the first or the second legislature. Thus, Robespierre, Pétion, Sieyès, François Buzot, Philippe-Antoine Merlin de Douai and Jean-François Reubell, to name only those already embarked upon significant careers, returned to office, while the mandates of Brissot, Vergniaud and Couthon were renewed without interruption. On the benches of the old royal riding school, which had served as the chamber since November 1789, they were joined by men who had yet to become national and international figures: the young ex-nobleman, Antoine Saint-Just; Georges Danton, who had resigned as a minister; Camille Desmoulins and Jean-Paul Marat, the fiery street-level journalists; Fabre d'Eglantine and Collot d'Herbois, both dramatists; and Billaud-Varenne. But would these individuals be able to work together? Many of those named had been chosen by the electorate of Paris, and their past went ahead of them, so to speak. Some were Cordeliers militants who had graduated to the Jacobin Club; a few were even suspected of involvement in the prison massacres which had taken place earlier in the month. How would they respond to the pressures for partnership in government? The democratisation of public life that was now under way implied a radical revision of policy objectives. Then there was the question of 'terror': should it be employed solely as a means of preserving the nation from its growing list of enemies, or as a tool with which to forge a new and purer society?

A JACOBIN REPUBLIC

The decision to turn France into a republic was taken in about a quarter of an hour at the inaugural session of the National Convention, when most of the deputies were still making their way towards the capital. We can assume that the Paris electoral delegation – Jacobin stalwarts almost to a man – played the major role, although there is no reason to suppose that Brissot and his close allies were opposed to the move. All of the contenders for power were members of the Jacobin Club at this stage, in any case, and it would be several months before sharply defined political groupings emerged in the Convention.

After the alarums of early September, the tide of war had shifted dramatically in favour of the Brissotins. Just as the deputies were assembling, Generals Kellermann and Dumouriez halted the Prussian advance at Valmy a few miles to the west of Sainte-Menehould. Since the enemy chose to withdraw, the French advanced and, by the end of October, Dumouriez was able to cross over the border into the Austrian Netherlands, while General Custine in the east proceeded to occupy the Rhineland. At Jemappes, an infinitely greater battle was fought – and won – on 6 November, that threw open Belgium and even the Netherlands to French forces. Meanwhile, another army under General Montesquieu had occupied Savoy and Nice. After the disappointments of the previous spring, Brissot's liberationist rhetoric seemed to be taking on substance at last and his popularity soared.

Yet even the encouraging news from the frontiers could not disguise the fact that the people's representatives were far from united. Many of the newly arrived deputies found the radical atmosphere of Paris to be deeply troubling, and they were particularly incensed by the 'insolence' of the Sections, whose brief experience of power during the summer had whetted political appetites. Ruault remarked upon the intimidatory climate in his own Section, where militants were insisting on 'out loud' voting. In the Convention, Buzot tried to pin the blame for the effervescence on the deputies of the Paris delegation and even went so far as to suggest that the Convention would be prevented from deliberating freely if it remained in Paris. This was the germ of a subversive idea, for it expressed a widespread feeling in the country that the people of Paris were taking over the revolution, heedless of the fact that they only constituted a tiny fraction of the 'sovereign' nation. The question of the fate of the king escalated this tension and would also be instrumental in the 'separating out' of the Convention into two mutually antagonistic wings (known as the Girondins and the Montagnards), plus a large body of uncommitted deputies (known as the Plain).

In prison and dethroned, Louis's person appeared to be inviolable unless it could be demonstrated that he had broken his oath to the constitution.

Plate 1 'The Day of the Tiles', Grenoble, 7th June 1788

Source: Debelle, Alexandre (1805–97) Musée de la Révolution Française, Vizille, France/The Bridgeman Art Library Nationality/copyright status: French/out of copyright

Plate 2 Model of the Bastille made from the stones of the Bastille

Source: Palloy, Pierre François, Musée Carnavalet, Paris, France/Giraudon/The Bridgeman Art Library Nationality/copyright: French/out of copyright

Plate 3 The Festival of the Federation, as depicted on a 5 sol token

Source: Courtesy of Sue Tungate/The Birmingham Assay Office Collections

Plate 4 The Planting of a Liberty Tree

Source: Alamy Images

La Femme du Sans Culotte
Rue du Theâtre Francois N.º 4.

Plate 5 A female sans-culotte
Source: Musée de la Ville de Paris, Musée Carnavalet, Paris/Archives Charmer/The Bridgeman Art Library Nationality/copyright status: French/out of copyright

Plate 6 A gang of brigands pillaging an inn

Source: Bibliothèque nationale de France, Paris, QB-201(138)-FOL-Hennin

Plate 7 Danton led to his execution

Plate 8 The Port au Blé and the Pont Notre-Dame, 1782

Source: Lespinasse, Louis-Nicolas de, Musée de la Ville de Paris, Musée Carnavalet, Paris, France/Lauros/Giraudon/The Bridgeman Art Library Nationality/copyright status: French/out of copyright

However, the Constitution of 1791 no longer existed in practice. Moreover, compromising evidence had come to light of potentially treasonous correspondence between Louis (and Marie-Antoinette) and foreign powers. A trial appeared to be the solution, although many questioned whether such a straightforward procedure might not become a dangerous hostage to political fortune. What court of law could be considered competent to judge a king, albeit an ex-king, in whose name the law itself had been administered until 10 August? What fate lay in store for those who had overthrown the monarchy if Louis were found to be innocent of the charges laid against him? And what if he were found guilty? The penalty prescribed for treason was death. Saint-Just, in his maiden speech, argued that the office of kingship was inherently culpable, and Robespierre agreed that the only question requiring deliberation was the sentence. In the light of the September prison massacres, Louis himself entertained no illusions and expected death to come by one route or another. Nevertheless, the majority of the deputies concluded that a trial was necessary and that only the legislative body was competent to serve as a court. The trial of Louis Capet, formerly King of the French, began on 10 December and he was found guilty of treason. After procedural manoeuvres, first to refer sentencing to the electorate (the *appel au peuple*) and then to suspend the death penalty, had failed, Louis was executed on 21 January 1793. The patriot Palloy celebrated the event that evening by eating a meal of stuffed pig's head with his family.

appel au peuple: A popular referendum to decide on the punishment of Louis XVI.

The behaviour of Brissot, Buzot, Vergniaud, Roland and company during the ballots on sentencing incurred the suspicion that they had wanted to save Louis, with the result that the trial greatly exacerbated the factionalism afflicting the Convention. On 6 February 1793, Nicolas Ruault reported to his brother: 'We now have two sorts of Jacobins or patriots who hate each other as desperately as the original Jacobins and royalists used to hate each other. The latest kind of Jacobins refer to themselves as Girondins, or Brissotins or Rolandists' (Ruault, 1976: 324). In fact, there is no reason to suppose that the latter were camouflaged moderates on this or any other issue. For as long as the war effort continued to go well, the Gironde could expect to remain in the ascendant in the Convention. As yet, none of the assembled deputies was showing much interest in the street-level political agenda, which was largely economic in content. In September, it is true, they had flinched in their ideological commitment to economic freedom, but once the armies of the republic had moved on to foreign soil, the argument for some kind of centralised control of prices and provisioning lost all purchase.

Thus, when a fresh round of attacks on Paris grocery stores materialised in February, Robespierre and Marat – supposedly the deputies closest to the common people – dismissed the calls for a price 'ceiling', or Maximum, to be fixed for commodities of everyday consumption in the same vein as everyone else. This was a risky response, for it suggested that the overwhelmingly bourgeois deputies had not yet grasped the implications of the 'second revolution' of 10 August if they supposed that a popular front could be nourished on a diet of military expansionism and repressive legislation against priests and *émigrés* alone. If no one was willing to speak on their behalf in the Convention, the Sections were quite capable of finding leaders of their own. These *enragés* (Roux, Varlet, Leclerc, etc.), as their opponents dubbed them, were no respecters of persons or reputations and, as tension increased between the Gironde and the Mountain, it became apparent that they could not be ignored indefinitely.

REACTIONS IN THE DEPARTMENTS

The shocks administered to provincial public opinion since the events of the summer of 1792 should not be underestimated. Although peasant unrest subsided nearly everywhere once the feudal regime had finally been laid to rest, small-town Jacobins found themselves facing a steep learning curve. They were expected to endorse, in rapid succession, the abolition of the monarchy, the proclamation of the republic, and then the trial and execution of Louis XVI. The correspondence of Louis Louchet, a little-known deputy sent to sit in the Convention by the voters of the department of the Aveyron (see Map 2), enables us to plumb the political fissure which was now opening up between Paris and the provinces. The pained silence of the local authorities of Rodez spoke volumes and, in October, he pleaded with them to issue an 'energetic and laconic' address congratulating the Convention on its decision to proclaim a republic (Louchet, 1792–94). More coaxing letters were required to induce the Jacobin club to accept the authority of the supreme legislative body in the matter of the trial of the ex-monarch; to allay its fears that even oath-swearing clergy were now under threat; and, finally, to persuade club members that the Parisian insurrection of 31 May–2 June 1793 had been perpetrated in the public interest.

The pace of events was also testing loyalties in the great cities, particularly in centres such as Lyons, Marseilles and Bordeaux, where the regeneration of France as a single, undifferentiated nation had dented regional pride. Bordeaux had not done well out of the administrative reforms of 1789–90. The legal bourgeoisie considered the city's role as administrative seat of the new department of the Gironde to be poor compensation for the loss of their ancient Parlement, and the merchant community reacted with understandable alarm when, in February and March, the Convention added to the list of enemies with declarations of war on both Britain and Spain.

March was a critical month on several fronts, in fact. The momentum of French military success in the Low Countries was finally halted when the Austrians counterattacked and forced the evacuation of Aix-La-Chapelle. Dumouriez, the general whose victories had earned the Brissotins huge political capital, was badly beaten at Neerwinden on 18 March. His desertion to the enemy a few days later, having failed to persuade his army to march on Paris and restore the monarchy, did immense damage to all those who had harnessed their political fortunes to Brissot's policy of military adventurism over the past year or so. The populations of the north-eastern departments, Louchet noted with relief and satisfaction, remained utterly unmoved in the face of Dumouriez's blandishments. In the west, however, the news was far from reassuring, for the activities of recruitment officers seeking to bolster the strength of the army had provoked a rash of riotous incidents.

The deputies were too preoccupied to pay much attention to these outbreaks at first, but by April it was becoming apparent that a rural counter-revolution, centred on the department of the Vendée, was in the making (see Map 2). It was in this context of crisis at home and abroad that much of the institutional fabric of the Terror came to be put in place. On 9 March, the Convention voted to send out around 80 deputies as *représentants en mission* to revolutionise the departments – in other words, to enforce the vision of the revolution as perceived in Paris. The following day, a special court (the Revolutionary Tribunal) was set up to try conspirators. On 21 March, police committees (*comités de surveillance*) with powers of summary arrest were enacted; on 26 March, the disarmament of 'suspects'. Then, on 6 April, a powerful new body which blurred legislative and executive responsibilities – the Committee of Public Safety – was brought into being.

représentants en mission: Deputies who were commissioned by the National Convention to tour the departments and enforce government policy.

In sullen or disaffected departments, the arrival of *représentants en mission* often proved to be the last straw. François Chabot and Jean-Baptiste Bo, the two colleagues of Louchet who were sent out to the Aveyron and the Tarn departments, strutted around like pro-consuls, commandeering whatever they needed, arresting and imprisoning individuals on the slightest pretext. The legally constituted authorities were powerless to intervene, for an emergency concept of law and order that was rooted in considerations of 'public safety' was starting to take over, and it had no time for procedural niceties. Indeed, the highly decentralised local government system that the committees of the National Assembly had devised in 1789–90 now appeared to be a luxury that the revolution could barely afford. In a sense, therefore, the provincial reaction to any further browbeating of the deputies by the militants of the Paris Sections would not have been too difficult to predict. In his letters of April and May, Louchet mingled indignation at the military reverses, reassurances as to the freedom of action of the Convention, and veiled comments that certain deputies appeared to lack the stamina for the stern measures that the political situation now demanded.

In fact, the tacticians of the Mountain had no more desire than the Gironde to enlist the populace of Paris in their feud. Yet they were in a parliamentary minority, as Louchet acknowledged on 6 May in a letter to the Jacobins of Rodez – not least because the majority of the *représentants en mission* had been selected from among their ranks. In the end, it was Robespierre and his closest associates who took the gamble and accepted, with misgivings, the help of the Sections to engineer a political outcome that could not be achieved by any other means. After an abortive mobilisation on 31 May, the armed forces of the Sections returned to the task two days later. Compliantly, Couthon drew up a list of deputies who were to be placed under house detention, although few of the individuals named were actually present in the Convention at the time.

The news that, on 2 June 1793, the Convention had been forcibly purged of 27 Girondin deputies caused consternation. The 'anarchists' of Paris had got their way again! In what has become known as the Federalist Revolt, perhaps half of the departments in the country expressed varying degrees of outrage at the turn of events. Only a handful of local authorities took steps to organise a more concrete response, though. In Bordeaux, there was a feeble attempt to march an expeditionary force against Paris in response to the outlawing of several of the city's deputies. It proceeded barely 50 kilometres before disintegrating. Marseilles, too, launched an armed force, which advanced up the Rhône valley as far as Orange. Potentially more serious was the regrouping of Girondin deputies in the Norman town of Caen, much closer to Paris, which included François Buzot, among others. But forces loyal to the Montagnard Convention removed the threat in mid-July. For all their hostility to the Paris Sections, the majority of the Federalists had no desire to see the republic overturned, whatever Montagnard propaganda may have asserted. This hampered their effectiveness, for only occasionally – as in the case of Lyons – did they make common cause with counter-revolutionaries. However, such distinctions became almost meaningless once the Terror was up and running.

The proscription of representatives of the people who had been legally elected and were entitled to parliamentary immunity from prosecution was a grim first for the revolution. However, it is probable that neither side actually willed the lethal outcome of the expulsions. During the *journées* in question, the deputies of the Mountain also felt threatened. They showed little desire to pursue their opponents initially, and the situation only seems to have become irretrievable towards the end of June (Whaley, 2000: 155–63). The arrest warrant against Brissot was only issued three weeks after the intervention of the Sections – by which time most of the proscribed deputies had fled Paris. The news that they were inciting various forms of resistance in the departments caused a distinct hardening of opinion in the Convention, however. The shock of Marat's assassination on 13 July by a female royalist who, if not a Federalist, came from Normandy, completed this process.

TERROR

The abiding image of the Terror is the guillotine. This beheading machine was proposed initially as a humane replacement for the hangman's noose, though, as we have noted, witnesses complained that it delivered death too swiftly and failed to ensure that victims suffered. Punishment and suffering were integral to the period of the Terror, the beginnings of which can be traced back to the war emergency and September Prison Massacres in Paris and Versailles (see Part Three). But if arbitrary arrest, imprisonment and summary justice were hallmarks of the Terror, it would be wrong to suggest that the whole country succumbed to these phenomena as early as September 1792. The great mass of French men and women did not come into contact with the politics of Terror until the autumn of 1793, and the ending of Terror as an instrument of central government can be fairly precisely dated to the upheaval of 9 Thermidor II (27 July 1794), which removed Robespierre and his supporters from power. Although violent repression at the hands of roving *représentants en mission* continued in several departments after this date, in most of the country the removal of Robespierre and his faction brought relief.

What we have termed the 'politics' of the Terror developed informally and without much central direction between September and December 1793, whereas Terror as a deliberate instrument and weapon of government was chiefly a feature of the winter, spring and early summer months of 1794. For the so-called Federalists and the many other categories of political 'suspect' that the revolution had left in its wake by this time, the difference was mainly one of emphasis, however. Autumn victims of the Terror were rounded up locally and dealt with locally, but once the institutions of Revolutionary Government had been put in place [**Doc. 17**], victims were more likely to be judged centrally – albeit no less savagely – and within a framework of legal, or rather quasi-legal procedure. Perhaps half a million men and women saw the inside of a prison cell during the period of the Terror, and around 16,000 mounted the steps to the guillotine. However, many thousands more were killed during spectacular acts of collective repression, in Lyons, in Toulon and in the villages of western France. The civil war fought in the Vendée is reckoned to have cost between 200,000 and 300,000 lives alone (Lyons, 1994: 84) [**Doc. 18**].

Since historians have concluded that no one set out consciously to create the Terror, we are bound to ask where this uniquely punitive mentality came from, and how it came to be incorporated into the apparatus of government. Just as foreign invasion, fear of the 'enemy within', and a general sense of embattlement helped to trigger the prison massacres of September 1792, it can be argued that the threats facing the republic during the summer of 1793 gave birth to the Terror. Even those historians who believe that extremism and the rejection of compromise were embedded in the revolution from the very start (see Part Three) would accept this argument of circumstance to some degree. There can be no doubting that the situation facing the purged Convention immediately after the insurrection mounted by the Paris Sections on 31 May–2 June was extremely serious. Throughout June and July, the news reaching the capital was uniformly bad: half of the departments were complaining loudly about the expulsion of the Girondin deputies; the Austrians were preparing to invade from the north-east; the Prussians through Alsace; Vendean rebels were probing the defences of the republic along the river Loire; and British fleets were prowling in the Caribbean and also in the Mediterranean. In Lyons, Marseilles and Toulon, hostility to Jacobinism was positively visceral and, by the late summer, visibly tinctured with counter-revolutionary sentiment. Marseilles would make its peace with the Convention at the eleventh hour, but both Lyons and Toulon broke away from the revolution and would only be returned to the fold by force of arms.

Grim tidings on this scale were enough to engage the repressive reflexes of the Committee of Public Safety – the nerve centre of government for the next 12 months – on their own. But the punitive mentality was also fuelled at street level, and the combination of studied savagery from above and impulsive brutality from below created a tension in the Terror that was never entirely resolved. Having hoisted the Mountain into power on 2 June, the activists in the Paris Sections, or **sans-culottes** [**Doc. 15**] as they had taken to calling themselves, expected to receive something in return. Indeed, they were prepared to barrack the deputies, and even to threaten them with another revolutionary *journée*, until they obtained satisfaction. The popular 'programme' had come a long way since 1792 and now consisted of a relatively sophisticated mix of political and economic demands that depended on public vigilance – not to say terror – for their enforcement [**Doc. 16**]. The *sans-culottes* clamoured for the expulsion of all the deputies who had voted for the *appel au people* after the trial of Louis XVI, the speedy transfer of the Girondins before the Revolutionary Tribunal, and the arrest of anyone who had signed a motion in support of them. They demanded that the offices of government be purged of former nobles and anyone else who manifestly did

sans-culottes: Literally 'those without knee-breeches'. Artisan militants of the Sections of Paris.

not need, or deserve, to be supported by the state. They wanted the prices of all foodstuffs and articles of everyday use to be fixed invariably. As a deterrent to hoarding, they insisted that the deputies enact a law making the practice punishable by death, and they called for the creation of institutions of repression (a blanket 'suspects' law, civilian militias, etc.) that could be mobilised against the economic as well as the political enemies of the people.

Faced with a huge array of responsibilities – not the least of which was the need to keep 750,000 fighting men in battle order on the frontiers – the Committee of Public Safety preferred to avoid actions that would cause disruption and quite likely increase the number of the nation's opponents. Yet the Sections were formidably organised by the late summer of 1793 and in no mood to back down. The news of Toulon's 'great betrayal' (the surrender to British Admiral Hood's Mediterranean squadron), which arrived in Paris on 2 September, proved to be the final straw. Three days later, a noisy demonstration that might easily have turned into an insurrection browbeat the Convention into compliance. In the days and weeks that followed, most of the demands enshrined in the programme that the enragés had been the first to formulate, and which Hébert and his clique had taken over in the late summer, were turned into law. To all intents and purposes, the Committee of Public Safety was now the executive arm of the revolution, and destined to remain so until such time as peace was restored and conditions made possible the implementation of the new Constitution that had briefly seen the light of day in June 1793. The September crisis had taught it a valuable lesson in the art of partnership government. Robespierre replaced Danton as the dominant personality in late July, and in September Billaud-Varenne and Collot d'Herbois, two deputies who had spoken in favour of the Terror agenda of the Sections, were taken on board. It seemed safer to have such men inside the government than on the outside. Thereafter, the composition of the body that controlled the destiny of France for the next 11 months scarcely altered.

That autumn was the heyday of sans-culotte power in Paris. Terror had been proclaimed the 'order of the day' (on 5 September) and the Sections vibrated with militancy and activism. The Convention more or less gave up any attempt to navigate and allowed itself to be swept along on the tide of events. With Marie-Antoinette, the Duke of Orleans, the Girondins, the Feuillants and the flower of the ancien régime aristocracy queueing at the foot of the scaffold, it would have been dangerous to have behaved otherwise. As the Committee of Public Safety had anticipated, the implementation of the popular programme resulted in a substantial loss of central control over the nature and direction of the Terror. Only with the enactment of the law of 14 Frimaire (4 December) did it become possible to redress the balance

[**Doc. 17**]. Even so, the pruning and disciplining of the Terror as it had evolved in the departments proved to be a protracted and delicate exercise. *Représentants en mission* and those to whom they had delegated their powers had to be called to order; the excesses of police committees, military commissions and sundry militias curbed; and the chain of command linking the institutions of government reconfigured.

REPRESSION

One of the most bizarre episodes of the 'anarchical' Terror was the dechristianisation campaign, which resulted in the closure of churches throughout the country from November onwards. The trend towards secularisation is not difficult to understand, nor is the revolutionaries' impatience with the Catholic Church. By the summer of 1793, even obedient, oath-swearing clergy found themselves relegated to the margins of public life, and in October the Christian calendar was replaced by a secular version in which the years were counted from the date of the proclamation of the republic. But the closing down of churches, the forcible defrocking of priests and heavy-handed attempts to deny Christian revelation in favour of a state policy of atheism (the worship of 'reason') belonged more to the politics of the Terror than to anything that had gone before. Left to their own devices, the Committee of Public Safety would probably not have countenanced such a move, and it is significant that the first steps towards the deliberate 'dechristianisation' of the republic were taken by deputies 'on mission' to the departments. Joseph Fouché began the purge in the department of the Nièvre early in October, ordering local officials to secure the termination of Christian worship in parish churches and to put up notices outside cemeteries proclaiming that 'Death is an eternal sleep'. Other *représentants en mission* followed suit, and, at the instigation of Chaumette and Hébert, militants in the Sections jumped on to the bandwagon as well. Jean-Baptiste Gobel, the constitutional archbishop of Paris, was induced to resign, and on 10 November the cathedral of Notre-Dame was reconsecrated as a Temple of Reason during a festival of liberty. In the weeks that followed, all the churches in the capital were shut down.

Even if 'dechristianisation' was popular in Paris, it seems unlikely that the policy attracted much bedrock support in the provinces. In government, opinion was divided. The offices of the Police Ministry (known as the Committee of General Security) contained enthusiastic anti-clericals, but the senior Committee, whose responsibilities were more wide-ranging, adopted a reserved attitude. Robespierre, like most educated men of his generation, held broadly Rousseauean beliefs in matters to do with religion and regarded atheism as a vice of the aristocracy. In any case, he was suspicious of the individuals who had instigated the frenzy of church closures. Randomised and gratuitous Terror, he felt, was more likely to weaken than to strengthen the republic.

But were Terror and blanket repression still needed as the autumn of 1793 turned into winter? Following successes against an Anglo-Dutch force outside Dunkirk and against the Austrians at Wattignies, the military situation on the north-eastern border had eased. True, the Army of the Rhine was still badly demoralised, having nearly lost control of Strasbourg, but Saint-Just and Philippe Lebas were restoring discipline and, by the end of the year, enemy forces would be almost totally cleared from Alsace. The Convention was also regaining the initiative in the struggle against its internal opponents. Federalism had been quelled everywhere by October, and Lyons was finally overrun on the 9th of that month. In the Vendée, however, the fortunes of war see-sawed alarmingly throughout September and October. A victory at Cholet on 17–18 October gave the advantage to the forces of the republic, but the rebels were not crushed beyond all hope of recovery until 23 December (battle of Savenay). Almost simultaneously, the news came through that the forts overlooking the harbour of Toulon had been recaptured, and that the British were finally evacuating this port city.

The pressure for a moderation – or perhaps we should say a de-escalation – of the Terror has been attributed to Robespierre, to Danton and to Camille Desmoulins, the talented journalist and Cordeliers militant turned Montagnard deputy. The involvement of the latter in the campaign for 'indulgence' is not in doubt, whereas the motives and behaviour of the others are harder to work out. Robespierre wanted to bring the 'dechristianisers' to heel, whereas Danton may only have been trying to protect a number of politically vulnerable friends. Be that as it may, disagreements over the Terror and the justification for repression once the immediate danger to the republic had passed would end up destroying a government that had no opponents except those of its own making, whether in the Convention or in the country at large. What alarmed deputies and dispassionate observers such as Nicolas Ruault was the way in which the bloodshed continued unabated, notwithstanding the easing of the military situation. In the aftermath of the fall of Lyons, *représentant* Couthon oversaw a moderate repression, which resulted in the judicial execution of around 200 individuals. But Couthon was recalled and replaced in late October by Fouché and Collot d'Herbois, who proceeded to organise mass shootings and guillotinings that took a further 1,667 lives. It was the same story in the Vendée. Although the rebels no longer posed a threat, General Turreau laid waste the countryside from January onwards, while *représentant* Carrier ordered or connived at the mass

drownings and shootings of Vendeans, refractory priests and common crim-
inals who had been incarcerated in the prisons of Nantes.

The diary of another dispassionate observer of public events, Célestin
Guittard de Floriban offers us a glimpse of the extent to which the repressive
reflex became normalised in the spring and summer of 1794. From early
April until late July, he noted down the executions carried out daily in Paris,
pausing only to reflect when the tumbrels contained a number of women
victims. As the Terror entered its final paroxysm in mid-June, he stopped
systematically recording the names and contented himself with a recital of
raw figures instead (Figure 5.1). On 31 July, as the score-settling of Thermidor
reached its term, he awoke from the blood-soaked trance and noted with
surprise, 'there have been no executions today' (Aubert ed., 1974: 441).

The difficulty faced by Desmoulins when denouncing, in veiled terms, the
excesses of that autumn and winter in the columns of his *Vieux Cordelier*
newspaper was that the mind-set of the Terror made 'moderation' and
'counter-revolution' bedfellows. Moreover, anyone who had carried out
brutal deeds at a time when no questions were being asked had an obvious
personal investment in the continuation of a policy of stern measures. When
Collot d'Herbois received reports that the Convention and even the Jacobin
Club were talking about releasing suspects and relaxing the Terror, he rushed
back to Paris in order to justify himself and, by extension, all the other
représentants en mission, Section and club militants whose activities laid them
open to reproach. How far the Committee of Public Safety as a whole was

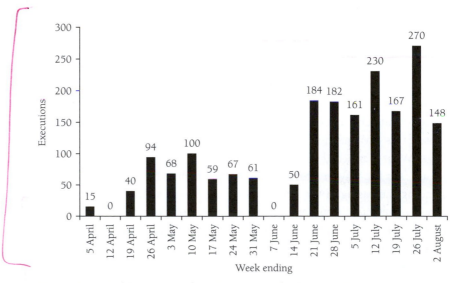

Figure 5.1 Weekly executions in Paris – April–August 1794
Source: Aubert, R. (ed.) (1974) *Journal de Célestin Guittard de Floriban, bourgeois de Paris
sous la Révolution*, published by Editions France-Empire, pp. 333–441.

prepared to countenance a retreat from the Terror is difficult to fathom, though. After all, it knew all about the activities of Turreau's 'infernal columns' in the Vendée [Doc. 18]. If we may judge from the law that spelled out the workings of Revolutionary Government (14 Frimaire II / 4 December 1793), the Committee were planning to concentrate and centralise the punitive will of the nation, not to weaken it.

These divergent visions of the direction in which the revolution should proceed, together with the gradual breakdown of trust between individual members of the two Committees, help us to understand why a government constructed in adversity could not long survive in the less testing conditions of the late spring and summer. Having witnessed the furious reaction of the 'ultras' to the campaign for clemency waged in the pages of the *Vieux Cordelier*, Robespierre quickly grasped that the future of the Montagnard hegemony was itself at stake. The balance between the contending groups had been lost, however. Amid fears that the supporters of Hébert in the Cordeliers Club and their allies in the Sections might exploit a recrudescence of food shortages and launch an insurrection, the Committee carried out a pre-emptive strike against them in March [Doc. 19]. Hébert, Ronsin, Vincent, Momoro and 14 lesser known figures from the Sections were accused of involvement in a 'foreign faction' and executed on 24 March 1794.

However, this embittered their allies in the Committees and made it difficult to resist calls for equivalent action against more highly placed 'plotters' – notably a group of deputies linked closely to Danton who were suspected of financial misdemeanours. Some of these *pourris* were already in detention, but the remainder were arrested on the night of 29–30 March. Because the deputies who had been calling for a relaxation of the Terror (Desmoulins, Delacroix, Philippeau and Danton) could not be easily, or safely, separated from them, they were arrested, too. As the printer of the *Moniteur* newspaper, Nicolas Ruault was able to watch what was going on from close quarters, and on 1 April he reported to his brother that the 'patriots' were waging a fierce struggle among themselves. After a show trial, the embezzlers and the 'indulgents' were jointly sentenced to death. They mounted the steps of the scaffold together four days later.

In the cart on the way to the guillotine, Danton expressed frustration that he was going to die six weeks before Robespierre (Ruault, 1976: 350) – a reminder to us that the revolution was now heading the way of so many dictatorships. In fact, the Committee of Public Safety, as constituted the previous September, lasted another 16 weeks before it fell prey to a lethal bout of infighting which caused the authority of the Committee of General Security to be destroyed as well. Robespierre did indeed aspire to some form of dictatorship in the weeks that followed the extermination of the factions.

The so-called Great Terror, as chronicled by Guittard de Floriban, became almost entirely disconnected from political necessity. The Paris Sections, whose vitality had been ebbing ever since the start of the year, were now largely excluded from the decision-making machinery of government; activism waned and French men and women were enjoined to turn away from participatory politics and find fulfilment in the worship of the Supreme Being instead. Jacobinism (Plate 5) in its female variant had been on the defensive ever since the autumn, when the Société des Républicaines Révolutionnaires had succumbed to criticism both from deputies in the Convention and from women of the central markets.

The final bloodbath of 9–10 Thermidor II (27–28 July 1794) seems to have been brought about by the entirely human reflex of fear rather than major differences of policy or ideology. Having withdrawn from the day-to-day business of government several weeks earlier, Robespierre threatened to denounce his opponents in the two Committees. This caused the survivors of the opposing factions – extremists and moderates – to band together and organise a counterattack. On 10 Thermidor and days following, it was the turn of Robespierre, Couthon, Saint-Just, Lebas and 100 others to clamber aboard the executioners' carts. Few, if any, of those participating in the *coup* sought explicitly to end the Terror, but the Convention moved quickly to exploit the resulting power vacuum and a progressive dismantling of the institutions of repression was the consequence.

6

The Search for Stability, 1795–99

The Jacobin levelling experiment of 1793–94 left in its wake an embittered society. As the reaction to the events of Thermidor gathered momentum, the country appeared to divide into those who had been involved in the Terror and those who counted themselves among its victims. The readmission to the National Convention of the surviving Girondins, together with those deputies who had protested against the purge carried through by the Montagnards and their street supporters, only exacerbated the tension. Before long, the stern figures in the two Committees who had helped to dislodge Robespierre (Billaud-Varenne, Collot d'Herbois, Vadier, Amar, etc.) would be called to account as 'terrorists' in their turn. The task facing France's legislators from 1795 was an exceptionally difficult one, therefore. They had to find a means of repairing the damage done by the Terror to the social fabric of the nation, whilst at the same time devising a system of rule that would enshrine both freedom of parliamentary expression and solid guarantees against dictatorship by the executive arm of government. Their failure to settle the bitter legacy of the Terror is the reason why historians tend to neglect these years, as though nothing durable or productive took place between 1795 and 1799. Better, therefore, either to 'end' the revolution with the fall of Robespierre, or to treat the regime brought into being by the Constitution of 1795 as an extended chronological prelude to the arrival in power of Napoleon Bonaparte.

It is true that the *dramatis personae* of the period did not change very much. On taking office in October 1795, the Executive Directory would find itself confronted by intransigent royalists, *émigrés*, non-oath-swearing priests and Jacobins who regretted the eclipse of the Terror. In this regard, little of substance had altered since the events of Thermidor in the Convention. France's foreign adversaries had not greatly changed either, nor had the arguments in support of war. Was the Directory therefore little more than a chaotic transitional regime located between two periods of robust, single-minded government? The most recent research suggests that this view needs to be modified. It has been pointed out that the Directory was the first regime to

build upon the achievements of 1790–91 and, for a time, to make democratic institutions actually work. Thanks to a broad franchise, a vibrant press
and frequent elections, Frenchmen served an extended apprenticeship in the
values of representative democracy during these four years [**Doc. 20**]. The
regime also gestated institutions of financial administration, tax raising and
local government, which anticipated and foreshadowed innovations more
commonly associated with the rule of Napoleon Bonaparte. Indeed,
researchers who have paused to consider the Directory in its own right go
further and propose a periodisation that blurs somewhat the traditional focus
on Bonaparte's anti-parliamentary coup of 18–19 Brumaire VIII (9–10
November 1799) as the single most important event of these years. It is true
that contemporaries were not as impressed by the significance of Brumaire as
generations of historians have been subsequently. They were all too aware
that the transition from a politics rooted in debate and the free exchange of
ideas to one rooted in authoritarianism was under way even before a victorious general decided to try his hand at government.

A THERMIDORIAN REPUBLIC

The best way to make sense of the complex events of these years is to divide
the period into two. From the summer of 1794 until the summer of 1797,
objectives that were closely entwined preoccupied the men of the revolution:
how to dismantle the Jacobin dictatorship without at the same time clearing
the way for a revival of domestic royalism that might serve as the curtain-raiser
to a Bourbon restoration. But from the autumn of 1797 until the summer of
1802 when Bonaparte, as First Consul, was prolonged in office for life (see
Chapter 7), the emphasis increasingly shifted from constitutionalism to
authoritarianism. Thanks to the *coup* of 18 Fructidor V (4 September 1797),
which was carried out with the assistance of the army, the political threat of
resurgent royalism declined. Instead, Directorial republicans and their suc-
cessors in the councils of the Consulate grew to fear that neo-Jacobins – the
men who had last held power during the Terror – would take over the regime
from within. In order to stop them, they resorted to blatantly unconstitutional
actions of which General Bonaparte's intervention was merely the most arresting
example. The Executive Directory can therefore be visualised as a see-saw
regime which was periodically assailed by individuals representing the extremes
of the political spectrum spawned since 1789. To be sure, its upholders were
committed republicans, but they were also firmly attached to the philosophy
of political liberalism. The challenge they set themselves was to detach the
idea of the republic from its embattled and blood-soaked origins and to harness

it instead to the principles of the early revolution. Their ultimate failure to achieve this synthesis was not a failure of political will so much as a reflection that the nation – post-Thermidor – appeared irretrievably divided.

The speed of the reaction against Jacobinism in the Convention and all it stood for once the powers of the Committee of Public Safety had been curtailed surprised everyone. The Paris Sections were prevented from holding meetings, legislation banned collective petitioning by the clubs or any other corporate bodies, and brawling between moderates and militants was used as a pretext to shut down the mother Jacobin club altogether. All the irksome policies to which the deputies of the Plain had agreed under duress were now put into reverse. The savage law of 22 Prairial II (10 June 1794), which pushed the conviction rate in the Revolutionary Tribunal to 80 per cent, had already been rescinded, and during the autumn all the restraints that had been placed on the economy under pressure from the Sections were removed. Price control was abandoned, the stock market reopened, and merchants and contractors recovered the freedom to go about their business unhindered. The consequences were immediate and predictable. Galloping inflation destroyed the purchasing power of the *assignat*, and the cost of living spiralled. By January 1795, real prices for day-to-day commodities were very nearly six times higher than they had been five years earlier. The savage winter of 1794–95 only made matters worse. Distress rose to levels without parallel in the cities. Suicide became commonplace: in Rouen the death rate doubled in the year after Thermidor. Famine and even starvation accompanied the retreat from the Terror, then, and provided fuel for political resentments. From the spring, the deputies began to receive reports from the south and south-east of the country concerning the activities of extra-legal punishment squads (the so-called 'White' Terror). These gangs were systematically targeting for violence and intimidation anyone who had held office during the climactic phase of Revolutionary Government.

The dilemma that ran like a thread through these years was already apparent by the summer of 1795, therefore. Each act of relaxation and would-be reconciliation appeared simply to reinforce the extremes. The deputies sought to pacify their armed opponents in the west (known as *chouans*) with an amnesty that included the freedom to worship as they pleased. In fact, a general law of religious pacification was introduced not long afterwards, which for a time restored to both juring and non-juring priests the use of churches all over the country. But the loosening grip of the Convention served only to encourage the western rebels to renew their struggle against the republic. The late king's one surviving son had died in prison and his uncle, the Comte de Provence, now claimed the succession. Styling himself Louis XVIII, Provence issued a grudging Declaration from Verona which made it clear that whilst 'constitutional' royalists might hope to secure control of France by parliamentary means, the 'pure' royalists remained committed to counter-revolution via the armed struggle. The failure of the Quiberon Bay expedition, when British warships landed a large force of *émigrés* on the coast of Brittany, demonstrated the futility of this approach. Indeed, the deputies were far more alarmed by the insidious spread of royalism as priests returned from exile and churches reopened. With a new constitution in the making and elections impending, the royalists saw the chance to weave together the many different strands of discontent. But the Convention also spotted the danger and riposted with decrees requiring that two-thirds of the new representatives be chosen from among the existing deputies. A prudent move to maintain continuity in a context of accelerating political reaction, or a cynical manoeuvre to save their own skins? Both, probably, and the measure was greeted with a violent royalist insurrection on the streets of Paris and with extreme distaste in the country at large.

France finally emerged from the limbo of Revolutionary Government and returned to the path of constitutional legality on 28 October 1795 in the shape of a regime known as the Executive Directory. During the preceding months, a new constitution (the Constitution of the Year Three) had been voted and ratified, which reinstated a broad franchise based on a threshold tax qualification. If not exactly universal manhood suffrage, around $5\frac{1}{2}$ million adult males out of some 8 million were entitled to participate in primary electoral assemblies. Significantly, it was accompanied by a re-issued Declaration of the Rights and the Duties of Man which referred not to *natural* rights (as in 1789 and 1793), but to rights acquired in *society*. In other words, the architects of the new regime were now stepping back from the universalistic claims which had served as the launchpad for the revolution. The emphasis on equality and sovereignty as a power rooted in the people was watered down. In fact, the clause 'Men are born, and always continue, free and equal in respect of their rights' was quietly dropped. These changes had the virtue of aligning constitutional theory with hard-won experience and some historians therefore detect in the transition of 1795 a fundamental shift in the political culture of the revolution (Jainchill, 2008: 30). It is true that deputies on the Left were in no doubt that a retreat had been sounded from the values that had sustained the revolution until now. But this is to pre-judge the new regime and to deny it any capacity to evolve. Whatever the Thermidorian architects of the Directory may have intended, it would not lack democratic credentials.

As always, however, the declared aim was to begin afresh. Two days prior to its dissolution, the Convention voted to rename the Place de la Révolution, where the guillotine had once stood, the Place de la Concorde. Moreover, in a more tangible gesture of reconciliation, a final decree granted an amnesty to those who had been charged with political crimes in the aftermath of the Terror. If only in terms of structure, the Directory was a very different regime from those that had preceded it. Such was the fear of dictators and dictatorial

Committees that the constitution was built on the principle of a rigorous separation of powers. In order to curb the domineering tendency of the legislative arm of government, provision was made for two chambers on a model first proposed by the *Monarchiens* back in the summer of 1789. The authority to initiate and to examine legislation was entrusted to a Council of Five Hundred, whereas parliamentary approval of bills was lodged with a senate of more senior deputies, known as the Council of Elders. The executive arm comprised five individuals, who were selected by the Council of Five Hundred to all intents and purposes, and who were known as Directors. While the Directors appointed the Ministers and the Commissioners – that is to say, the agents of the government in the departments – they had no authority to make or shape legislation. On the other hand, the power to conduct diplomacy, to supervise the armies and to handle appointments gave them very considerable scope to influence the formulation of policy. In the event of a stalemate or paralysis in the mechanisms of government, a procedure for constitutional revision could be invoked; however, a minimum delay of nine years was laid down before any changes could take effect. True, the Directors were subject to annual renewal, but one by one, and by random ballot. Constitutional revision was all but impossible, therefore, which helps to explain why the Directory both resorted to illegal acts and fell prey to the illegal acts of others.

As we have seen, the democratic credentials of the Directorial regime rested on a broad franchise. It is true, however, that voting remained indirect. Also, electors had to satisfy fiscal conditions that were much stiffer than they had been in 1790 and 1791. But the opportunities to vote at the primary level were now more numerous, since the constitution required that ballots would be held every year in the month of March. After the studied conformism of Revolutionary Government, some vigour and vitality returned to national political life, in consequence. However, the Councils proceeded to cut one of the tap roots of revolutionary spontaneity in a bid to discourage the more anarchical features of mass political mobilisation. Elective village councils were abolished and replaced by canton-level municipalities instead.

Notwithstanding the hunger, the economic dislocation and the fragility of law and order in the south and the west, the early Directory years did prove conducive to the growth of a practice of participation rooted in electoral assemblies, newspaper readership and, for city dwellers, the reappearance of clubs. Some historians have even detected signs of the development of embryonic political parties in this period. However, the combination of elections and a vigorous marketplace for oppositional ideas also tended to provide a platform for those occupying the margins of the political spectrum – the more so as the Directory was not yet willing to use force against its opponents. The 'républicains fermes', as the Directory's latter-day Jacobins were called, had benefited from the amnesty law, and although the royalists

third: Prior to its dissolution, the Convention passed an electoral law to ensure a degree of political continuity. Voters were required to select two-thirds of the new deputies from the ranks of those who had served in the Convention. Thereafter, these deputies would stand down, a third at a time, each year.

proved to be the chief gainers from the elections to fill the places of the outgoing '**third**', these neo-Jacobins posed the more palpable threat. Their clubs were infiltrated and their newspapers harassed; in fact the Pantheon Club, which regularly attracted many hundreds of nostalgic supporters of the politics of the Terror, was closed down by the government in February 1796. This action provoked a more sinister development, though. Led by Gracchus Babeuf, the publisher of *Le Tribune du Peuple* and a man who had dabbled in democratic politics since the start of the revolution, a small group of enthusiasts for the advanced social and democratic agenda outlined in the Constitution of 1793 began to plot an insurrection – or, more properly, a *coup* – against the regime. Babeuf's 'Conspiracy of the Equals' was betrayed within a matter of months and it never amounted to much in any case. Nevertheless, the Directory made the most of the 'threat', put the plotters in the dock and dressed up the case as a trial of Jacobinism as a whole. Babeuf and a fellow conspirator were guillotined in May 1797.

Despite the precautions taken by the Convention during its final weeks, the main beneficiaries of regime change turned out to be the royalists. The elections that launched the Directory in October 1795 returned over 100 to parliament, although they were by no means all 'purs' (i.e. counter-revolutionaries). On the contrary, many would have been content with a return to constitutional monarchy on the 1791 pattern, or something similar. But at least the citadel of government was held firmly by the moderate republicans: the deputies who had been prolonged in office took care to make sure that the executive was filled by men of their own stamp. All five of the Directors had supported the death sentence meted out to Louis XVI in 1793. Still, the royalists had achieved an important bridgehead and would draw strength from the fact that the rampart constructed around the republic by the Convention could only erode in the years to come. When the next electoral renewal fell due in March 1797, the royalist leaders made a supreme effort of organisation and propaganda, and they swept the board. Only 11 of the 216 retiring deputies were re-elected and, in total, about 180 of 260 seats being contested were taken by royalist candidates of one persuasion or another. This diluted considerably the political complexion of the Councils, with the regicides among the deputies now numbering barely one in five. As a consequence, the regime entered a phase of protracted crisis.

'LA GRANDE NATION'

From the late spring of 1794, the logistical efforts of the Committee of Public Safety, which had enabled the armies to expand to 750,000 men, began to bear fruit. Victory against the Austrians and the Dutch at Fleurus reopened the road into Belgium in June, and before the year was out, Austrian forces had been pushed back across the Rhine as well. By the time the Directory came to power, the territory of the republic was not even remotely under threat from foreign enemies. On the contrary; the 'natural' frontiers of France (the Rhine, the Pyrenees) had been secured, and her armies were encamped on German, Spanish and Italian soil. How much this fortunate state of affairs owed to enhanced combat effectiveness deriving from the coupling of military service and citizenship is a matter for debate among historians. Yet the structural weaknesses which had bedevilled French military performance in 1792 had certainly been remedied by 1794. Even if the troops were not necessarily the missionaries of liberty of Brissotin rhetoric, a truly national and omnicompetent fighting force had come into being. This applied to the navy as well. When the Russell sisters of Birmingham were captured in the Channel by a French frigate as they were heading for America that summer, they were struck by the calm efficiency of the crew and the cameraderie between officers and sailors. Most of all, however, they were impressed by how they all sang the 'Marseillaise Hymn' morning, noon and night (Jeyes, 1911: 66–7).

Between 1795 and 1802, France proceeded to annex Belgium, the Rhineland and Piedmont, thereby enlarging the republic by a fifth (see Map 4). It was difficult to confine these expansionist moves to the realm of foreign policy, however. As in 1792–93, the successes (and failures) of the armies directly impacted on the domestic political debate. Many deputies were fearful that the acquisition of territory for its own sake would undermine the republic and open the way to empire and despotism. Whilst liberty would probably survive the securing of 'natural' frontiers, any further expansion might place it in jeopardy. Why, then, did the Directory proceed to set up eight 'sister republics' in these years? Until the summer of 1796, the armies were kept on a fairly tight rein, the Directory believing that their successes should be used chiefly in order to bring France's adversaries (primarily Austria) to the conference table. After all, a weakened Sardinian monarchy on France's south-eastern border might make better sense than a democratic republic of Piedmont. However, the thinking in Paris shifted radically the following year – no doubt in response to General Bonaparte's stunning successes in northern Italy. The concept of the sister republic seemed to offer an alternative to outright annexation, and it enabled the regime's architects to persuade themselves that they were not, after all, embarking on the acquisition of a land-based empire. It also enabled the Directory to accommodate home-grown republican movements, which were particularly vigorous in Italy. Nevertheless, we should be under no illusion as to the nature of the relationship. It was entirely one-sided – not a partnership [**Doc. 21**]

The 'grande nation' was coming into being willy-nilly, then. Yet the combination of victory and peace continued to elude the Directory. Whilst

Prussia, Holland and Spain were all brought to terms in the course of 1795, Britain and Austria fought on. Indeed, Russia was induced to join the anti-French coalition once the third partition of Poland had been completed. Not until October 1797 would the Habsburgs agree terms for peace (Treaty of Campo Formio), thereby securing for France recognition of her annexation two years earlier of the Austrian Netherlands. Britain, meanwhile, remained at war with France until March 1802 (Peace of Amiens).

France owed her military achievements during these years to a number of factors in addition to sheer fighting ability. Wherever French generals and civil commissioners went, they introduced reforms that tended to boost their own self-belief and sap that of the army commanders arrayed against them. Liberationist rhetoric would turn out to be an immensely powerful weapon of war. However, it was probably sheer experience and military competence that turned them into such redoubtable foes by 1795. The novice volunteer recruits of 1791 and 1792 had become battle-hardened, and systems had been put in place to blend old troops with new, and to ensure that only the most capable individuals were selected for command positions. In the process, the old royal army with its aristocratic officer elite almost entirely disappeared. By 1798, only a tiny fraction of the soldiers had service records dating back to the *ancien régime*. France also possessed a considerable reservoir of manpower which could be tapped in a relatively straightforward manner, thanks to the administrative reforms of the revolution. Informal conscription had been introduced with the **levée en masse** decree passed on 23 August 1793, and from 1798 it became routine and bureaucratic in the sense that all single males aged between 20 and 25 were automatically registered as liable for military service. This Jourdan Law encountered opposition and its enforcement in the west was delayed for a time. However, systematic and open-ended conscription ensured that a further 280,000 men could be enrolled in the armies of the republic by the summer of 1800.

Of course, the professionalisation of military life meant that the close bonding with the Jacobin 'nation in arms' of 1793–94 tended to weaken as well. Soldiers with long years of service both behind and ahead of them increasingly identified with the unit or the army corps to which they belonged. Thus, the Army of the Rhine and the Moselle commanded by Pichegru and then Moreau acquired a reputation for crypto-royalist sympathies, whilst in Italy the troops commanded by Bernadotte clashed with Masséna's ostentatiously republican division. The Army of Italy under General Bonaparte's command, by contrast, remained identifiable by virtue of its Jacobin affiliations. Bonaparte had already made himself useful to politicians struggling to overcome the domestic royalist threat on several occasions, and in March 1796 he was sent to Italy to take over from Schérer. In the absence of a decisive breakthrough on the Rhine front, the exploits of

levée en masse: Proclamation of a 'mass levy' of able-bodied men to rush to the defence of the revolution.

this modest-sized army, commanded brilliantly by its 27-year-old general, rapidly attracted the attention of the Directory back in Paris. In a whirlwind campaign, Bonaparte split the Austrian and Piedmontese forces, causing Victor Amadeus III to relinquish control over Nice and Savoy. He then headed into the Po valley in pursuit of the Austrians, who were badly mauled at Lodi. On 15 May 1796, the French entered Milan and subjected the city to a huge ransom. Bonaparte paid his troops in cash, an unheard-of gesture, before advancing with what amounted to a private army towards Modena, Tuscany and the most northerly Papal States. A long siege of the fortress of Mantua followed, during which Bonaparte inflicted further defeats on the Austrians (Arcola, Rivoli). Mantua fell early in 1797, enabling the Army of Italy to continue its rampage. The Austrians were pushed back to Leoben, where an armistice was signed (18 April), whereupon the French proceeded to occupy Venetia.

By this date, the government was beginning to lose the power to control its generals. Bonaparte, in particular, realised that he could act pretty much as he pleased, provided that the flow of money and resources being sent back to Paris was maintained. Parleying with the Austrians at Leoben, just 100 miles short of Vienna, had been his own idea and the terms of the armistice were presented to the Directors as a *fait accompli*. No doubt there was considerable relief in the corridors of political power when, the following year, this immensely popular general with apparently impeccable republican – if no longer Jacobin – credentials decided to take an army to Egypt. Britain's naval superiority in the Channel had forestalled the plan to launch an invasion against France's one remaining adversary, and so the decision had been taken to try to cut her trade routes to India instead.

RULE BY *COUP*

By the spring of 1797, the political problem that had bedevilled all previous revolutionary regimes – namely, the striking of a balance between the executive and the legislative arms of government – was beginning to reassert itself. The solution (tried out originally in the Convention) appeared to be to engineer a balance by means of *coups* and purges. But the removal of 'disloyal' deputies (and Directors) simply risked weakening the loyalty of everyone to the solution devised in 1795. Since the allocation of powers within the government could scarcely be altered by constitutional means, the whole regime was brought into disrepute. Bonaparte's final *coup* pushed at an open door, therefore. It seems unlikely that it could have succeeded if those with executive authority had chosen to resist.

The landslide victory of the royalists in the elections of 1797 set the scene, if only because the number and temper of the new royalist deputies (who included men with links to the Pretender, such as Pichegru and Imbert-Colomès) galvanised the moderates into action. With Pichegru at the helm of the Council of Five Hundred and a pliant tool (Barthélemy) elected to the Directory in the place of the outgoing Le Tourneur, the royalists secured the lifting of the disabilities imposed on the relatives of *émigrés* and a substantial repeal of the persecutory legislation that still affected non-oath-swearing clergymen. They also manoeuvred to deny the Directors control over expenditure, a crucial issue at a moment when the government was in the throes of withdrawing paper currency and reliant on the remittances from Italy in order to stave off bankruptcy. On 4 September, in consequence, Parisians awoke to find troops loyal to one of Bonaparte's most trusted commanders encamped in the capital. Barthélemy and 53 deputies were expelled (and condemned to the 'dry guillotine' of deportation), and the election results achieved earlier that year in 49 departments were overturned.

The use of the army in order to resolve a parliamentary crisis set a worrying example. However, it was not without precedent and was not inconsistent with the creeping militarisation of public life that was taking place during the Directory years. In the late winter of 1795, the Thermidorians had broken the taboo and called out troops to put down disturbances outside bakers' shops. In April of the same year, during a final hunger-driven uprising of the Sections, the deputies had responded by sending soldiers and cavalry into the *faubourg* Saint-Antoine to enforce compliance with the will of government. Those involved in this Prairial insurrection (20–23 April), together with six ex-Montagnard deputies who had compromised themselves, were then sentenced using the expedient of a military commission. Just before the dissolution of the Convention, troops had again been called out – this time to quell a mobilisation in Paris of royalists protesting against the two-thirds law. In principle, however, the architects of the regime deplored military intervention in domestic politics. General Augereau would twice offer himself as a candidate for the Directory and would be turned down twice. By 1797, though, the army was no longer a pliant tool. The generals had largely emancipated themselves from civilian control when on campaign, and the politicians knew that they were playing with fire when soliciting help to overturn the wishes of the voters.

The coup of 18 Fructidor V would prove to be a defeat for royalists of all persuasions, and one from which they would never recover. But it was indubitably a defeat for the Directory as well, since it demonstrated that the adherents of the regime lacked the courage of their liberal convictions. Setting aside the legally expressed wishes of the electorate was no way for a parliamentary democracy to behave. All over the republic, priests and *émigrés* who had slipped back into the country in the hope of better times repacked their bags. In nearly half of the departments, large numbers of elected and non-elected officials were summarily dismissed in a purge reminiscent of the days of the Terror. Journalists who had helped to mobilise royalist opinion were arrested, and 42 Parisian and provincial newspapers forced to close down. But if the triumvirate of Directors who had been chiefly responsible for the *coup* (La Révellière, Barras and Reubell) supposed that it would enable the political 'centre' to regain the initiative, they were mistaken. The main beneficiaries in the country at large were the 'firm republicans' (that is to say the neo-Jacobins) and, as the new round of legislative elections approached, it began to look as though they would come to pose the next parliamentary challenge.

By any standards, the elections of March 1798 represented a huge gamble for a regime that had yet to accept the logic of political pluralism. Not only had the final 'third' of outgoing deputies from the Convention to be replaced, but all the seats left vacant by deaths, resignations and purges had to be filled as well. In short, a contest involving 437 candidates was looming. With feelings running high against royalism, the neo-Jacobins naturally thought that their moment had come. Political clubs reopened and stern measures against priests, *émigrés* and ex-nobles were demanded. There was even an attempt to rehabilitate some of those who had been swept up in the wake of Babeuf's quasi-communist conspiracy of the year before. However, the government remained obsessed with the royalist menace, and only belatedly recognised that reliance on the neo-Jacobins in order to defeat the royalists might place the regime at risk from forces located at either end of the political spectrum. A law permitting the Councils to scrutinise the validity of the electoral results was introduced and, a month before the poll, the Directors alerted the electorate to the danger of 'royalism in a red bonnet' and started to close down neo-Jacobin press organs and clubs.

Notwithstanding the exhortations of the government, the voters turned out in smaller numbers than the year before: cynicism was beginning to take its toll. Yet those who did, gave strong support to the candidates with left-of-centre credentials. All in all, some 162 individuals who had sat in the Convention were returned, 71 of whom were on the record as having voted for the death of Louis XVI. Whilst scarcely overwhelming in number, the neo-Jacobins now constituted sizeable minorities in each of the two Councils. However, the government showed its mettle in its treatment of the results of disputed ballots, of which there were no fewer than 178. The elections of candidates who were thought to be hostile were systematically invalidated. And when this laborious process began to run out of parliamentary time, the Directors intervened (on 11 May 1798) and simply annulled results en masse. Around 127 deputies were denied the right to take up their seats, of whom roughly 60 per cent would have counted as neo-Jacobins.

The Fructidor *coup* had been carried out against a well-substantiated royalist threat. But no one pretended that the neo-Jacobins were bent on overthrowing the regime. The intervention of 22 Floréal VI would appear to demonstrate, therefore, that the Directory could not even reconcile itself to the existence of a constitutional opposition. The government did its best to prepare the elections of the following year (March 1799) as well. Far better to secure the election of its own candidates than to resort to yet another damaging administrative intervention *post facto*. Clearly, it suited the Directory to depict the neo-Jacobins as nostalgic throwbacks to the Year Two (1793–94) whose unsavoury links to the Paris *sans-culottes* had not yet been broken. Whether this picture is entirely accurate is a matter for debate. Some historians argue that neo-Jacobinism should be recognised as a maturing political force (if not yet a party), which would have occupied a niche within the Directorial system of government had the events of 1799 not determined otherwise (Gainot, 2001: 1–25).

At least the army had not been involved in the efforts to set aside the more inconvenient results of the elections of 1798. Yet the electorate drew its own conclusions. In March 1799, turnout dropped to the lowest level of the decade. By this time, the terminal crisis of the regime was fast approaching. With their most talented general cut off in Egypt following Rear-Admiral Nelson's destruction of the French fleet in Aboukir Bay, the Directory suffered reverses in Italy that brought Austria into the fray once more. By June 1799, nearly all of Bonaparte's achievements in the peninsula had been wiped out; moreover, defeat in southern Germany had forced General Jourdan's army to retreat back across the upper reaches of the Rhine and into Switzerland. Emboldened by the re-election of some of the deputies who had been removed the year before, the Council of Five Hundred attacked the Directors for their mishandling of the war effort and succeeded in carrying out its own purge. Sieyès had already been elected in the place of Reubell, who had drawn the unlucky ball in the annual renewal ballot, but then Treilhard, Merlin de Douai and La Révellière were forced out in rapid succession. This was serious, for Merlin and La Révellière had been the only true believers left in the Directory, while Sieyès, the perpetual dreamer of constitutions, was known to disapprove of that of 1795.

In an atmosphere of incipient military disaster and civil emergency reminiscent of the spring and the summer of 1792, the final countdown began. Despite all the administrative meddling, a sizeable minority of between 135 and 150 neo-Jacobin deputies had survived in the two Councils. With the support of others who *had* lost confidence in the regime, they were able to secure punitive laws against *émigrés* and former nobles, and a 'forced loan' was imposed on the rich. The clubs briefly revived and a motion was even put on 13 September to have 'the fatherland in danger' declared. The motion was defeated, for it prompted the deputies to take stock and to ask themselves whether their irritation with the Directors was worth risking a return to the Terror. The neo-Jacobin offensive ground to a halt amid a slight easing of tensions on receipt of the news that General Masséna had decisively beaten the Austro-Russian army in the second battle of Zurich. The threat of a concerted counterattack in the south-west and the west had receded by this time as well, although the *chouans* of Brittany and Normandy remained on a hostile footing. Nevertheless, these multi-pronged assaults prompted even the most sanguine supporters of the Directory to wonder how much longer it would be possible to steer a political course between the extremes. Sieyès, who felt no compunction about discarding the constitution, had already made contact with General Joubert, but he was killed at the battle of Novi. Bonaparte was by no means the politicians' first choice of instrument for the strengthening of executive authority, it should be said. In any case, he was in Egypt – or was he? On hearing of the disasters in the European theatre of war, he abandoned his army and hurried back to France, where he arrived on 9 October 1799.

OPPONENTS

The neo-Jacobin programme might or might not have offered a viable alternative to the *coup* of Brumaire if the Directory had been granted time and political space in which to evolve. Nevertheless, by 1799, the revolution as a whole had generated an impressive list of opponents. The first casualty had been Charles-Alexandre de Calonne. Following his fall from grace as Côntroleur-Général in April 1787, he was threatened with prosecution by the Parlement of Paris and withdrew to London. Hopes of a recall at the time of the Estates-General were never realistic, and he would become the first of the servitors of absolute monarchy to join in the emigration. The ministers, such as Barentin and the Baron de Breteuil, who had conspired to oust Necker and overawe the embryonic National Assembly with a display of force in the summer of 1789 were the next to go. Most left the country soon after the fall of the Bastille. They included the king's brother, the Comte d'Artois (future Charles X), the Princes de Condé and de Conti, the Duc de Bourbon and powerful courtier families such as the Polignacs. The Comte de Provence, his other sibling, would not depart until June 1791, whilst the king's aunts (Victoire and Adélaide) made a controversial journey out of the country in February 1791. Like Louis, they would be stopped on route by a vigilant municipality, but the Assembly could find no grounds on which to restrict their freedom to travel, and they were allowed to head towards Turin unimpeded.

All these men and women refugees formed nuclei of a political and physical emigration which would define itself as explicitly hostile to the revolution. Most gathered in European capitals such as London, Turin and Verona to await the turn of the political tide. Few could have imagined in 1790 or 1791 that their self-imposed exile would last a decade and more.

Not all opponents became *émigrés*, of course. As early as the autumn of 1789, a trickle of deputies had chosen to absent themselves from the legislature on the grounds that the pace of political events had far outstripped what they, or their constituents, could tolerate. After the defeat of the *Monarchiens'* proposal for an upper house and an absolute veto, Jean-Joseph Mounier and the Marquis de Lally-Tollendal – their chief parliamentary spokesmen – quit in disgust. Many other deputies also requested passports in the aftermath of the October Days. Some managed to live obscurely and safely by keeping their opinions to themselves and trusting neighbours not to denounce them. The same is true of the aristocracy – or rather, the ex-aristocracy – since the legally enshrined status of noble had been abolished by the National Assembly. The majority did *not* emigrate. Instead, they lived quietly on their estates in the hope that the wheel of political fortune would one day turn again in their favour.

Until 1792, and the descent into war with the rest of Europe, it was not absolutely certain that France *had* crossed the political Rubicon in any case. A prudential attitude, such as that adopted by the (ex-)Marquis de Ferrières, therefore seemed justified. Although historians often overstate the extent to which harmony and a sense of common purpose prevailed throughout the year 1790, the notion that the country faced malevolent opponents only began to take shape in the aftermath of the king's covert departure from the Tuileries Palace in June 1791. The Flight acted as a catalyst. It forced the Great Powers to act; it unleashed fears of a war of intervention the following spring; and it triggered, albeit indirectly, a renewed wave of despairing emigration when Louis appended his signature to the constitution. For the first time, ordinary men and women began to discuss the possibility of a 'counter-revolution'.

Once the deputies of the Legislative Assembly had got the political bit between their teeth, emigrant nobles really were put on the spot. The **Elector of Trier**, whose territories touched France's eastern border, was advised that he should stop sheltering *émigrés* in Koblenz, whilst the Comte de Provence was warned to return on pain of being excluded from the succession. When the essentially personal decision to express hostility to the train of events by leaving the country was made an offence punishable by law, the issue was clarified for many nobles: return and accept the revolution and all its works, or stay abroad and pay the price. With seizure of property, imprisonment and even execution the likely price, the decision to join an armed counter-revolution became an easier one to take.

Elector of Trier: The ruler with territory west of the river Rhine who provided shelter to *émigrés*.

Clerical opponents of the revolution were granted much less time in which to mull over their options, for the National Assembly forced the issue by demanding that all clergy swear an oath of loyalty early in 1791. However, the result was more poignant, for most of the clergy had been conspicuous supporters of the new regime from the outset. The oath legislation split clergymen into two roughly equal groups. Those who refused the oath swiftly became irreconcilable opponents of the revolution. Many fled the country in fear of arrest and imprisonment. As a result, it became hard to distinguish them from a counter-revolution of courtiers and nobles who regretted the passing of the *ancien régime*. However, the requirement to swear successive oaths of allegiance made political hostages of the 'constitutional' or juring clergy as well. By the time of the Terror, the revolutionaries had lost interest in building a state church with a dedicated priesthood. Coerced into abandoning their spiritual vocation and pushed onto the margins of public life, if not actively persecuted, it is probable that many constitutional clergy ended up in the opposition camp as well. In fact, the separation of church and state was formally promulgated early in 1795, and the Directory years would see an exuberant flowering of cults, not to mention 'do it yourself' religion pioneered in parishes with neither juring nor non-juring clergy to hand [**Doc. 22**]. The latter were frequently treated as outlaws by the authorities and were liable to deportation or worse if captured, but the erstwhile jurors were subjected to intermittent harassment as well.

Much, perhaps too much, has been made of counter-revolution by historians in recent years. As the decade of the 1790s drew to a close, most men and women were still glad that the *ancien régime* had come to an end. The Directory's opponents, like the opponents of previous regimes, were not necessarily counter-revolutionaries. With the exception of well-defined areas, such as Brittany and the Vendée, there never seems to have been much support for counter-revolution inside the country. The repeated failure of outlaw clergy and roving emissaries of the Princes to trigger royalist insurrections acknowledges as much. Another such attempt occurred in the summer of 1799, when inhabitants of villages and small towns in the vicinity of Toulouse responded to a call to arms. But it is far from certain that the mobilisation was inspired by the royalist agenda and, in any case, it soon fizzled out. No doubt many country dwellers had grown tired of the revolution by this date, but impatience at the reappearance of tax collectors, frustration at the absence of priests, and hostility to requisitions and military service would not turn them into counter-revolutionaries.

7

Consolidation, 1799–1804

Most survey histories of the French Revolution end in 1799; some even end in 1794. Why, then, do we continue the story until 1804 and Bonaparte's coronation as Emperor of the French? The question should be answered at several levels. For a start, the republic remained in existence until 1804. It was a system of government that could accommodate hugely divergent interpretations of how power should be exercised. However, it could not accommodate the hereditary rule of one man. Moreover, France's infant republic was in the throes of an evolution in 1799, as we have seen, and it would be arbitrary to curtail its life cycle purely on the grounds a *coup* happened in Brumaire.

It seems unlikely that the mass of French men and women would have regarded the events of that autumn as somehow out of the ordinary, in any case. After all, they were informed that the intervention had taken place in order to make the republic more secure. The sense of a new beginning – one indissolubly associated with the name of Bonaparte – only began to develop after the victory at Marengo (14 June 1800) brought some solidity to the new regime. As for General Bonaparte personally (from 1802 official proclamations referred to him as Napoleon Bonaparte), his relationship to the revolutionary past may have been ambiguous, but it was not rooted in deep-seated hostility. Witness the declaration to the public that accompanied the issuing of the new constitution: 'Citizens! The revolution is established upon the principles with which it began: it is over' (Crook, 1998: 73).

Napoleon regarded himself not as the enemy of the revolution, but as its consolidator. The fact that others begged to differ (not least historians), simply tells us that the heritage of the revolution meant different things to different people by 1800. For Napoleon, the enduring legacy of the revolution lay in the victory over 'privilege' achieved in 1789, the institutional and administrative reforms initiated by the first two legislative Assemblies, and the social regrouping in the corridors of power that these achievements had made possible. He was scornful of radical schemes to recast society, and regarded undiluted sovereignty of the people as tantamount to anarchy. Yet most thinking people would probably have shared these views in 1799, even while continuing to think of themselves as beneficiaries of the revolution.

BRUMAIRE

Despite the annual drama of elections, the Directory had, by the autumn of 1799, lasted longer than any of the previous governments put in place by the revolutionaries. The electoral hustings held in March of that year had not added to the injuries inflicted in 1797 and 1798, and the regime might have continued to evolve had it not been destabilised by the military crisis of the summer. The news of Bonaparte's return was taken to be a good omen; he would roll back the republic's external and internal enemies once more and curb all the alarmist talk insinuating that the nation's survival could only be guaranteed by a return to something resembling the politics of the Terror. His involvement in the schemes to strengthen executive authority being mooted by Sieyès and others was consistent with these expectations. The *coup*, when it came on 18 Brumaire, was not a determined bid for personal power. On the contrary, Bonaparte turned out to be a rather ham-fisted plotter and the assault launched against the Directory very nearly ended badly for him.

As in the case of all previous *coups* and insurrections, the aim was to achieve change by legal means if possible and to use force only as a last resort. Early on the morning of 9 November, a number of deputies in the Council of Elders, who were no doubt privy to what was afoot, were advised of the discovery of a terrifying neo-Jacobin 'plot'. If plausible, the allegation was nevertheless entirely bogus; its purpose was to induce the deputies to agree to the transfer of the legislative bodies to a place of 'safety' outside the capital. Bonaparte, meanwhile, was empowered to take charge of all the troops in the Paris military district, and three of the five Directors resigned (Sieyès, Ducos and Barras). To forestall any opposition, Bonaparte's brother Lucien, who had been elected president of the Council of Five Hundred only a couple of weeks earlier, cut short the discussion in his chamber; but no attempt was made to arrest any neo-Jacobin deputies at this stage.

The next day, the legislative bodies reconvened in the former royal palace of Saint-Cloud, six miles distant from the capital. Realising that they had been hoodwinked, some of the deputies began to show signs of a willingness to defend the regime – an eventuality that appears to have caught the plotters unprepared. Impatient at the delay, Bonaparte barged into the meeting place of the Elders and harangued the deputies in a manner that made it all too obvious that he was the instrument chosen to overthrow the government.

But worse was to follow, for he then entered the chamber of the Five Hundred, accompanied by an escort of grenadiers, only to be greeted with shouts of 'Down with the dictator!' After some rough handling, he beat a retreat. This setback forced the conspirators into a life or death struggle, for a vote to outlaw Bonaparte and his collaborators would have caused the *coup* attempt to collapse. Lucien saved the day with remarkable presence of mind. Having also been ejected from the chamber, he harangued the waiting troops, claiming that the majority of deputies were being held hostage by 'miserable offspring of the Terror' (Woloch, 2001: 22), adding that an attempt had been made to stab their commander to death. For good measure, he insisted that he would rather stab his brother himself than allow him to betray the nation's freedom. On this appeal from the president of the Five Hundred, the guards cleared the hall of the deputies, with regular troops providing a back-up force. That evening, a rump legislature voted to abolish the Directory and to substitute a three-man executive comprising Sieyès, Bonaparte and Ducos. Around 60 neo-Jacobin deputies were expelled from the Council of Five Hundred with immediate effect, and plans were put in hand to draw up a new constitution.

In the country at large, the events of Brumaire were poorly diagnosed. Public opinion in Rouen interpreted the news as simply another Directory *coup*, although decrees issued in the aftermath of the proroguing of the Councils made it clear that a provisional 'Consulate' had been set up. In Toulouse and Grenoble, the *coup* was perceived as having an anti-Jacobin animus, even though Bonaparte issued an announcement insisting on the non-partisan character of the action taken against the Directory. Paris remained non-committal at street level, a fact for which the plotters had reason to be grateful. The stock exchange rallied on the other hand – presumably because the strengthened executive moved swiftly to abolish the 'forced loan' and the draconian legislation imposed on the families of *émigrés* during the summer. It would be a year before the change of government managed to reverse the breakdown of law and order in the countryside, though. Highwaymen, draft-evaders and unruly priests generated a climate of insecurity which in the south-east of the country, particularly, had never seemed greater (Plate 6). Only in the west did the authorities score an early success when the *chouans* agreed to an armistice. Like the Pretender and his *émigré* Court, they were watching events closely in an effort to determine the political significance of Brumaire.

The speed with which the legislative commissions appointed immediately after the *coup* produced a constitution betrays the anxiety of all concerned to bring to an end the makeshift character of the new regime. Constitutions of the revolutionary era habitually took months – if not years – to draft, but the founding document of the Consulate was drawn up and issued in six weeks – that is to say, on 15 December 1799. In practice, it was devised by

Bonaparte himself, who liked to do everything quickly. As such, it was short, obscure and notably lacking in a preliminary statement of rights. Sieyès, whom everyone assumed would have a ready-made draft in his pocket, contributed general ideas, including the notion that 'confidence comes from below and authority from above' (Jainchill, 2008: 227), but was ignored by the overbearing General on the issue of power sharing. Bonaparte wanted to concentrate executive power rather than to divide and disperse it in order to achieve balance. Only by sublimating the freedom of all into a singular source of authority that would stand above party, he believed, could the revolution be brought to a successful conclusion. He therefore borrowed an idea from the lawyer-deputy Boulay de la Meurthe for a 'First Consul' who would exercise power for a ten-year term with the help of two other Consuls. However, their role would be consultative, for the decision of the First Consul alone counted, and the text of the constitution specifically allocated the office of First Consul to Bonaparte. The problem of the Directory's weak executive – designed as such in reaction to the Terror – had been resolved.

Legislative arrangements under the Constitution of 1800 retained more traces of Sieyès's ideas, though. Two chambers came into being: a small body, known as the Tribunate, was empowered to discuss proposals put forward by the government, but could not vote on the measures, whereas a rather bigger Legislative Body (Corps Législatif) was entitled to vote on legislative proposals, but could not debate them beforehand. However, all bills were subject to prior scrutiny by a Senate acting as a kind of constitutional court. The right to initiate legislation was vested in the Consuls, needless to say, and the First Consul alone had the power to submit amendments. To aid in the preparation of legislation, a Council of State was set up, the members of which would bring proposals before the Tribunate and the Legislative Body and defend them as necessary. None of these bodies was directly elected – Bonaparte believed that direct elections nurtured factional strife – and neither the Consuls nor the ministers were responsible to the two-chamber legislature.

The constitution as a whole should have been submitted to the outgoing Councils of the Directory for ratification. But this would have been to invite a critique of the very considerable powers now concentrated in the hands of one man. Instead, Bonaparte decided to hold a plebiscite or referendum, although this did not prevent the Consuls from putting the constitution into effect in anticipation of the results of the popular ballot. The voters scarcely had much of a choice since both the *coup* and the extinction of the Directory were *faits accomplis*. According to the results announced on 7 February 1800, over 3 million endorsed the constitution and 1,562 rejected it. In fact, the returns were padded in the bureaux of the Interior Ministry, which was controlled by Lucien Bonaparte: only about 1.5 million adult males out of a potential 7 million turned out to declare their support for the regime.

BUILDING AFRESH

If the *coup* of Brumaire was not intended to be a repudiation of the principles of the revolution, there was general agreement among supporters of the
new regime that a certain amount of rebuilding would be required so as to
remedy defects that had come to light since 1789. In many spheres, the Directory
had already begun this work, of course, although Bonapartist propaganda
went to some pains to obscure the fact. Decisive action in the budgetary
domain had largely sorted out the problem of financial insolvency, which had
hindered the actions of the politicians ever since the time of Calonne. In the
aftermath of the Fructidor coup, Ramel-Nogaret, the Finance Minister,
reneged on two-thirds of the public debt, thereby cutting it at a stroke from
about 250 million to 80 million *livres*. Converted into treasury bonds, the
remaining third soon lost value, with the result that the debt came to repres-
ent only about 10 per cent of annual income, whereas in 1789 it had stood
at 250 per cent. The experiment with a paper currency had also been
brought to an end, which vastly increased the value of receipts from taxation.
The Consulate was only too happy to build on these reforms, and it built,
too, on the trend towards the recentralisation of tax collection. A law passed
within days of the *coup* created a specialist tax administration in each department. With the gradual return of law and order to the countryside, overhead
costs went down, and by 1801 it proved possible actually to collect tax liabil-
ities in the year in which they fell due. For most of the previous decade, taxes
had been paid in arrears, often in depreciated paper notes and vouchers.

The Directory had also started to address some of the defects inherent in
the devolved local government system put in place by the National Assembly.
Individual village municipalities – one of the prime sources of revolutionary
vitality – had been abolished in 1795, as we have seen. Likewise the District
administrations, which were replaced with consolidated, or canton-based,
municipalities. The Constitution of 1795 also made the first breach in the
principle that local officials should be democratically accountable, inasmuch
as the Commissioners of the Executive Directory – the main cogs in the
Directorial apparatus of local government – were appointed, not elected.
Within months of taking office, the Consuls radically overhauled this system
and resolved its ambiguities. Democratic accountability was no longer to
form part of the heritage of the revolution. The Bonapartist synthesis of
liberty and authority required the initiative to come from above, rather than
below. Individual villages retrieved their mayors and municipal officers, it is
true, for power-sharing at the level of the canton had not proved a satisfactory compromise. But local officials were all appointed by, and answerable to,
the government in the person of a 'prefect'. The opportunities for municipal
councils to meet and deliberate were curtailed, too, for the First Consul

considered assemblies and elections to be the twin sources of the party strife that had stood in the way of consolidating the work of the revolution.

The key figure in the post-1799 system of local government was the prefect. In each department the First Consul nominated an agent, whose responsibilities were all-embracing. With the help of sub-prefects residing in divisions of the departments known as *arrondissements*, he was to supervise police activities, village affairs, hospitals, public works, conscription, tax raising and much else besides. Vestigial assemblies, reminiscent of the old Department and District councils created in 1790, operated alongside the prefects and sub-prefects, to be sure, but they had no powers of their own. The prefects are sometimes compared with those agents of absolute monarchy, the intendants. Yet the prefects were far more powerful figures – if only because the abolition of corporate privilege had removed all rival sources of authority from the regions in which they administered. They were also utterly loyal to the central government and to a concept of law that placed them above and beyond the reach of factional politics.

The Consulate's greatest act of consolidation occurred in the religious domain, however. Despite the abandonment of the Civil Constitution of the Clergy in 1795 and the tentative moves towards toleration, the Directory had never felt entirely at ease with the policy of religious pluralism. The link between the activities of the non-oath-swearing clergy, the *émigrés* and internal counter-revolution was too obvious to ignore. Besides, the regime had its own liturgy of civic festivals and adhered doggedly to the republican calendar that the Convention had introduced in 1793. When one of the first acts of the Brumaire plotters was to curtail the elaborate programme of secular feast days, exiled clergy all over Europe pricked up their ears, therefore. Indeed, large numbers of non-jurors returned to their parishes during the winter of 1799–1800 in the belief that a relaxation of the proscription laws was only a matter of time. However, the regime needed the kind of solidity and legitimacy that could only be earned on the field of battle before it felt able to contemplate a move in this direction. On the eve of the decisive engagement at Marengo, Bonaparte appeared to acknowledge that the goal of a consolidated civil society would prove illusory without the reinforcement of religion, and that this, in turn, would require a rapprochement with the pope. 'In religion', he later commented, 'I see not the mystery of the incarnation, but the mystery of the social order' (Ellis, 1997: 235).

Since the policy of clerical persecution (not to mention that of dechristianisation) had manifestly failed, the advantages of a policy of pacification – sincerely undertaken – were not difficult to spell out. It would cut the tap-root of peasant resistance (in the Vendée; in Brittany); it would force the *ancien-régime* bishops, who had spent ten years fishing in the troubled waters of the revolution from the safety of exile, to choose between the interests of the monarchy and those of religion; it would make the future expansion of the 'grande nation' into Catholic parts of Europe easier to carry through; and, above all, it would bring to an end the rift of 1790–91, and provide a further source of legitimacy for the regime in the making. In return, Pope Pius VII would regain control over Europe's largest Catholic state, a chance to restore the fabric of the Church and the opportunity to rechristianise the population [**Doc. 22**]. To be sure, this 'control' came at a price which many in the hierarchy considered excessive: Catholicism would not be the state religion, but merely 'the religion of the great majority of French citizens' (Buchez and Roux, 1838: vol. 38, 465), and the corporate privileges of the old Gallican Church had to be given up without any hope of recovery. The tithe remained abolished and the sales of Church property (***biens nationaux***) would not be reversed, nor compensation paid.

biens nationaux: Confiscated property formerly belonging to the Church and to individuals who had fled the revolution, which was put up for sale.

A question mark hung over the fate of the oath-swearing bishops and clergy, however, for the pope was most reluctant to have them back in the fold on a 'forgive and forget' basis. Yet the constitutional Church was far from moribund and the treatment meted out to it represented a test of the government's commitment to genuine reconciliation. Bonaparte would advise his Minister of Ecclesiastical Affairs to 'mix the constitutional priests with the others in such a way that no party seems to be triumphing at the expense of the other' (Lyons, 1994: 91). However, at the moment the Concordat was signed on 15 July 1801, this matter was still not fully resolved.

Nor was that quite the end of the saga, for the deal struck with the papacy remained secret for many months and Bonaparte used the pause to add further 'organic articles' to the outline agreement. These additional clauses enhanced the authority of the secular power in matters to do with the clergy, yet the authority of the bishops over the parish clergy was reinforced also. Under the new regime, they would be appointed by their ecclesiastical superiors rather than elected by the laity, and could be moved at will. When the Concordat was finally made public in time for Easter Sunday 1802, the tolling of church bells was heard across the republic for the first time in eight years. Jacobin sympathisers who could remember the glory days of 1793 and 1794 were not impressed. At the solemn Mass held in the presence of the government and the diplomatic corps in Notre Dame cathedral, General Delmas is reported to have exclaimed: 'all we need are the 100,000 men who got themselves killed to be rid of all this' (Lyons, 1994: 88).

A NEW ORDER

Although the resolving of the unfinished business of the revolution in matters of faith and conscience proved more robust than anyone could have anticipated, it was not the most enduring achievement of the Consulate. The

Civil Code, which was promulgated in 1804, must be regarded as the supreme act of consolidation to emerge from the *coup* of Brumaire. Even at the time, this synthesis of *ancien régime* and revolutionary legal wisdom was hailed as the cornerstone of the new post-1799 social order. Bonaparte would come to regard it as a greater victory than any he had won on the battlefield. The Code became one of the primary instruments of French domination in Europe, and its clauses remain embedded in the constitutions of a number of states – France included – to this day. Diversity and jurisdictional diversity, in particular, had been one of the defining features of the corporate society of the *ancien régime*, as we have seen. Indeed, Lamoignon, the Keeper of the Seals, was preparing to tackle this legal tangle when he fell from power in 1788. The revolutionaries never doubted the need for a codification of the law, then, but it had not been their top priority. In the meantime, however, another 30,000 decrees were committed to the statute book in the course of the decade.

Two problems faced the legislators of the 1790s. They needed to decide among themselves which aspects of *ancien-régime* jurisprudence, if any, they wished to preserve and, having decided, they needed a powerful executive authority to push the work to fruition. Although the Thermidorian deputies made some headway, the Directory lacked the authority to initiate legislation, with the result that little was achieved. The task fell to the men of Brumaire, therefore, but opinion differed as to how much of the legal heritage of the revolution should be retained and how much discarded. An initial draft was criticised in the Tribunate, and it was only after Bonaparte removed his opponents from that body in 1802 that the work of codification moved to a conclusion.

The Civil Code (or Napoleonic Code as it was known from 1807) gave legal expression to the social gains of the revolution [**Doc. 24**] – or, at least, to those gains that seemed, from the vantage point of 1804, to be the most important and the most worthy of preservation. Enshrined in the Code were statements guaranteeing the equality of all in the eyes of the law (and therefore the abolition of privilege); the inviolability of individual ownership (and therefore the validity of the sales of Church and *émigré* property); the freedom of contract; the freedom of careers; and the secular nature of the law. With its thoroughly modern conception of property rights and economic relationships, it should not surprise us that the Code became a veritable charter for the liberal-bourgeois world of the nineteenth century. However, the document also laid out a systematic framework of law applicable to rights and obligations within households (dowries, divorce, adoption, wardship, etc.) and to inheritance, and in these areas it was more cautious and compromising. The authority of husbands and fathers within the family was reinforced in a manner that curtailed and even reversed some of the liberalising impulses of the revolution.

This what states the was in civil Code.

Divorce, for example, was made harder to obtain, particularly for women. The remarkably egalitarian law of 1792 was repealed and provisions were introduced which restricted divorce by mutual consent and imposed a 'double standard' test of adultery, to the advantage of husbands. In the city of Lyons, the frequency of divorces dropped from 87 annually prior to the implementation of the Code to 7 after 1805 (Lyons, 1994: 100). But at least divorce was still possible. Indeed, Napoleon made use of the legislation himself to put away Joséphine de Beauharnais in 1809. In 1816, the Bourbons would remove the facility of divorce altogether. The Code also marked a retreat from the strictly egalitarian inheritance legislation of the Terror, which had drawn no distinction between the rights of legitimate and illegitimate offspring. In recognition of the custom of male primogeniture widely practised in the southern provinces of the kingdom before 1789, the drafters devised a solution that acknowledged the rights of the family group as well as those of the individual. Testators were allowed to will freely a portion of their assets, while the remainder had to be shared equally between (legitimate) heirs.

Bonaparte understood better than most of his collaborators that the work of consolidation required the creation of a social elite whose loyalties were anchored firmly to the new status quo rather than to one or more of the failed regimes of France's recent past. In 1802, he argued that the reforms being undertaken by the Consulate should provide a 'granite substratum' (*masses de granit*) binding the nation together. Whether the social bedrock was made up of groups that had been rich and powerful under the *ancien régime*, or groups that had risen to prominence during the revolution, did not much matter, as long as their primary allegiance was focused on the regime. In a marked departure from past republican practice, *émigrés* were allowed to return to France, although there was no question of them recovering possessions that had already been sold, and they were required to take the oath of allegiance to the constitution. By 1803, all but the most notorious royalist exiles had been offered the chance to return. Jacobins of 1793 vintage were allowed to rally to the regime, too, on condition that they had not been involved in subversive activity during the Directory years, or in the Opera Plot which very nearly succeeded in killing Bonaparte with his entire entourage in December 1800. Most kept their distance though: the governing bodies of the Consulate contained very few regicides. In the country at large, the regime tried hard to nurture a class of 'notables' who would act as a pool of socially acceptable and non-partisan recruits for public office and positions in the bureaucracy. It is at this level that the rallying of former stalwarts of the Terror is most noticeable.

Whether the emerging new order in the metropole carried a largely positive charge in France's overseas territories is open to question, however. The

Convention's abrupt slave emancipation decree of 1794 had improved the republic's military position in Saint-Domingue, even if it was too late to prevent the loss of Martinique to Britain for eight years (1794–1802). The Constitution of 1795 had re-affirmed, moreover, that France's colonies 'are integral parts of the republic and are subject to the same constitutional law' (Jainchill, 2008: 144). Bonaparte, on the other hand, had more flexible opinions on the slave issue and was feeling his way on colonial policy. In the event, the post-Brumaire constitution signalled a retreat from universalist rhetoric inasmuch as it abandoned the principle that the colonies were to be governed by the same law as the metropole. The strategic situation had evolved and the immediate priority was now to strike a deal with Britain that would make possible the recovery of Martinique (where slavery had never been abolished). When a definitive peace treaty was finally signed in March 1802, the Consulate's overseas policy became clearer: a law declared that, in the colonies returned to France, 'slavery will be maintained in conformity with the laws and regulations anterior to 1789' (Dubois, 2004: 370). French vessels would also be permitted to resume slave trading. Dispatches bearing this news and ordering the re-imposition of slavery in Guadeloupe and Saint-Domingue arrived from Paris in September 1802. However, this was not the final act in the story of citizenship in the French Caribbean, for the republic had first to recapture Saint-Domingue. Despite initial successes, the military capability of a large section of the black population proved decisive, and in 1804 the victorious ex-slaves were able to proclaim the founding of the new nation of Haiti.

TOWARDS DICTATORSHIP

For all the attempts to embed the regime, Bonaparte had no illusions as to its long-term viability if statesmanship at home was not accompanied by generalship abroad. 'My power is dependent on my glory, and my glory on my victories', he later remarked, and 'my power would fall if I did not base it on still more glory and still more victories' (Brown and Miller eds, 2002: 32). The men of Brumaire would have emphatically agreed: it was the victory at Marengo in Piedmont and the success of Moreau's Rhine Army at Hohenlinden (3 December 1800) that permitted the experiment of the Consulate to go ahead. Between the summer of 1799 and the spring of 1801, the balance of European warfare swung dramatically in France's favour once more. The left bank of the Rhine was recovered, as was northern and central Italy. At Lunéville (February 1801), the Austrians were brought to the conference table and obliged to accept French control over Venice and the

Dalmatian coastline, the reinstatement of the sister republics, and the annexation of Piedmont. The following year, favourable terms were reached with Britain also. At the Peace of Amiens, which was signed on 25 March 1802, France remained in possession of all of her continental conquests, although the British government withheld recognition of the satellite republics. For the first time since 1792, all military activity ceased in Europe.

These foreign policy successes, together with the prospect of internal peace following the publication of the Concordat, brought the regime to a turning point in the spring of 1802. Intransigent royalists had already begun to ask themselves whether Bonaparte might not be persuaded to play the role of herald for a monarchical restoration. Indeed, the self-styled Louis XVIII had already raised the subject, only to be told: 'You must not hope for your return to France; you would have to walk over one hundred thousand corpses' (Lyons, 1994: 131). In fact, the nation's 'saviour' was more interested in perpetuating his own authority than in making way for someone else. Despite some expressions of unease as to the direction of government policy, the Tribunate was induced to make the suggestion that the powers of the Consuls be extended to ten years. But this was not quite what Bonaparte had in mind. Instead, he intervened – discreetly – to ensure that a rather different proposition be worded and placed before the electorate for ratification: 'Shall Napoleon Bonaparte be named First Consul for life?' This alarmed liberal republicans in the Tribunate, the Legislative Body and even the Senate, for it indicated that Bonaparte's authoritarian ambitions might well extend beyond what was needed to consolidate the revolution. Thibaudeau, one of the deputies who had supported the Brumaire *coup*, warned: 'The impression of the revolution is still too fresh and this transition too abrupt' (Woloch, 2001: 94).

Nevertheless, the results of the referendum on the Life Consulship proved to be highly satisfactory to its sponsor inasmuch as a little over half of the electorate actively declared themselves in support of the proposition. On this occasion, there was no need to falsify the returns. The voters were certainly endorsing the reforms undertaken since 1799, but whether they were also giving Bonaparte a licence to transform the regime into a personal dictatorship is another matter. At any event, the immediate consequence was to usher in a modification of the constitution introduced only two years earlier. Napoleon Bonaparte, as he was now styled, remained First Consul, but for life, in common with the Second and Third Consuls. However, the latter were to be chosen by the First Consul (through the intermediary of the Senate) and he was empowered to appoint his own successor also. Only the Senate, as guardian of the constitution, could have impeded what amounted to quasi-prerogative powers vested in the person of the First Consul. But Bonaparte took steps to remove the doubters from this body, whilst the

Tribunate and the Legislative Body could simply be put into abeyance. With the Senate now a docile tool, its power to issue decrees (*senatus consulta*) that bypassed the legislature fell into Bonaparte's hands as well.

In the aftermath of the constitutional revision of August 1802, few could have mistaken the direction in which the governance of France was now tending. Already, in May, an honours system had been established which would reward military valour rather than civic virtue (the Legion of Honour). Protesters in the Tribunate objected that it infringed the 'bedrock' principle of equality. The constitution made provision, moreover, for Napoleon's effigy to appear on coins, just like the kings of old, and an embryonic Court began to take shape in the Tuileries Palace – the First Consul's official residence. Slowly, the political culture of the revolution was receding from public memory, or rather from official public memory. While the tricolour flag was retained, the red bonnet of the emancipated slave that had often accompanied it in 1793 disappeared from view and was replaced with the image of an eagle. The Marseillaise was heard less and less often, and citizens reverted to the practice of addressing one another as 'Monsieur'. Opposition from within dwindled. On grounds of state security, censorship of the press was reimposed, with the result that the number of political newspapers published in Paris dropped from 60 to 13. 'Journals', a police report noted approvingly, 'have always been the tocsin of revolutions' (Aulard ed., 1903, vol. 1: 96). Following the attempt to kill Bonaparte with a huge bomb (the Infernal Machine Plot) as he was making his way to the opera, many street-level neo-Jacobins were deported. In fact, the attack had been the work of royalists, and it was the continuing threat of plots and assassination attempts from this quarter that would set the stage for the ultimate transformation of the Consulate.

The peace signed at Amiens lasted only 14 months and with the return of Britain to the fray, royalist efforts to topple Bonaparte were renewed. Georges Cadoudal, the former *chouan* leader who had fled to England in order to escape the pacification of the west in 1801, seems to have played the key role. A plan was hatched for him to make contact – in Paris – with the royalist General Pichegru, who had managed to return from deportation following the Fructidor *coup*, and General Moreau, the conqueror of the Austrians at Hohenlinden. On a signal of the arrival of a Bourbon prince in France, the conspirators would kidnap, or kill, the First Consul. But no royal prince seems to have been prepared to risk what would have been an extremely hazardous mission; Moreau's dislike of Bonaparte did not extend to co-operating in a Bourbon restoration; and, in any case, Cadoudal was betrayed. The government responded decisively and, in the view of many, outrageously. The young Duke of Enghien (grandson of the Prince de Condé), who was assumed to be the princeling in question, was kidnapped on foreign territory, brought to Paris and court-martialled. He met his end before a firing squad in the fortress of Vincennes on 21 March 1804, just a few days after the promulgation of the Civil Code.

The murder of Enghien, the suspect 'suicide' of Pichegru in his prison cell and the exiling of Moreau formed part of Bonaparte's balancing act. Royalists had been warned that the road back to the *ancien régime* was definitively closed; sincere republicans were reassured, temporarily, as to the fundamental character of the regime; and the generals were put on notice to stay out of politics. Yet the Cadoudal Plot also reminded many of the extent to which the Consulate was willing to play fast and loose with the rule of law [**Doc. 23**]. It was a reminder, too, of how much now depended on the survival of one man. Only a hereditary system of government, it was suggested, could develop the qualities of robustness required to withstand and overcome the constant threat of political assassination. A week after Enghien's execution, a Senate rendered docile by rewards and bribes 'invited Napoleon Bonaparte to complete his work and make himself immortal like his glory' and, a month or so later, the Tribunate urged quite explicitly that he be proclaimed 'hereditary emperor of the French' (Boudon, 1997: 49). Thereafter, events moved swiftly: the Senate drew up a modified constitution on 18 May and, in keeping with the practice followed since 1800, the proposal to confer the dignity of hereditary emperor on Napoleon Bonaparte and his direct descendants was submitted to the electorate. A resounding vote in favour was recorded (3,572,329 'Yes' and 2,569 'No'), although close analysis of the turnout figures suggests that support for the regime among ordinary voters may actually have fallen when compared with the ballot on the Life Consulate in 1802.

The Constitution of 1804 nowhere stated that the republic had been formally abolished. It simply declared that an Emperor would take over the reins of government, and that the current First Consul would become Emperor. However, the new incumbent was required to swear an oath to uphold, among other things, civil and political liberty, the freedom of religion and the irreversibility of the property transfers of the revolutionary era. He was also required to govern with a view solely to the happiness and glory of the French people. No question any longer of the division of powers; the various bodies of the state were to be activated by the will of Napoleon Bonaparte alone. The imperial coronation took place at the end of the year and it completed the metamorphosis of the Consulate into a dictatorship that was intended to be permanent. Yet this would be no ordinary dictatorship: Bonaparte enjoyed a large measure of public support; he did not owe his elevation to the generals; and he could claim, with some plausibility, that his regime remained in the furrow ploughed by the revolution.

PART 3

8

The Assessment

The French Revolution can best be understood as a huge release of civic energy. The flow began in 1787, reached a peak between 1789 and 1795, and then ebbed slowly. Only in a very superficial sense is it accurate to describe this phenomenon as a series of events. In reality, the revolution was a process which had at its core the realisation by ordinary men and women that the human condition was not fixed until the end of time but could be changed, provided that sufficient amounts of effort, ingenuity and – yes – suffering were brought to bear. The shock of this realisation gripped the whole of French society; at intervals, it gripped large parts of continental Europe too; even in 1814–15, when throne and altar partnerships were restored in many states, it was not entirely eradicated. Once the French Revolution had happened, no government could find safe refuge in 'the length of its continuance' alone (Burke, 1790/1973: 149). The people were now poised to become the prime actors in their own historical drama. In this sense, the French Revolution marks the dividing line between the medieval and the modern eras in the western world.

What shape did this monumental energy burst take? The revolution should be regarded as one of the key episodes in the history of freedom. What happened in France between 1787 and 1804 opened up a new range of possibilities as to how society might be organised, and at the forefront of these possibilities was the aspiration for democracy. Before France's great revolution, 'democracy' was pretty much an abstract concept; it had little purchase on the 'here and now' world of politics. But no one would have ventured such a statement as the nineteenth century commenced. For all the brave talk among Europe's elder statesmen after the defeat of Napoleon about turning the clock back, democracy was here to stay. The word had entered common vocabulary, both as a noun and in adjectival form, and a whole generation of Europeans had come into being who would have understood the meaning of the verb to 'democratise' (Dunn, 2005: 16–17). Whether they would have approved of this seismic shift in understanding of the relationship between state and society is another matter, of course. It is true that the first trial of democracy had not been an auspicious one. A democratic franchise did not translate neatly into a democratic state, as events between 1792 and 1794 had demonstrated. Many decades and further revolutions would come to pass before this paradox could be resolved. Nevertheless, it is undeniable that the French Revolution gave the aspiration for democracy a motive power which it has never subsequently lost. In the process, it expanded hugely the arena of attainable civil and political freedom.

How, then, did this energy come to be released? Historians have looked for the origins of the revolution in many quarters. Indeed, the question of origins can lead students into a maze from which only the most clear-sighted stand any chance of emerging. For much of the twentieth century, social and economic factors played the principal role in historians' explanations of the outbreak of revolution. According to this scenario, a society organised around the legal fiction of 'orders' (or 'estates') was being transformed into a society increasingly shaped around the emerging socio-economic reality of classes. Class formation was thus the remote control of revolution, and the frustrations and ambitions of an expanding bourgeoisie its immediate trigger (Soboul, 1988). The middle class found in the ideas of the Enlightenment the arguments they required to challenge the structures of the *ancien régime*. Needless to say, this interpretation drew its inspiration from the political philosophy of Karl Marx, and it was buttressed by plentiful evidence to show that the economy of the *ancien régime* was also entering a phase of protracted crisis in the 1770s. An obvious drawback of this diagnosis, however, is that it presupposes that the very considerable diversity of eighteenth-century society can be neatly marshalled into classes which indulged in conflict. It also requires us to conclude that the 'energy' that made possible the break-through in 1787–88 emanated primarily from the middle class. These are not insuperable problems, as some historians have demonstrated; however, the traditional social interpretation of the origins of the revolution nowadays tends to incur a more substantial objection. It deflects attention away from 'non-class' social and political explanations of how the old regime came to be replaced with something new.

Since the 1980s, historians have tried to redress this imbalance. In particular, they have begun to investigate more closely the workings of the Bourbon state, the construction of platforms or arenas for political expression, the coming together of an ideology to counter absolutism, and the impact of shifts in material culture during the second half of the eighteenth century, in an effort to probe beyond the frame of analysis formulated by Marx. As a result, a largely political interpretation of how the revolution came about now challenges the schematic certainties of class-based analysis. There are two main variants of this approach: one which still allows scope for individual social actors and one which does not.

Now that the state – the machinery of government and its functionaries – has been released, so to speak, from the essentially passive role allocated to it in the class-driven model of how change takes place, a number of historians have argued that the revolution was essentially a product of the breakdown of a system of government that tried to reform itself, and failed. Thus, the chronic fiscal embarrassments of the Bourbon monarchy become not a symptom, but a prime cause. If contemporary critics concentrated their fire on Court extravagance and pecuniary privilege, it can only have been because they knew little about the true state of royal finances. A few historians might rest their case at this point, denying the instrumentality of any other factor in the collapse of the *ancien régime*. However, most would still find some room for economic causation, while insisting that the bleak outlook of the later 1770s and 1780s would not have brought down the regime of its own accord. It is true that historians who now identify the monarchy itself as the primary force for change do not always agree on how to depict that institution. Are we dealing with a proto-modern, bureaucratic and administrative state by the 1770s, or one still caught in a Renaissance time warp where the Court was the fulcrum of politics and every minister first and foremost its creature?

At least some sense of human agency and responsibility for the outbreak of the revolution is retained in this interpretation, even if we are now trying to unravel the behaviour of Louis XVI and his reforming ministers rather than the collective stance of a thrusting and impatient bourgeoisie. The alternative is to discount the 'social' altogether and to seek agency in the autonomous operation of ideas. This contribution to the debate about the origins of the revolution came from intellectual historians in the main, and it attracted considerable interest around the time of the bicentenary (1989). Rather than seeking to anatomise the society that gave birth to the revolution, in the belief that it should be possible to uncover the signs of terminal illness, they suggested that researchers might do better to start with the language and styles of discourse that became commonplace during the revolution and to ask themselves where they originated. Language, after all, does help to shape social and political reality, even if the reverse is more often the case in practice. Perhaps the process of revolution was somehow 'scripted' (Baker ed., 1990: 86–106) in a language of resistance to the claims of absolute monarchy long before a crowd of angry Parisians managed to clamber into the inner courtyard of the Bastille. Yet a proto-revolutionary language still requires real people to deliver it, and to be influenced by it. The growth, after 1750 or thereabouts, of a critical state of mind among educated men and women surely must have contributed to the outbreak and subsequent direction of the revolution. Even so, it is far from clear how this approach might stand in place of a social interpretation and constitute an explanation sufficient on its own.

The energy that launched the revolution was by no means entirely male. Yet the contributions made by women are usually treated as 'unscripted', either because the evidence tends to be overlooked altogether, or because (male?) historians have failed to discover a meaningful pattern in the partici-patory activities of women. During the later *ancien régime* decades, there can be no doubt that a few women were able to play a quasi-public role in the salons and masonic lodges found in Paris and the larger regional capitals. This has prompted some historians to judge that the French revolutionaries failed women on two counts: on the one hand, they curtailed the promising developments of the Enlightenment; on the other, they refused to admit the logic of their own universalist rhetoric and to extend political rights to female citizens. One might ask how far the Enlightenment genuinely embodied a promise of liberation for women, for there are methodological dangers in taking a handful of Parisian blue-stockings as representative of the position of women in general (Goodman, 1994).

As for developments after 1789, it is undeniable that women were never formally admitted to the public space of the revolution, though they were never formally excluded from it. Women did not wait to be asked (or told) what to do: they participated in revolutionary politics willy-nilly – whether marching to Versailles in order to fetch the king, raiding grocers' shops, resisting the closure of churches, or raucously shouting down deputies whom they disapproved of from the spectator benches of the Convention. There were self-consciously female *sans-culottes* and, despite efforts to dismantle their club network, they played a significant role in sustaining the Terror. When the Thermidorian Convention sounded the retreat from the controlled economy during the winter of 1794–95, the trigger for insurrec-tion came not from men, but from ordinary Parisian women. The deputies obliquely acknowledged the role they had played by excluding them from the galleries of the Convention and from the meetings of the Sections. This was the closest any of the revolutionary Assemblies came to legislating against women as such (Godineau, 1988: 319–31). And lest it be supposed that the revolution offered nothing concrete to women, we should not over-look the marked improvements in their legal status that took place in the 1790s. It is true that this trend came to a halt, and was even put into partial reverse during the Consulate. The answer to the question: 'Did women have a revolution after 1789?' must be 'Yes', therefore. Even as the provisions of the Civil Code took effect, more women enjoyed more freedom than they had ever possessed at the end of the *ancien régime*.

The character of the early revolution was indelibly marked by the social conflicts that immediately preceded the surrender of absolute monarchy.

Historians who find the class approach unpersuasive when applied to pre-industrial societies, point to the considerable evidence of a convergence of elites by the end of the *ancien régime*. Aristocrats, bourgeois and the senior prelates of the Church were all growing more alike, whether in terms of economic status or cultural outlook. They fight shy of terms such as the 'pre-revolution', the 'aristocratic revolution' and the 'revolutionary bourgeoisie' in consequence – terms which belong more properly to a class analysis of the origins and inception of the revolution. These terms do now seem redundant and have been used sparingly – if at all – in this introductory survey. If the aggressive destabilising force of the late 1770s and 1780s was, in fact, the monarchy, it does not seem appropriate to schematise the resistance of the Parlements in 1787–88 as an 'aristocratic revolution'.

However, this approach is less successful in accommodating what actually happened between 1789 and 1791. Even though the structuring of the Estates General scarcely facilitated a fusion of elites, the deputies were painfully aware of what divided them almost from the outset. Noble and bourgeois representatives kept their distance from one another: if the desire to punish the aristocracy as a caste was largely absent from debates before the summer of 1791, there was no real meeting of minds either. Commoner deputies continued to think of themselves as 'unprivileged' and of nobles as 'privileged', even though, objectively speaking, 'privilege' no longer existed.

Were the deputies so unexpectedly brought together in 1789 political novices? The question is important, for the answer may touch upon our understanding of the Terror as well as the transition from reforming abso-lutism to constitutional monarchy. Some historians believe that educated Frenchmen did not have much of a political vocabulary before 1789 – a plausible hypothesis since political activity, under absolute monarchy, was largely confined to the king, his councillors and the Court. However, we know that the king and his advisors were ceasing to define the monarchy in this strict sense by the 1780s – in fact, they were actively casting around for a safe means of enlarging the sphere of consultation and participation. In the event, a sizeable minority of the Third Estate's deputies were able to bring political experience to bear in the debates in the Estates General and the National Assembly, thanks to the provincial assemblies reforms pushed through by Necker, Calonne and Loménie de Brienne. The elite on whom power devolved in the summer of 1789 may have been new to office, then, but they were scarcely untried enthusiasts. Nor, indeed, were their counter-parts in the provinces; that is to say, the men who would colonise the new machinery of local government set up in 1790. Many could call upon experi-ence gleaned in seigneurial courts or the lowest municipal tier of the assem-blies established by Brienne. Of course, the deputies and their collaborators liked to clothe their actions in regenerationist rhetoric, but in this instance a focus on language is apt to mislead. The achievements of the National Assembly sprang from the spirit of pragmatism that animated its committees, not from a parliamentary free trade in disembodied ideas culled from the Enlightenment.

Nevertheless, the historians who have renewed our understanding of the Terror place particular emphasis on the alleged political immaturity of the deputies who took power in 1789. Borrowing from the seminal study of the *ancien régime* by Alexis de Tocqueville, they depict these first-generation legislators as self-taught *philosophes* whose abstract mode of reasoning did not combine well with the realities of holding and sharing political power. As Rousseauean intellectuals, they believed that the nation had inherited the absolutist pretensions of the old monarchy and must therefore speak with one voice. This discourse of the 'general will' (Baker ed., 1994: xix) could tolerate no opposition or dissent, thus leading to the conclusion that the potential for the Terror lay embedded in the language of the revolution from the very start.

Terror and violence were intrinsic to the revolutionary mentality, therefore, not the deviant products of civil war and military emergency. The relentless head-chopping of the Revolutionary Tribunal in the spring and summer of 1794 was prefigured in the prison lynchings of September 1792, which, in turn, were foreshadowed in the bestial violence which accompanied the seizure of the Bastille in July 1789. Several objections can be raised against this line of argument, however. For a start, it seems unlikely that the Third Estate deputies in the Estates General – or anybody else, for that matter – were particularly avid readers of the political writings of Jean-Jacques Rousseau and, as we have seen, they were scarcely unskilled novices either. As for the appropriation of the absolutism of the unreconstructed monarchy, this is an idea whose semantic neatness is its chief defect. Absolutism is not the same as totalitarianism, even if measured by the yardstick of Louis XIV's reign. In any case, the lessons that future revolutionaries might have absorbed from the later years of the reign of Louis XVI would have been lessons in quasi-constitutional, not absolutist, practice. Historians who have examined closely the political and judicial practices of the National Assembly also find little evidence of the mindset of the Terror. On the contrary, they emphasise the restraining effect of the humanitarian ideas of 1789. If the terrorist mentality can be located anywhere at this date, it is in the popular approach to justice and retribution pioneered by crowds in Paris and elsewhere.

Still, it remains the case that the deputies had trouble learning how to agree to disagree. Unanimity was prized in the belief that nobody could possibly *not* wish to participate in the regeneration of the kingdom. The line between loyal opposition and subversive disagreement was therefore hard to tread, and even harder to police. For as long as the revolutionaries showed themselves to be capable of solving their political problems, the divergence of opinion did not matter too much, but with the religious schism, the outbreak of war and the descent into armed rebellion in the west, dissension in the ranks became harder and harder to tolerate. Most historians (like most contemporaries, indeed) would agree that a distinction has to be drawn between the early 'liberal' revolution (up to the summer of 1792), and the 'authoritarian' republic of 1792–94, then. The war was perceived as a struggle for survival – particularly once the Vendée insurgency had demonstrated the potential of an armed counter-revolution – and it gnawed away the middle ground in domestic politics.

That said, it is beyond dispute that the politics of extremes developed a life of its own. Just as the rationale for a people's war began to fuse with France's traditional foreign policy objectives, so the reasons for Terror became confused with plot paranoia and the ambition to found a virtuous republic cleansed of all impure social elements. Mild expressions of anti-revolutionary sentiment that would have bothered no one in 1790 or 1791 became loaded with counter-revolutionary menace. Simple thefts of property would lead to accusations of treason now that a bell rope, a harness or a bit of metal left over from the demolition of a wayside cross could be construed as material vital to the war effort. It is at this point that an enquiry into the self-sustaining logic of the Terror ought legitimately to begin.

If the Terror impulse can be detected first and foremost in the behaviour of the crowd, is it safe to explain this reflex as mindless bloodlust, as some historians have argued? The judicial shedding of blood was as instrinsic to the old regime as it was to the new: there was nothing 'modern' about it. One has only to read the accounts of eighteenth-century travellers to know that mangled and broken corpses spread-eagled on cartwheels were a familiar and (for English travellers) a disturbing sight at road intersections. Crowd violence nearly always occurred in a judicial setting as well, albeit one that frequently bypassed the formal institutions of repression. The crowds of the 1790s were rarely 'mindless' in any of their activities, in fact, and as the revolution developed, they became more and more 'purposive' (Lucas, 1988: 259) – that is to say, better organised and better able to determine the dosage of pressure and violence required in order to achieve their aims. Collective violence would be used in the name of the sovereign people to punish and to purify, but it would also be used to consolidate and defend the revolution.

The *sans-culotte* phenomenon can be understood in this context as the ultimate refinement of the purposive crowd. Indeed, it was the political sophistication with which the crowd exploited its capacity for violence by 1793–94 that alarmed the deputies as much as the violence itself. In a sense, therefore, the bureaucratisation of the Terror following the consolidation of

Revolutionary Government amounted to an attempt to substitute measured state violence for the violence of unruly or independent-minded crowds. A cycle of violence in Paris that had begun with informal lynching from lamp posts ended with the tumbrels of the Revolutionary Tribunal being routed through the most plebeian districts of the capital for the edification of spectators.

The disarray – not to say, discomfiture – of historians when confronted with the problem of violence in the revolution helps to explain the renewal of interest in the period of the Directory. For the task of finding the escape route from the Terror fell to the deputies of the Thermidorian Convention and the Councils of the Directory. Institutions were renewed or replaced, yet it proved immensely difficult to eradicate the mentality of 1793–94 with its characteristic ingredients: the plot, the purge and exemplary punitive justice. Nevertheless, historians have tried hard to redeem the regime from its reputation as 'one of the most chaotic periods in modern French history' (Sutherland, 1985: 279) in the belief that, beneath the surface, it continued the work of consolidating the revolution. After the interruption of the Terror, democratic political practice resumed its faltering progress; there were even some signs that a public space sufficient to accommodate embryonic political parties was starting to open up. In the country at large, the various factions of the revolutionary elite began to draw together once more as the political animosities born of the early years shaded into an overarching recognition of a common post-1789 heritage. The latter development proved more fruitful than the former, though, for the Fructidor *coup* (4 September 1797) demonstrated that the regime was still searching for the elusive escape route towards a politics of normality. In the view of some historians, therefore, the real turning point of these years was not 1799 but 1797. Fructidor launched the republic on a new trajectory, that is to say, the quest for a method of synthesising authority and liberty. The solution would be found in the person of Napoleon Bonaparte.

The elite that was slowly acquiring a collective identity by the later 1790s was none other than the 'granite substratum' of the Consulate and the Empire. Thanks to considerable research undertaken in the 1970s and 1980s, historians now agree on its composition, but tend to differ in how they label it. For some, the 'notables' are a vindication of the proposition that the revolution was launched and consummated by the bourgeoisie or middle class. Others point out that the 'notables' resembled nothing so much as the parallel elites of the *ancien régime* whose fusion had been so rudely interrupted in 1789.

It is true that, if we carry out an occupational and status analysis, the results are rather surprising. The revolution did not wipe out the nobility and titled – or formerly titled – families appear in some strength in the electoral lists of 'notabilities' drawn up during the Consulate. Although this is an area in which it is hard to generalise, it does seem that the majority of the wealthiest landowners in 1802 came from families which would have been regarded as noble in 1789. Of course, many émigré nobles had been granted permission to return home by this date, but the real import of the finding lies in the fact that the revolution did not undermine irretrievably the economic strength of the old Second Estate. On current best estimates, provincial nobles may have lost about one-fifth of their lands and one-third of their income as a result of the events of 1789 and subsequent years. To give a concrete example, the nobility of the district of Bordeaux lost about 30 per cent of its property during the Terror (Figeac, 1995: 540–41). There had been 824 noble families in the district in 1789, of whom 102 were imprisoned and 397 fled abroad (thereby risking the forfeiture of their lands).

However, the 'notables' were not the elites of the *ancien régime* reheated. For a start, the outworn social categories of the eighteenth century had been abandoned, or legislated out of existence. Landowners, whether noble or bourgeois, were now labelled 'proprietors'. Analysis of the electoral list for 1810 (totalling 66,735 individuals) shows that 25 per cent were owners of land, 34 per cent held administrative posts and 14 per cent were members of the liberal professions (attorney, advocate, medical practitioner, etc.). No more than 11 per cent made a living from commercial activity (Lyons, 1994: 162). A composite elite, then, but an open elite as well. The 'notables' of the Consulate and the Empire earned their admission to the rank not on the basis of birth and ancestry, but by virtue of their wealth and social utility.

The modest presence within this post-revolution elite of families engaged in trade and industry ought not to surprise. *Ancien-régime* France had been a land-based society – a fact that an intensely political revolution was not going to alter overnight. But the lists of 'notables' compiled under the Consulate do reveal that a much broader conception of the economic foundations of political authority had taken root. Whether we label the post-revolution elite a middle class is a matter for individual historians. Some would find no tension in the phrase 'the bourgeois revolution of property owners' (Lewis, 1993: 35), whereas others operate with stricter criteria as to what constitutes a 'bourgeois revolution'. Yet there can be little doubt that the men who voted Napoleon Bonaparte into power and worked the levers of his government machine had a radically different cast of mind from that of their *ancien régime* predecessors – a cast of mind that it would not be inappropriate to describe as 'bourgeois'.

The mixed character of the power elite that took on institutional form during the Consulate is only one of several phenomena that make Bonapartism extremely difficult to pigeonhole. A regime that managed to combine father-figure authority with outward respect for the principle of popular sovereignty necessarily points in two directions. Bonaparte and his officials could behave illiberally, even despotically, yet they worshipped the rule of law and pursued the rationalisation of public administration unflinchingly – goals that liberals all over Europe admired and supported. They despatched armies across the face of the Continent in the name of self-determination, only to define freedom as the entitlement to furnish tax revenue and military manpower for the greater glory of the new French Empire. Feudal privilege and the corporate status of the Church were attacked wherever these armies marched, yet at home Bonaparte would strike a deal with the papacy, and take steps to re-create a hierarchy of privilege.

Is it any wonder, therefore, if historians experience difficulty in deciding where to draw the line between the revolution and the regime that took shape from Brumaire onwards? Many would not stray beyond the year 1799 in their bid to survey comprehensively the French Revolution, whereas others regard the vote on the Life Consulship of 1802, or the founding of a dynastic empire in 1804 as the proper terminus. Equally, an argument could be made in favour of 1808 (the creation of the Imperial nobility), 1810 (the Habsburg marriage), or 1812 (the Russian campaign). This survey has opted for 1804 on the ground that the substitution of an hereditary empire in the place of an increasingly threadbare republic dispelled any lingering illusions that Napoleon Bonaparte might not be striving for personal dictatorship. Ever since the summer of 1789, voices had been heard declaring that the revolution was now over. By 1804, it really was at an end.

What, then, were the enduring consequences of this revolution that both inspired and traumatised a whole society? The psychological imprint of the rituals of citizenship (voting, oath-taking, enrolment in the national guard, the wearing of a liberty cap, etc.) is hard to specify. However, it would not be safe to assume that it was transient and that the aspiration towards freedom for the individual had been snuffed out by 1804. The anaesthetic of Bonapartism wore off, and as the Empire went into a painful decline (1811–14), the language of popular sovereignty and national defence would be heard again. Napoleon Bonaparte soon followed the republic into oblivion, but the immensely powerful and centralised state that the revolutionaries had brought into being survived. The long-meditated project of monarchs to bring their subjects under administrative control had finally been accomplished. Whilst its origins may have been suspect, the restored Bourbons were certainly not going to repudiate this legacy. They were scarcely going to repudiate the economic, financial and fiscal changes that had occurred during the revolution either. Louis XVIII went out of his way to guarantee the property transfers that had taken place in the 1790s, just like Napoleon Bonaparte before him. Purchasers of church and *émigré* property could rest easily in their beds, although recent research has indicated that less land and property changed hands than was once assumed (under 10 per cent of the total stock) (Bodinier and Teyssier, 2000: 8).

But the revolution had some economic effects that no one anticipated. Civil disturbance, inflation followed by deflation and 22 years of near-continuous warfare dislocated industry and commerce. Growth was checked, leading sectors of industry under the *ancien régime* went into decline for a period, and the centre of gravity of commercial activity moved from the south and south-west to the north and north-east, in line with the shift northwards of the international trading economy. Since much capital had been absorbed by the land transfer operation, and inflation had killed off the credit market, France initially found herself ill-prepared to meet the challenges of the modern industrial age. Not until around 1800 did industrial output return to the level recorded in 1789, while the volume of external trade by the end of the Empire was still only half of what it had been in 1784–88. Yet new economic structures were emerging which, in the view of some historians, would facilitate the growth of a uniquely French form of capitalism (Horn, 2006). Bourbon France had been trying to kick-start a structural transformation of the economy ever since the time of Calonne and had not wanted for entrepreneurs. What had been cruelly lacking in the 1780s was an entrepreneurial climate. Without anyone having anticipated, or planned, the development, a new model of partnership between the state and the entrepreneur had emerged out of the Terror. The Directory, and then the Consulate, would build on these foundations. It is true that Bonaparte's imperial ambitions halted and even undermined this development for a time. But France's characteristic formula of a state-led approach to industrial progress would reassert itself once the era of continental warfare had come to an end.

The macro-economic impact of the revolution does not tell us much about how ordinary men and women computed their gains and losses, though. The ending of fiscal privilege meant that everybody was now taxed according to their wealth, rather than their birth, occupation or place of residence – a huge psychological gain. But discrepancies of fiscal 'load' between the various regions of the country took much longer to sort out, and it is not at all certain that French men paid less tax overall as a result of the revolution. More likely, the sense of fiscal well-being derived from the fact that tax obligations to the state had been avoided altogether, or else settled in depreciated paper money, coupled with the fact that payments to the Church (the tithe) and to former seigneurial overlords had come to an end. Working men and women had reason to feel grateful to the revolution inasmuch as real wages rose across the period, thanks mainly to labour shortages. On the other hand, the livelihood of the semi-destitute poor was thrown into question by the withdrawal of alms following the abolition of monastic vows and the sales of Church endowments. Farmers benefited from a run of good harvests in the later 1790s and early 1800s, but the conscription of labour, along with requisitions (fatstock, horses, fodder, etc.) for the armies, had a braking effect on agricultural yields.

In truth, it is probable that the biggest gains for ordinary people were the deeply personal ones. They concerned the way individuals assessed their life chances and viewed their relationships with one another. Unfortunately, such changes can only be detected indirectly. We know that the practice of marriage fairly took off – after all, parental consent was no longer required. But so, too, did the practice of family limitation. In the words of one historian, couples emerged from the revolution more 'egotistical and calculating' (Dupâquier, 1979: 118). Men stopped going to church like sheep every Sunday – and, of course, these two cultural traits may well be linked. Despite all the attempts at moral rearmament by the post-Concordat clergy, the Catholic Church had lost its capacity to compel. Now that it had been demonstrated that the human condition was not fixed, men and women were exploiting the new freedoms and quietly taking charge of their own lives.

PART 4

DOCUMENTS

Document 1 A ROYAL REPRIMAND

Louis XV had been offended by a gratuitous suggestion emanating from the Parlement of Rouen that he had sworn an oath to the nation at his coronation. The following extract is taken from a rebuke that the king caused to be read out before the Parlement of Paris on 3 March 1766. It became known as the Discourse of the Flagellation and would be treated almost as a doctrinal statement of absolutism for the remainder of his reign.

[. . .] to set about erecting into matters of principle such pernicious innovations is to do injury to the body of the magistrature, to betray its interests, and to mistake those laws that are really fundamental to the state. As if it could be overlooked that it is in my person alone that sovereign power resides, the true character of which is founded in conciliation, justice and reason; as if it could be overlooked that the courts owe their existence and authority to me alone; that this plenary authority, exercised in my name, remains forever attached to me and can never be turned against me; that legislative power is vested in me alone, without any subordination or subdivision; that the officers of my courts undertake not the fashioning of the laws but their registration and publication on my sole authority, albeit with permission to make remonstrance as befits good and loyal counsellors; that all public order stems from me and that I am its supreme custodian; that my people are at one with me; and that the rights and interests of the *nation*, which some have dared to constitute as a body separate from that of the monarch, are necessarily united with my rights and can only reside in my hands. The officers of my courts will, I am persuaded, never lose sight of these sacred and immutable maxims, which are inscribed in the hearts of all faithful subjects [. . .]

Source: Antoine, M. 'La Monarchie absolue', in Baker, K.M. (ed.) *The French Revolution and the Creation of Modern Political Culture. Volume 1: The Political Culture of the Old Regime* (Pergamon Press, Oxford, 1987), p. 6. Copyright Elsevier 1987. Translated by Peter Jones.

Document 2 IMAGINING THE *ANCIEN RÉGIME* BODY POLITIC

This description of French society is taken from a remonstrance of the Parlement of Paris dated 12 March 1776. It shows how vested interests within the kingdom chose to visualise the institution of absolute monarchy.

All of your subjects, Sire, are divided into as many different *corps* as there are different estates of the realm: the Clergy, the Nobility, the sovereign courts; the inferior courts, the officers attached to these tribunals, the universities, the academies, the companies of finance and of commerce; all present and existing throughout the State, these *corps* may be regarded as the links in a great chain of which the first is in the hands of Your Majesty, as chief and sovereign administrator of all that constitutes the *corps* of the Nation.

Source: Cavanaugh, G.J. 'Turgot: the Rejection of Enlightened Despotism', *French Historical Studies*, vol. 6 (spring 1969), p. 32, note 4.

———————◀●▶———————

FUNDAMENTAL LAWS ACCORDING TO THE PARLEMENT OF PARIS   **Document 3**

The news that Lamoignon, Keeper of the Seals, was preparing a root-and-branch reform of the judiciary had leaked out in April 1788. Fearing the worst, the magistrates restate their understanding of the constitution of the kingdom.

The court, with all the chambers assembled and the peers present, amply warned by public knowledge and notorious fact of the coup d'état which threatens the nation by striking at the magistrature [. . .] and leaves the nation no other resource but a precise declaration by the court of the maxims it is charged with maintaining [. . .]

Declares that France is a monarchy governed by the king in accordance with the laws. That of these laws several are fundamental and that these include:

The right of the reigning house to succeed to the throne in the male line according to primogeniture with the exclusion of females and their descendants.
The right of the nation to grant taxation freely in an Estates General regularly convoked and of fixed composition.
The customs and capitulations of the provinces.
The irremovability of magistrates.
The right of the courts in each province to verify the king's legislative volition and to proceed to its registration only in so far as it is conformable to the basic laws of the province as well as the Fundamental Laws of the state.
The right of every citizen, whatever his offence, to appear only before his peers as defined by law.
And the right, without which all the others are of no avail, to appear before the competent judge immediately after arrest, no matter on whose orders.

The said court protests against any future violation of the above principles.

Source: Hardman, J. *The French Revolution: the Fall of the Ancien Régime to the Thermidorian Reaction, 1785–1795* (Arnold, London, 1981), p. 55.

———————◀●▶———————

Document 4   DEFINING THE NATION

Penned by a priest Emmanuel-Joseph Sieyès around the time of the Assembly of Notables, the pamphlet What is the Third Estate? *was published early in 1789. It was one of the most widely read contributions to the debate on the composition of the forthcoming Estates General.*

The plan of this work is quite simple. There are three questions that we have to ask ourselves:

1. What is the Third Estate? *Everything.*
2. What has it been until now in the existing political order? *Nothing.*
3. What does it want to be? *Something.*

[. . .]

First we will see whether these answers are correct [. . .]

Who would then dare to say that the Third Estate does not, within itself, contain everything needed to form a complete nation? It resembles a strong, robust man with one arm in chains. Subtract the privileged order and the Nation would not be something less, but something more. What then is the Third? Everything; but an everything that is fettered and oppressed. What would it be without the privileged order? Everything, but an everything that would be free and flourishing. Nothing can go well without the Third Estate, but everything would go a great deal better without the two others.

[. . .]

It is pointless for the Third Estate to expect joint action by the three orders to restore its *political* rights and all its civil rights in their full entirety. The fear of seeing abuse reformed has inspired more of a feeling of alarm than a desire for liberty among the aristocrats. Faced with a choice between liberty and a few odious privileges, they have opted for the latter. The privileged soul has aligned itself with the favours granted to servility. They are as afraid of the Estates General today as they were once so vigorous in calling for them. As far as they are concerned, everything is fine. Their only cause for complaint is the spirit of innovation. Nothing, it seems, is now wanting. Fear has given them a constitution.

In the light of these changes in matters and moods, the Third Estate has to see that it has to rely solely upon its own vision and courage. Reason and justice are on its side. It ought to aim, at the least, to secure their full support. The time for working for a conciliation between the parties is over. What hope of agreement can there be between the energy of the oppressed and the fury of the oppressor? It is they who now have dared to launch the word 'secession' and use it as a threat against both the king and the people. Ah! dear God, how happy a day it would be for the Nation if that great and desirable secession was to be accomplished and made final. How easy it

[handwritten margin notes:] This priest has a very radical view. He is saying that the third estate could be a nation on its own. He is saying that if the third estate succeeded it would be a good thing.

He says that it would even be easy to exist without the upper two estates.

would be to do without the privileged orders! How difficult it will be to induce them to become citizens! [. . .]

Source: Sonenscher, M. (ed.) *Emmanuel Joseph Sieyès: Political Writings* (Hackett Publishing Company, Indianapolis, 2003), pp. 94, 96,145.

FIXING A FRAMEWORK FOR THE ESTATES GENERAL

Document 5

Having returned in triumph to its courthouse, the Parlement of Paris declares on 25 September 1788 that the forthcoming Estates General should be convened in accordance with the precedents established in 1614.

The court, continuing in the principles which inspired its resolutions of 3 and 5 May last [. . .] orders that the said declaration be registered on the rolls of the court to be implemented according to its form and tenor but with the following provisos: that it cannot be argued from the preamble or any of the articles of the said declaration that the court needed to be restored in order to resume functions which violence alone had suspended; the court cannot be prevented, by the silence imposed on the king's *procureur-général* in matters relating to the execution of the Ordonnances, Edicts and Declarations of 8 May last, from taking cognizance of offences with which the court would have been obliged to deal; that it cannot be argued from articles 4 and 5 that the judgements mentioned there are not subject to appeal or that any of those who have not been examined and sworn in by the court, should be allowed to exercise the functions of judge in the lower tribunals. Finally the said court, in conformity with its resolution of 3 May last, maintains its insistence that the Estates General designated for next January be regularly convoked and composed, and that according to the forms observed in 1614.

Source: Hardman, J. (ed.) *The French Revolution: the Fall of the Ancien Régime to the Thermidorian Reaction, 1785–1795* (Arnold, London, 1981), p. 70.

SWANSONG OF THE ARISTOCRACY

Document 6

With no end to the press debate on 'privilege' in sight and deadlock – or disarray – within the ministry as to how to respond to the demands being made by Third Estate pamphleteers, the Princes of the Blood become seriously alarmed. This Memorandum was despatched to the king on 12 December 1788.

When Your Majesty forbade the Notables to discuss the memorandum submitted to them by the Prince de Conti, Your Majesty declared to the 'Princes of the Blood that when they desired to communicate to him that which might be useful to the good of his service and that of the state, they might address him'.

The Comte d'Artois, the Prince de Condé, the Duc de Bourbon, the Duc d'Enghien and the Prince de Conti consider it their duty to respond to this invitation from Your Majesty.

It particularly behoves the Princes of the Blood to tell you the truth: by rank, they are the first of your subjects; by their condition, your natural advisors; by their rights, most interested in defending yours; and they consider likewise that they owe you an account of their feelings and of their thoughts.

Sire, the state is in peril. Your person is respected, the virtues of the monarch assure him of the nation's homage. But, Sire, a revolution is being prepared in the principles of government; it is being accomplished through the turmoil in men's minds. Institutions which were considered sacred and which have enabled this monarchy to flourish for so many centuries have been put into question or even decried as unjust.

The writings which have appeared during the [second] Assembly of Notables; the memoranda which have been submitted to the princely signatories, the demands formulated by various provinces, towns, *corps*; the subject matter and style of these demands and memoranda all herald, all prove that there is a deliberate plan of insubordination and of contempt for the laws of the state. Every author sets himself up as a legislator; eloquence or a facile pen – even devoid of study, knowledge or experience – seem sufficient authorisation to regulate the constitution of empires. Whoever advances a bold proposition, whoever proposes to change the laws is assured of readers and sectaries.

So fast does this deplorable mania develop that opinions, which a short while ago would have appeared most reprehensible, today seem reasonable and just [. . .] Who can say where the audacity of opinions will stop? The rights of the throne have been called into question; opinion is riven over the rights of the two orders of the state; soon the rights of property will be attacked; inequality of wealth will be presented as something which needs to be reformed; already it has been proposed that feudal dues be abolished as representing a system of oppression, a barbarous survival.

Derived from these new theories, from the intention to change rights and laws, is the claim advanced by several sections of the Third Estate that their order should have two votes in the Estates General whilst each of the two leading orders continues to have but one.

The princely signatories will not repeat what has been developed by several committees [of the Notables], namely the injustice and danger of innovations in the composition of the Estates General; the host of resultant claims; the ease with which, if votes were counted by head and not by order, the interests of the Third Estate – better defended by the existing arrangements – would be compromised by corrupting members of the Third Estate; the destruction of the equilibrium so wisely established between the three orders and of their mutual independence.

It has been demonstrated to Your Majesty how important it is to preserve the only method of convoking the Estates which is constitutional, the mode hallowed by law and custom: the distinction between the orders, the right to deliberate in separate chambers, equality of votes [between them] – these unchangeable foundations of the French monarchy [. . .]

Source: Hardman, J. (ed.) *The French Revolution Sourcebook* (Arnold, London, 1999), pp. 69–70.

FORWARD-LOOKING NOBLES

Document 7

Nobles could be as concerned about civil liberties as educated members of the Third Estate, a fact which serves to remind us that the liberal attack on arbitrary government had aristocratic roots.

Cahier of the nobility of the *bailliage* of Nemours

1. The wish of the nobility of the *bailliage* of Nemours is that places in the meeting hall of the Estates General be occupied without distinction of province or deputation, so as to avoid anything that might be interpreted as conferring pre-eminence on one province or another.
2. That the president of the order of the nobility in the Estates General be freely elected by and in his order, without distinction of province or rank.
3. That the persons of the members of the Estates General be declared inviolable and that in any case they may not answer for what they have said or done in the Estates General to any but the Estates General.
4. That the wish of the order of the nobility of the *bailliage* of Nemours is that the vote be by order.
5. But in the case that voting by order be absolutely rejected by the Estates General, and the deputies of the *bailliage* see that further resistance to voting by head would be useless, they will ask that voting by head be done in the separate chambers of each order and not in a general assembly of the three orders together.

   That the Estates General decide how many votes beyond half will constitute a majority.

Voting by head can never be allowed in matters concerning only one of the three orders.

6. That the nobility of the *bailliage* wishes to declare at the outset to the Estates General that its intention is that taxes be generally and equally divided among individuals of the three orders.

And that, always wishing to set an example of the most entire obedience to the laws of the realm, the nobility ask that criminal and civil laws which ought to protect all citizens equally should apply to everyone, without regard to rank or birth.

7. That the nation having come together in the assembly of the Estates General, it regains all its rights and, as a consequence, all taxes presently established must be declared null and void, as not having been voted by the nation, which alone has the power to do so.

[. . .]

9. That the wish of the nobility of the *bailliage* is that individual freedoms be guaranteed to every Frenchman, before any other matters are dealt with. . .

[. . .]

13. That freedom of the press be granted, with such exceptions as may be determined by the Estates General.

[. . .]

15. That agriculture, industry, arts and commerce enjoy the greatest freedom and be delivered from the monopoly resulting from excessive privileges.

[. . .]

17. That the Estates General be constituted according to just proportions among the three orders, and that legislative power be given them in its entirety. Therefore in order to have full force, this legislative power need only be sanctioned by the Royal Assent.

[. . .]

Source: Kaplow, J. *France on the Eve of Revolution: a Book of Readings* (John Wiley & Sons Inc. New York, Toronto, 1971), pp. 155–6. Translated by Susan Kaplow.

Document 8   BACKWARD-LOOKING NOBLES

The Cambrésis, a frontier province annexed to France in 1678, enjoyed substantial fiscal advantages, not to mention a royal tobacco monopoly. All social groups – not just the nobility – anticipated that they would be the losers if privileged enclaves were asked to make sacrifices in the name of the common good.

Cahier of the nobility of Cambrai and the Cambrésis

[. . .]

1. That the Estates General attends first and foremost to the drawing up and passing, in collaboration with His Majesty, of a body of constitutional law which will be recorded for ever more in a national statute book; no deliberations on taxes or loans until such time as all the elements of this code have been definitively drafted, approved and promulgated as constituting the foundation of the constitution of France.

2. That it shall be established as fundamental maxims that the government of the kingdom is monarchical; that the throne is hereditary; and that females may not succeed to it. The Estates General is requested also to rule immediately on the issue of the regency in case of an [unanticipated] event.

3. *[Concerning] constitutional laws; the forming of a national assembly, and the frequency of meetings.*
    That it be declared that national assemblies are integral to government; and that in consequence they will always be made up of the three separate orders, and will be summoned invariably every three years.

4. *[Concerning] the summoning of national assemblies.*
    That the manner of convocation of national assemblies, the number of deputies [allocated to] each province, and finally all matters relating to organisation be determined by the assemblies themselves – in the light of any injustices that the present meeting might throw up, and in accordance with whatever circumstances might dictate over time.

5. That no law take on the status of constitutional law without the consent of the nation.

6. *[Concerning] voting by order.*
    That in all debates votes be counted by order and not by head.

7. *[Concerning] the renouncing of exemptions and privileges.*
    These matters having been dealt with in outline, the nobility of the Cambrésis, while sacrificing its pecuniary interests and willingly submitting to the strictly equal distribution of taxes, confines itself to asking for the maintenance of the constitution and privileges of the province, as specified and endorsed by our monarchs.
    [. . .]

16. *[Concerning] the new civil code.*
    [. . .]

17. That seigneurial assize courts in the Cambrésis be confirmed as forming part of the [original] enfeoffment, with the power to judge definitively cases to the value of 500 *livres*, with appeal to the Parlement for cases in excess; all intermediate justices to be abolished in consequence.
    [. . .]

38.   That letters of nobility no longer be granted, save in the case of conspicuous service to the fatherland, and only then at the request, and on the attestation, of the *corps* of nobility of the Provincial Estates where the [candidate] resides.

Signed: Marquis d'Estourmel; Cordier de Caudry secretary.

Source: Marchand, P. (ed.) *Florilège des cahiers de doléances du Nord* (Centre d'histoire de la région du nord et de l'Europe du nord-ouest, Université Charles de Gaulle – Lille III, Lille, 1989), pp. 219–20; 223. Translated by Peter Jones.

Document 9   PARISH GRIEVANCES

The choosing of the deputies and the drawing up of the cahiers de doléances of the Third Estate took place in two stages. Villagers articulated their thoughts in parish assemblies, whereupon individuals were appointed to take these 'preliminary' grievance lists to the neighbouring town. There, a much larger assembly of delegates fused the grievances into a single document and chose the deputies who were to carry it to Versailles.

Grievances and complaints which the inhabitants of the *bourg* and *prévôté* seat of Chaumont-sur-Moselle humbly request His Majesty to address, and which they expect their deputies to the *bailliage* [assembly] of Vézelise and their representatives to the Estates General to place a firm emphasis upon.

1.   They demand and will always demand [the setting up of] Provincial Estates with control over all branches of the administration;
2.   That no taxes ever be established without the prior approval of the Estates General, and only then for a fixed duration;
3.   That their representatives in the Estates General consent to no new taxes unless they judge them to be essential to the needs of the state, and then only after the subtraction of all useless and extravagant expenditures – excluding from this description those linked to the splendour and majesty of the throne – and only after the reduction in both the number and the scale of pensions, the arbitrariness of which has weighed down the state.
4.   That all the pecuniary burdens known as taxes, subventions or subsidies – and under whatever label they might feature in the future – be distributed among all citizens, notwithstanding distinctions of order, or privilege, but in proportion to their property and ability to pay.
5.   That the price of salt be cut by half, [since] its extreme dearness often forces the rural poor to do without; it is from this privation that many

of the illnesses which frequently afflict them stem, and it makes it impossible for farmers to maintain and to increase their stock.

6. The abolition of [the offices of] valuers-and-auctioneers whose exorbitant charges and fees, which they alone know how to multiply, all too often swallow up the greater part of the inheritances falling to minors; and who keep the subjects of His Majesty in thraldom by virtue of their exclusive privilege to estimate the value of chattels and to carry out sales, whether forced or voluntary.

7. That all monopolies, and particularly that of the wine press, be abolished; or, at least, that owners of vines be allowed to have their own presses as is the case in territories belonging to the king, in return for a payment to the seigneurial overlord of 2 *francs* per *jour* of vines; this abolition would prevent the spoiling or loss of a large quantity of wine.

8. That the inhabitants be free to employ any competent distiller they please for the manufacture of their eau-de-vie, not those designated for the locality; on the ground that all exclusive privileges are contrary to the public interest. This demand is founded, moreover, on the Edict of 13 August 1782, article 3, which requires owners wishing to have distilled their wine and grape pressings to employ any suitable distiller, and not one designated for the locality in preference to another as the inspectors who supervise the production of eau-de-vie have claimed.

9. That they be relieved of the burden of contributing to the perquisites of the officers of the Parlement [of Nancy], on the ground that such a burden should be a matter solely for the litigants; that the intendants be abolished.

10. That those who tender successfully for timber from the communal forests be obliged to make payment directly to the sindics appointed for the purpose by the municipal assemblies so that the sums can be used to meet the needs of the community. The current practice of depositing the sums with the forestry receiver is just another pointless expense and burden for rural communities, not only because of the receivership duty that is debited, but also because of the difficulties and obstacles they have always encountered in trying to withdraw these monies when they are needed; not to mention the numberless journeys and efforts that the sindics are required to undertake for the purpose – all at the expense of their constituents.

11. That the stud farm set up in the province be abolished on the ground that its costs outweigh the meagre benefits it secures; besides, it would be much more preferable to distribute the stallions among substantial and well-regarded farmers who would be granted privileges in return

for their upkeep: by this means costs would be reduced almost to nothing and farmers would no longer moan about the pointlessness of concentrating all the stallions at Rosières; instead they would become very useful under this new arrangement.

12. That their dwellings and cellars be exempted from the excavations of the saltpetre inspectors in conformity with the paternal intentions of His Majesty as clearly laid out in his *arrêts* of 8 August 1777 and 24 January 1778 [. . .]

13. That the royal Letters-Patent concerning the amalgamation and redistribution of land holdings in the territory of [the community of] Chaumont dated 15 December 1770 be withdrawn, and that the free grazing of the common flocks be restored, as we always understood was to be the case.

14. The abolition of the duty on hides which has pushed up their price to such an extent that farmers and country dwellers can no longer obtain what they need.

15. That tendering for the community's work stint on the highways be conducted before the municipal assembly, and that it be allowed to arrange for the work to be undertaken by *corvée* if it chooses while standing guarantee for the solidity of the workmanship, thereby retaining the value of the tax levied for this purpose.

16. The abolition of the *corvées* and *tailles* demanded repeatedly by our seigneurs.

17. Knowing as our representatives do that the high price of wood derives from sales abroad and the consumption of the salt-works, amounting to a double charge on this province since it is providing the means of obtaining its salt [. . .] there should be some indemnification. By reducing the cost of salt by half, sales would increase by a quarter; the resultant price should then be set against this double tax load, which brings enormous sums into the country [. . .]

18. That seigneurs who insist on maintaining forges, glass-works and other work-shops do so using their own wood; and that the majority of these enterprises be abolished.

The said inhabitants have given authority to their delegates to present and make known all the articles in this *cahier*, and any others they judge to be consonant with their interests, those of the state and the public good; to combine with the other parishes and jurisdictions of the *bailliage* of Vézelise in order to elect upright and capable individuals to participate in the Estates General of the kingdom scheduled to take place in Versailles on 27 April next.

Drawn up in the court-room of Chaumont-sur-Moselle, on the 11 March 1789, and signed by all those present who are so able. [sixty-eight signatures, four illegible].

Endorsed by Lambert, seigneurial judge of Chaumont.

Source: Etienne, C. *Cahiers de doléances des bailliages des généralités de Metz et de Nancy.* Tome 3: *Cahiers du bailliage de Vézelise* (Nancy, 1930), pp. 56–61. Translated by Peter Jones.

———————————◆———————————

(Pay close attention to this one - it is a very important document)

THE NEW DOCTRINE OF RIGHTS   **Document 10**

Voted on 27 August 1789, this document was intended by the National Assembly to be a preliminary statement of the principles around which the constitution would be framed.

Declaration of the Rights of Man and of Citizens by the National Assembly of France.

The representatives of the people of France, formed into a National Assembly, considering that ignorance, neglect, or contempt of human rights, are the sole causes of public misfortunes and corruptions of government, have resolved to set forth, in a solemn declaration, these natural, imprescriptible, and inalienable rights: that this declaration being constantly present to the minds of the members of the body social, they may be ever kept attentive to their rights and their duties: that the acts of the legislative and executive powers of Government, being capable of being every moment compared with the end of political institutions, may be more respected: and also, that the future claims of the citizens, being directed by simple and incontestable principles, may always tend to the maintenance of the Constitution, and the general happiness.

For these reasons, the National Assembly doth recognise and declare, in the presence of the Supreme Being, and with the hope of his blessing and favour, the following *sacred* rights of men and of citizens:

1. Men are born, and always continue, free, and equal in respect of their rights. Civil distinctions, therefore, can be founded only on public utility.

2. The end of all political associations is the preservation of the natural and imprescriptible rights of man; and these rights are liberty, property, security, and the resistance of oppression.

3. The nation is essentially the source of all sovereignty; nor can any individual, or any body of men, be entitled to any authority which is not expressly derived from it.

Only men and also doesn't apply to slaves at first.

4. Political liberty consists in the power of doing whatever does not injure another. The exercise of the natural rights of every man, has no other limits than those which are necessary to secure to every *other* man the free exercise of the same rights; and these limits are determinable only by the law.

5. The law ought to prohibit only actions hurtful to society. What is not prohibited by the law, should not be hindered; nor should anyone be compelled to that which the law does not require.

6. The law is an expression of the will of the community. All citizens have a right to concur, either personally, or by their representatives, in its formation. It should be the same to all, whether it protects or punishes; and *all being equal in its sight, are equally eligible to all honours, places, and employments, according to their different abilities, without any other distinction than that created by their virtues and talents.*

7. No man should be accused, arrested, or held in confinement, except in cases determined by the law, and according to the forms which it has prescribed. All who promote, solicit, execute, or cause to be executed, arbitrary orders, ought to be punished; and every citizen called upon, or apprehended by virtue of the law, ought immediately to obey, and renders himself culpable by resistance.

8. The law ought to impose no other penalties but such as are absolutely and evidently necessary: and no one ought to be punished, but in virtue of a law promulgated before the offence, and legally applied.

9. Every man being presumed innocent till he has been convicted, whenever his detention becomes indispensable, all rigour to him, more than is necessary to secure his person, ought to be provided against by the law.

10. No man ought to be molested on account of his opinions, not even on account of his *religious* opinions, provided his avowal of them does not disturb the public order established by the law.

11. The unrestrained communication of thoughts and opinions being one of the most precious rights of man, every citizen may speak, write and publish freely, provided he is responsible for the abuse of this liberty in cases determined by the law.

12. A public force being necessary to give security to the rights of men and of citizens, that force is instituted for the benefit of the community, and not for the particular benefit of the persons with whom it is entrusted.

13. A common contribution being necessary for the support of the public force, and for defraying the other expenses of the government, it ought to be divided equally among the members of the community, according to their abilities.

[Handwritten margin notes: "A lot of them are about justice and punishment"; "This allows for the spread of ideas and allows also a sense of community"]

14. Every citizen has a right, either by himself or his representative, to a free voice in determining the necessity of public contributions, the appropriation of them, and their amount, mode of assessment, and duration.

15. Every community has a right to demand of all its agents, an account of their conduct.

16. Every community in which a separation of powers and a security of rights is not provided for, wants a constitution.

17. The right to property being inviolable and sacred, no one ought to be deprived of it, except in cases of evident public necessity, legally ascertained, and on condition of a previous just indemnity.

Source: Paine, T. *Rights of Man* (edited and with an introduction by H. Collins, Penguin Books, Harmondsworth, 1971), pp. 132–4.

———————◄●►———————

CHURCH REFORM   **Document 11**

Although the cahiers had signalled the need for church reform, the debate on the issue in the National Assembly swiftly moved beyond concrete grievances and necessary adjustments to become all-embracing.

The Civil Constitution of the Clergy, 12 July 1790

Chapter 1: ecclesiastical offices
Each department will form a single diocese and each diocese will have the same extent and the same limits as the department.

The seats of the bishoprics of the 83 departments of the kingdom will be fixed in accordance with the following table [. . .] All the other bishoprics present in the 83 departments of the kingdom which are not expressly mentioned in the present schedule are, and will remain, suppressed.

The kingdom will be divided into ten metropolitan provinces.
[. . .]

7. On the advice of the bishop and of the new district authorities immediate steps will be taken for a new division of all the parishes of the kingdom [. . .]
[. . .]

16. In towns where there are less than 6,000 souls, there will be only one parish; the other parishes will be suppressed and joined to the principal church.

Chapter 2: nomination to ecclesiastical offices

From the publication of the present decree there will be only one way of appointing to bishoprics and cures, namely election.

All elections will be conducted by ballot; the successful candidate will have an absolute majority of votes.

The election of bishops will be conducted in the form prescribed and by the electoral college provided for by the decree of 22 December 1789 for the nomination of members of the departmental administration.

[. . .]

19. The new bishop may not ask the Pope for confirmation; but he may write to him as the visible head of the Church Universal in token of the unity of faith and of communion he should maintain with him.
     [. . .]

21. Before the ceremony of consecration begins, the newly elected one, in the presence of municipal officers, the people and the clergy, will take a solemn oath to care for the faithful of the diocese which is entrusted to him, to be faithful to the nation, to the law and to the king and to maintain with all his power the constitution decreed by the National Assembly and accepted by the king.

Source: Hardman, J. *The French Revolution Sourcebook* (Arnold, London, 1999), pp. 115–6.

Document 12   WHAT THE KING REALLY THOUGHT OF THE REVOLUTION

Plans for the escape from Paris had been in the making for months. Louis left this Déclaration *in the Tuileries Palace to be found on 21 June 1791.*

As long as the king could hope to see order and the welfare of the kingdom regenerated by the means employed by the National Assembly, and by his residence near that Assembly in the capital, no sacrifice mattered to him; [. . .] but today, when his sole recompense consists of seeing the monarchy destroyed, all powers disregarded, property violated, personal security everywhere endangered, crimes unpunished, and total anarchy taking the place of law, while the semblance of authority provided by the new Constitution is insufficient to repair a single one of the ills afflicting the kingdom, the king, having solemnly protested against all the acts issued during his captivity, deems it his duty to place before Frenchmen and the entire universe the picture of his conduct and that of the government which has established itself in the kingdom.

[. . .]

But the more sacrifices the king made for the welfare of his people, the more the rebels laboured to disparage the value thereof, and to present the monarchy under the most false and odious colours.

The convocation of the Estates General, the doubling of the deputies of the Third Estate, the king's efforts to eliminate all difficulties which might delay the meeting of the Estates General and those which arose after its opening, all the retrenchments which the king made in his personal expenses, all the sacrifices which he made for his people in the session of 23 June [1789], finally, the union of the orders, effected by the king's wish, a measure which His Majesty then deemed indispensable for the functioning of the Estates General, all his anxiety, all his efforts, all his generosity, all his devotion to his people – all have been misjudged, all have been misrepresented.

The time when the Estates General, assuming the name of National Assembly, began to occupy itself with the constitution of the kingdom, calls to mind the memoirs which the rebels were cunning enough to have sent from several provinces, and the movements of Paris to have the deputies disregard one of the principal clauses contained in their *cahiers*, namely that providing that *the making of the laws should be done in concert with the king*. In defiance of that clause, the Assembly placed the king entirely outside the Constitution by refusing him the right to grant or to withhold his sanction to articles which it regarded as constitutional, reserving to itself the right to include in that category those which it deemed suitable; and for those regarded as purely legislative, reducing the royal prerogative to a right of suspension until the third legislature, a purely illusory right as so many examples prove only too well.

What remains to the king other than the vain semblance of monarchy?

[. . .]

Signed Louis

Paris, 20 June 1791

Source: Stewart, J.H. *A Documentary Survey of the French Revolution* (The Macmillan Company, New York, 1951), pp. 205–6 and 210.

PARTING OF THE WAYS ON THE CHAMP DE MARS   **Document 13**

Interrogation of a cook named Constance Evrard, who had been arrested on 17 July 1791 following an accusation that she had insulted the wife of a national guardsman.

Question: Has she been to the Champ de Mars?
Answer: Yes, she had been there with Madame Léon and her daughter.
Question: Why had she been there?
Answer: To sign a petition 'like all good patriots'.

Question: What was the petition about?

Answer: She understood that its aim was 'to organise in a different manner the executive power'.

Question: Did she often go to public meetings?

Answer: She had sometimes been to the Palais Royal and the Tuileries.

Question: Did she belong to any club?

Answer: She had sometimes been to the Cordeliers Club, although not actually a member.

Question: Had she been with any particular group in the Champ de Mars?

Answer: She had been on the 'altar to the fatherland' and signed the petition.

Question: Had she thrown stones or seen any stones thrown?

Answer: No.

Question: Who had invited her to sign the petition?

Answer: No one, but she had heard various people say that there was a petition to sign in the Champ de Mars.

Question: Was it true that her name had appeared in the papers?

Answer: Yes, her name had appeared in *Les Révolutions de Paris*, because she had expressed grief at the death of Loustalot.

Question: What papers did she read?

Answer: She read Marat, Audoin, Camille Desmoulins, and very often, *L'Orateur du Peuple*.

Source: Rudé, G. *The Crowd in the French Revolution* (Clarendon Press, Oxford, 1959), pp. 86–7.

Document 14   OVERTHROW OF THE MONARCHY

From a letter despatched by a national guardsman to a friend in Rennes.

Paris, 11 August 1792, Year Four of Liberty

We are all tired out, doubtless less from spending two nights under arms than from heartache. Men's spirits were stirred after the unfortunate decree which whitewashed Lafayette. Nevertheless, we had a quiet enough evening; a group of *fédérés* from Marseilles gaily chanted patriotic songs in the Beaucaire café, the refreshment room of the National Assembly. It was rumoured: 'Tonight the tocsin will ring, the alarm drum will be beaten. All the *faubourgs* will burst into insurrection, supported by 6,000 *fédérés*.' At 11 o'clock we go home, at the same instant the drums call us back to arms. We speed from our quarters and our battalion, headed by two pieces of artillery, marches to the palace. Hardly have we reached the garden of the Tuileries than we hear the alarm cannon. The alarm drum resounds through all the streets of Paris. People run for arms from all over the place. Soon the public squares, the Pont Neuf, the main thoroughfares, are covered with troops. The National Assembly, which had finished its debate early, was recalled to its duties. It only knew of some of the preparations that had been made for the *journée* of 10 August. First the commandant of the palace wishes to hold the mayor a hostage there, then he sends him to the mayor's office. The people fear a display of his talents! In the general council of the Commune it is decreed that, according to the wishes of the 48 Sections, it is no longer necessary to recognise the established authorities if dethronement is not immediately announced and the new municipal bodies, keeping Pétion and Manuel at their head, entrusted with popular authority. However, the *faubourgs* organised themselves into an army and place in their centre Bretons, Marseillais and Bordelais, and all the other *fédérés*. More than 20,000 men march across Paris, bristling with pikes and bayonets. Santerre had been obliged to take command of them. The National Assembly are told that the army has broken into the palace. All hearts are frozen. Discussion is provoked again by the question of the safety of the king, when it is learned that Louis XVI seeks refuge in the bosom of the Assembly.

Forty-eight delegates are sent to the palace. The royal family places itself in the middle of the deputation. The people fling bitter reproaches at the king and accuse him of being the author of his troubles. Hardly was the king safe than the noise of cannon-fire increased. The Breton *fédérés* beat a tattoo. Some officers suggested retreat to the commander of the Swiss guards. But he seemed prepared and soon, by a clever tactic, captured the artillery which the national guard held in the courtyard. These guns, now turned on the people, fire and strike them down. But soon the conflict is intensified everywhere. The Swiss, surrounded, overpowered, stricken, then run out of ammunition. They plead for mercy, but it is impossible to calm the people, furious at Helvetian treachery.

The Swiss are cut to pieces. Some were killed in the state-rooms, others in the garden. Many died on the Champs-Elysées. Heavens! That liberty should cost Frenchmen blood and tears! How many victims there were among both the people and the national guard! The total number of dead could run to 2,000. All the Swiss who had been taken prisoner were escorted to the Place de Grève. There they had their brains blown out. They were traitors sacrificed to vengeance. What vengeance! I shivered to the roots of my being. At least 47 heads were cut off. The Grève was littered with corpses, and heads were paraded on the ends of several pikes. The first heads to be severed were those of seven *chevaliers du poignard*, slain at 8 o'clock in the morning on the Place Vendôme. Many Marseillais perished in the *journée* of 10 August.

Source: Wright, D.G. *Revolution and Terror in France, 1789–1794* (Pearson Education Ltd, London, 1990), pp. 123–4.

Document 15   WHAT IS A SANS-CULOTTE?

A self-description. The Ami des lois *was a comedy fashionable in 1793 and* Chaste Suzanne *a light operetta. Gorsas was a Girondin journalist and the* Patriote françois *and* La Chronique *Girondin news sheets.*

Reply to an impertinent question: what is a sans-culotte?

A sans-culotte, you rogues? He is someone who always goes about on foot, who has not got the millions you would all like to have, who has no chateaux, no valets to wait on him, and who lives simply with his wife and children, if he has any, on the fourth or fifth floor. He is useful because he knows how to plough a field, to forge and file metal, to use a saw, to roof a house, to make shoes, and to spill his blood to the last drop for the safety of the republic. And because he is a worker, you are sure not to meet his person in the Café de Chartres, or in the gaming houses where others plot and wager, nor in the Theatre of the Nation, where *L'Ami des lois* is performed, nor in the Vaudeville Theatre at a performance of *Chaste Suzanne*, nor in the literary clubs where for two sous, which are so precious to him, you are offered Gorsas's muck, with *La Chronique* and the *Patriote françois*.

   In the evening he goes to the meeting of his Section, not powdered and perfumed and nattily booted in the hope of being noticed by the citizenesses in the galleries, but ready to support sound proposals with all his might and ready to pulverise those which come from the despised faction of politicians.

   Finally, a sans-culotte always has his sabre and belt with him, ready to cut off the ears of all mischief makers; sometimes he carries his pike about with him; but as soon as the drum beats you see him leave for the Vendée, for the Army of the Alps, or for the Army of the North.

Source: Wright, D.G. *Revolution and Terror in France, 1789–1795* (Pearson Education Ltd, London, 1990), pp. 126–7.

Document 16   THE POPULAR PROGRAMME

This petition was presented to the Convention by the Section des Sans-Culottes on 2 September 1793, just as frustration at the deputies' failure to address the social and economic grievances of ordinary people was approaching boiling point.

Delegates of the people – for how much longer are you going to tolerate royalism, ambition, egotism, intrigue and avarice, each of them combined with fanaticism, surrendering to tyranny our frontiers, whilst spreading devastation and death everywhere? How much longer are you going to suffer food hoarders spreading famine throughout the republic in the detestable hope of causing patriots to cut each other's throats and the restoration of the throne in the midst of bloody corpses and with the help of foreign despots? You must make haste for there is no time to lose [. . .] the whole universe is watching you: humanity reproaches you for the troubles that are laying waste the French republic. Posterity will condemn your names in centuries to come if you do not speedily find a remedy [. . .] Make haste, representatives of the people, to remove from the armies all former nobles; all priests, magistrates of the Parlements and financiers from all administrative and judicial posts; also to fix the price of basic foodstuffs, raw materials, wages, and the profits of industry and commerce. You have both the justification and the authority to do so [. . .] No doubt aristocrats, royalists, moderates and intriguers will retort that this is to compromise [rights of] property which should be sacred and inviolable [. . .] No doubt; but are these rogues unaware that property is constrained by physical need? Are they unaware that no one has the right to do anything that injures another? What is more injurious than the arbitrary power to attach to food a price that seven-eighths of citizens cannot possibly reach [. . .] Are they unaware, finally, that every individual making up the republic should employ his intelligence and the strength in his arms in the service of the republic, and should be prepared to spill his blood to the last drop for her? In return, the republic should guarantee to each one of its citizens the means of procuring sufficient basic necessities for his existence.

Have we not directed a fearsome law against hoarders, you will retort. But delegates of the people, do not be deceived [. . .] This decree, which forces those with large stocks of foodstuffs to make a declaration, tends to benefit hoarders more than it extinguishes hoarding: it puts all their stocks under the supervision of the nation, while leaving them to sell at whatever price their greed dictates. In consequence, the general assembly of the Section des Sans-Culottes, considering it to be the duty of all citizens to propose measures which seem calculated to bring about the return of plenty and public tran-quillity, resolves to ask the Convention to decree the following:

1. That former nobles be barred from military careers and every kind of public office; that former *parlementaires*, priests and financiers be deprived of all administrative and judicial posts.
2. That the price of basic necessities be fixed at the levels prevailing in 1789–90, allowing for differences of quality.
3. That the price of raw materials, the level of wages and the profits of industry and commerce be also fixed, so that the working man, the farmer and the trader will be able to obtain not only the materials essential to their existence, but also the means of making the most of their life chances.

4. That all those farmers who, by some accident, have not been able to bring in their harvest be compensated from public funds.

5. That each department be allocated sufficient public money so as to ensure that the price of basic foodstuffs will be the same for all citizens of the republic.

6. That the sums of money allocated to the departments be used to eradicate variations in the price of foodstuffs caused by transport costs across the republic, so that everyone enjoys the same advantage.

7. That leases be abrogated and returned to the levels prevailing in average years; and that a uniform *maximum* be set for food and basic commodities.

8. That a *maximum* on wealth be fixed.

9. That no individual may possess more than one *maximum*.

10. That no one be allowed to lease more land than is required for a given number of plough-teams.

11. That no citizen shall be allowed to own more than one workshop, or boutique.

12. That all those with purely nominal title to goods or land be deemed proprietors.

The Section des Sans-Culottes believes that these measures will restore plenty and tranquility and will cause to disappear, bit by bit, the excessive disparity in wealth, and will multiply the number of proprietors.

Source: [with re-translations by Peter Jones] Wright, D.G. *Revolution and Terror in France, 1789–1795* (Pearson Education Ltd, London, 1990), pp. 128–30.

Document 17 LEGISLATING REVOLUTIONARY GOVERNMENT

The law of 14 Frimaire II (4 December 1793) reasserted central control over the application of the Terror.

Section II: Implementation of laws

1. The National Convention is the sole centre of impulsion of the government.

    [. . .]

9. All established authorities and all public functionaries are placed under the immediate supervision of the Committee of Public Safety for measures concerned with government and public safety, in conformity with the decree of 19 Vendémiaire [10 October]; and for everything

relating to individuals and to general and internal police, this particular supervision belongs to the Convention's Committee of General Security, in accordance with the decree of 17 September last; these two committees are obliged to give an account of their operations to the National Convention at the end of each month. Each member of these two committees is personally responsible for the performance of this duty.

10. The execution of the laws is divided into surveillance and application.
     [. . .]

13. Surveillance over the execution of revolutionary laws and measures of government, general security and public safety in the departments is exclusively attributed to the districts, who are obliged to give a faithful account of their operations every ten days to the Committee of Public Safety for matters of government and public safety, and to the Convention's Surveillance Committee for matters of general and internal police and for individuals.
     [. . .]

15. The application of revolutionary laws and measures of government and general security is entrusted to the municipalities and to the surveillance (or revolutionary) committees, who are likewise obliged to give an account every ten days of the execution of these laws to the district [administrations] of their area, to whom they are immediately subordinate.
     [. . .]

18. It is expressly forbidden for any authority or public functionary to issue proclamations or to take measures which extend, limit or contradict the literal meaning of the law, on the pretext of interpreting or expanding it.
     [. . .]

21. In the place of the procurator-sindics of the District [administrations] and the procurators of the Communes and their deputies, posts which are abolished by this decree, there will be *agents nationaux* specially entrusted with requiring and enforcing the execution of the law and also with denouncing negligence in such execution and infringements which may be committed. These *agents nationaux* are authorised to move from the seat of administration and to travel round the area of their jurisdiction to exercise surveillance and to assure themselves more positively that the laws are being implemented to the letter.

Section III: Competence of the established authorities

5. [. . .] The hierarchy which placed the districts, municipalities or any other authority under the department [administration] is abolished as

regards revolutionary and military laws and measures of government, public safety and general security.

[. . .]

10.   All changes ordered by the present decree will be implemented within three days of its publication.

[. . .]

20.   No armed force, tax or loan (whether forced or voluntary) may be levied except in virtue of a decree. The revolutionary taxes of the representatives of the people will not be collected until they have been approved by the Convention, unless it be in enemy or rebel territory.

Source: Hardman, J. (ed.) *The French Revolution Sourcebook* (Arnold, London, 1999), pp. 187–8.

Document 18   SCORCHED EARTH TREATMENT FOR REBELS

A letter of Turreau, one of the generals put in charge of crushing counter-revolutionary resistance in the Vendée, to the Minister of War, 19 January 1794.

the peasant revolt

My purpose is to burn everything, to leave nothing but what is essential to establish the necessary quarters for exterminating the rebels. This great measure is one which you should prescribe; you should also make an advance state-ment as to the fate of the women and children we will come across in this rebellious countryside. If they are all to be put to the sword, I cannot under-take such action without authorisation.

All brigands caught bearing arms, or convicted of having taken up arms to revolt against their country, will be bayoneted. The same will apply to girls, women and children in the same circumstances. Those who are merely under suspicion will not be spared either, but no execution may be carried out except by previous order of the general.

this policy (plan) had public support.

All villages, farms, woods, heath lands, generally anything which will burn, will be set on fire, although not until any perishable supplies found there have been removed. But, it must be repeated, these executions must not take place until so ordered by the general.

I hasten to describe to you the measures which I have put in hand for the extermination of all remaining rebels scattered about the interior of the Vendée. I was convinced that the only way to do this was by deploying a sufficient number of columns to spread right across the countryside and effect a general sweep, which would completely purge the cantons as they passed. Tomorrow, therefore, these twelve columns will set out simultaneously, moving from east to west. Each column commander has orders to search and burn forests, villages, market towns and farms, omitting, however, those places which I consider important posts and those which are essential for establishing communications.

Source: Cobb, R. and Jones, C. (eds) *The French Revolution: Voices from a Momentous Epoch, 1789–1795* (Simon and Schuster, London, 1988), p. 206.

CRISIS IN THE SECTIONS OF PARIS **Document 19**

The Committee of Public Safety and the Committee of General Security received regular briefings from police agents on the public mood at street level in the capital as the winter of 1794 gave way to spring.

2 Germinal II (22 March 1794)

It is imperative to speed up the trial of Citizen Hébert. There's a muffled ferment which is hard to define. However much one talks to people, makes enquiries, asks questions in order to try and ascertain public opinion, everybody is negative and responds vaguely.

Nonetheless, it's easy to judge that many have been affected (by the trial) and I firmly believe that it is important to proceed to sentencing as quickly as possible. In the meantime as much publicity as possible should be given to the conduct of Hébert so as to pre-empt stirrings among a section of the populace who are strongly disposed in his favour.

I even think it necessary to post up the justification of the sentence before his execution.

Source: Markov, W. and Soboul, A. *Die Sansculotten von Paris. Dokumente zur Geschichte des Volksbewegung 1793–1794* (Verlag, Berlin, 1957), p. 338. Translated by Peter Jones.

CIVIC CULTURE IN THE MAKING? **Document 20**

Although both of these extracts come from official sources, they raise questions about the Directory's efforts to embed its particular vision of the political order within the population at large.

16 Ventôse IV / 6 March 1796

The Commissioner of the Executive Directory [of Neuviller] reported that the law of 3 Brumaire [25 October 1795] designated 10 Germinal [30 March 1796] for one of the seven annual festivals. The Municipal Administration deliberated on how to celebrate it, and resolved that nothing does more to strengthen and consolidate public spiritedness than the gathering together of citizens in order to rejoice together at the conquest of liberty [. . .] It considered moreover that festivals should not only be days for relaxation and entertainment, but employed principally for the purpose of developing [public] behaviour and leading hearts towards fraternity [. . .] It was resolved that on the occasion of the 10 Germinal Festival of Youth appropriate games would take place and that the organization of the national guard would be put in hand on the same day.

Source: Archives Departements de Meurthe-et-Moselle L2943 *bis*. Register of deliberations of the administration of the canton of Neuviller, 14 Nivôse IV–18 Floréal VIII. Translated by Peter Jones.

Ventôse VII / March 1799

National festivals have been set up, but I would not speak here of their celebration. Is there any sight more pathetic than a municipal body decked in its sashes of office and accompanied by four or five village urchins coarsely intoning around a dead [liberty] tree a few couplets which usually have nothing to do with the ceremony in question, before returning home in a similar procession? Yet this is what happens in three quarters of France. This way of celebrating festivals is an insult to the nation; to say the least it is manifestly contrary to the intentions of legislators.

Source: Report of the Commissioner of the Executive Directory [of Leintrey, Meurthe-et-Moselle]: Clémendot, P. *Le Département de la Meurthe à l'époque du Directoire* (n.p., 1966), pp. 293–4. Translated by Peter Jones.

Document 21   MANAGING 'LA GRANDE NATION'

The conquests and territorial expansion of France between 1795 and 1799 raised fundamental questions in the minds of the policy makers of the Directory. These were resolved, in part, by establishing a number of 'sister' republics.

Treaty between France and the Cisalpine Republic, 3 Ventôse VI / 21 February 1798

The French Republic recognizes the Cisalpine Republic as a free and independent power; it guarantees its liberty, its independence, and the abolition of every government anterior to the one which now administers it.

There shall be peace, amity and good understanding between the French and the Cisalpine Republic in perpetuity.

The Cisalpine Republic pledges itself to take part in all wars which the French Republic might wage, when requisition therefore has been made upon it by the Executive Directory of the French Republic; as soon as such requisition is addressed to it, it shall be required to put all its forces and resources into action. By notification of the said same requisition, it will be constituted de facto in a state of war with the Powers against which it has been requisitioned, but until such notification has been made to it, it will remain in a state of neutrality. The French Republic shall be required to include the Cisalpine Republic in treaties of peace which follow wars which it has engaged by virtue of the present article.

The Cisalpine Republic having requested the French Republic for an army corps sufficient to maintain its liberty, its independence, and its internal peace, as well as to preserve it from all aggression on the part of its neighbours, the two Republics have agreed upon the following articles in such connection.

Until otherwise agreed thereon, there shall be in the Cisalpine Republic a body of French troops amounting to 25,000 men, including the staff and administration. The said body shall be composed of 22,000 infantry, 2,500 cavalry, and 500 artillery, either horse or of the line.

The Cisalpine Republic will furnish annually to the French Republic, for payment and maintenance of the said troops, a sum of 18,000,000 [francs], which shall be paid, in twelve equal monthly instalments, into the funds of the army; and in case of war, the necessary supplement of supplies. [. . .]

The French Government may withdraw and replace the said troops at will.

The said troops, as well as those of the Cisalpine Republic, shall always be under the command of French generals

[. . .]

Separate articles

[. . .]

5. The Cisalpine Republic may not, without the consent of the French government, go to war with any Power friendly to, or allied with, the French Republic.

[. . .]

Source: Stewart, J.H. *A Documentary Survey of the French Revolution* (Macmillan, New York, 1951), pp. 721–4.

———————◄●►———————

STATE OF THE COUNTRY IN THE AFTERMATH OF BRUMAIRE   **Document 22**

These extracts are taken from reports commissioned by the First Consul a few months after the establishment of the Consulate. Theophilanthropy was a civic cult briefly fashionable during the Directory, whereas Jansenists, Molinists and Convulsionists were mutually antagonistic sects within the pre-1789 Catholic Church.

Report of state councillor Fourcroy on his mission to the departments of the 14th military division [Calvados, Manche, Orne] in the month of Floréal Year IX [April–May 1801].

V. Political, military and administrative situation of the three departments comprising the 14th military division.

[. . .] There exists a marked diversity of opinion among the inhabitants of the three departments. Some individuals express a wish for a return to the *ancien régime*; others would like the constitutional monarchy of 1791, and a few still hanker for the ochlocratic [democratic] government of 1793. There are those who regret [the passing of] the Constitution of the Year III [1795], but the great majority – friends of the revolution – have rallied with sincerity to the Constitution of the Year VIII [1800], which has provided France with internal peace and stable government.

These opinions are purely speculative. Among the avowed partisans of anarchy or royalty, no one wishes to run the risks of another revolution; and no one, above all, is inclined to take up arms or to foment disturbances in order to secure the victory of one or other of these parties. I have noticed merely that among the individuals currently employed in the prefecture of the Calvados who are attached to the Constitution of the Year III, some continuing hopes of appointing to posts all those who share their opinion. And in order to achieve this objective, they pursue the policy of informing and denunciation which proved successful so often during the time of revolutionary turmoils. The government should investigate this matter which breeds distrust between administrators and those whom they administer.

[. . .]

Mission in the Year IX [1800–1801] of General Lacuée, councillor of state in the 1st military division [Aisne, Eure-et-Loir, Loiret, Oise, Seine-et-Marne, Seine-et-Oise].

Sources of national and individual wealth.

Agriculture – before the revolution agriculture (in the six departments excluding the Seine) might have been in a flourishing state but for the tithe, the *champart* and the [problem of] game. It is estimated that game destroyed one-eighth of the sowings and one-tenth of the harvest; at least this was the case in the Seine-et-Oise.

Requisitions and the Maximum caused a lot of damage to agriculture during one period of the revolution, but these drawbacks have been more than compensated for by the subdivision of landholdings; the non-collection of taxes; the residence [on their estates] of landowners and the abolition of [exclusive] hunting [rights], the *champart* and the tithe. Thus appreciable steps towards a better state of affairs have occurred.

However, agriculture suffered badly during the Year VII [1798–99]. Apprehensive owners of national property farmed poorly and wastefully. But the 18th Brumaire rekindled hope, [the sowing of] fodder crops multiplied, land was cleared, trees planted, the quantity of stock increased, farm buildings repaired.

[. . .]

Religion – the needs of the people in this sphere seem at the moment to be limited, both in the towns and the countryside, to vain spectacles and ceremonies. Attendance at Mass, listening to the sermon, going to Vespers, that's good enough; but submitting to confession, taking communion, abstinence from meat, or fasting is nowhere commonplace, and practised only by a tiny number. In those parts of the countryside where there are no priests, a lay official (magister) officiates and everyone is well content. The priests in rural areas are mostly indifferent. In the towns this indifference can be found also, but it is less marked. Some prefer the constitutional [clergy], but only a few; those [priests] who have sworn the oath of loyalty have more adherents; however, it is those who have declined to swear any oath who are the most ardently followed.

The services of the constitutional clergy are the most basic, whereas those provided by clerics who have taken the oath of loyalty [to the regime] are more elaborate. The non-jurors operate clandestinely, and these latter are the only ones to complain about the obstacles posed by the laws. All the others are broadly content with the freedom they enjoy, particularly the clergy ministering to non-Catholics.

The Jews are few in number, and protestants can only be found in the [departments of] the Seine and the Loiret.

The Theophilanthropy cult is collapsing, or has collapsed, everywhere. There are still some Jansenists and Molinists around, and Convulsionists can even be found in Paris.

The constitutional clergy manage on their pensions and whatever surplice fees they can collect. All the rest get by on hand-outs and the yield of collections, although they are scarcely the poorer thereby – at least in the towns. The non-jurors brought money with them when they returned [to France], but most of it was spent on giving pomp to their services.

In the countryside the people prefer [the sound of] bells without priests, to priests without bells.

Source: Rocquain, F. *L'Etat de la France au 18 Brumaire d'après les rapports des conseillers d'état chargés d'une enquête sur la situation de la République* (Didier et Cie, Paris, 1874), pp. 179–80; 237–8; 253–4. Translated by Peter Jones.

———— ◆ ————

REGAINING CONTROL   **Document 23**

The establishment of special criminal tribunals was part of the government's strategy to overcome brigandage, but in the eyes of many observers the measure risked undermining the principles of the system of justice established at the start of the revolution.

Law of 19 Pluviôse IX / 29 January 1801

Title 1

A special tribunal will be established in departments where the government deems it appropriate for the repression of the crimes stipulated below.

This tribunal will consist of two criminal law judges, three military persons possessing the rank of captain or above and two citizens qualified to act as judges. Individuals in the last two categories will be appointed by the First Consul.

[. . .]

Title 2

6. The special tribunal will prosecute crimes and offences subject to corporal punishment or deprivation of civil rights committed by vagabonds, vagrants and convicts [. . .]

    [. . .]

8. The special tribunal will take cognizance of highway robbery involving violence, assault or other aggravating circumstances by whomsoever it is committed.

It will likewise take cognizance of theft in the countryside and from rural dwellings and buildings where breaking and entering has taken place, or where the offence involved the carrying of weapons and was committed by two or more people.

It will also take cognizance, concurrently with the ordinary courts, of cases of premeditated murder by whomsoever committed.

    [. . .]

24. On submission of an accusation, with supporting evidence [. . .] the tribunal will try cases within its competence without right of appeal [. . .]

25. The verdict will be notified to the defendant within twenty-four hours. The Government Commissioner will likewise send to the Minister of Justice within twenty-hour hours a notification for onward dispatch to the court of appeal.

    [. . .]

29. [Arguments for a stay of execution having been heard], the tribunal will sentence in the last instance and without appeal. Robberies of the type described in articles 9 and 10 will incur a death penalty. Threats and assaults directed against purchasers of national property will be liable to a punishment of imprisonment of not less than six months and not

exceeding three years, but with the option of more severe penalties in aggravated cases

[. . .]

Source: *Gazette nationale ou Moniteur universel* (Paris, 1789–1810), an VIII, pp. 545–6. Translated by Peter Jones.

MARKING OUT THE NEW CIVIL ORDER **Document 24**

The Civil Code of 1804 sought to combine the Customary and the Roman law of ancien régime France with the legislation passed in the 1790s. It lays out un-ambiguously the rights and responsibilities of individuals within the family and in matters relating to inheritance. The statement on property expresses the consensus verdict as to what had been achieved after a decade and a half of revolution.

CIVIL CODE

Preliminary title: on the publication, application and effects of general laws

[. . .]

2. The law applies to the future only; it has no retrospective effect.

Book One: on persons

Chapter One: on the enjoyment of civil rights
[. . .]

8. Every Frenchman shall enjoy civil rights.

Chapter Six: on the rights and responsibilities of married persons

212. Married persons owe to each other fidelity, succour and assistance.
213. The husband owes protection to his wife; the wife owes obedience to her husband.
214. The wife is obliged to live with her husband and to follow him wherever he may choose to reside; the husband is obliged to take her in, and to provide her with all of life's necessities, according to his means and his station.
215. The wife cannot plead in her own name without the authorisation of her husband, even though she should be a public trader, or not in community, or separate in property.
216. The authorisation of the husband is not required when the wife is prosecuted under criminal or police jurisprudence.

217. The wife, even though not in community or separate in property, cannot donate, give away, pledge or acquire, whether freely or at a cost, without the husband's agreement or written consent.

218. If the husband refuses to authorise the wife to plead in her own name, a judge can give such authorisation.
[. . .]

Title Six: on divorce

Chapter One: on the causes of divorce

229. The husband may demand divorce because of the adultery of the wife.
[. . .]
230. The wife may demand divorce because of adultery on the part of the husband where he has kept his mistress in the communal home.
[. . .]
233. The mutual and sustained consent of the married persons, expressed as prescribed by the law and in accordance with the conditions and tests which the law lays down, will be considered sufficient proof that communal living is no longer tolerable to the parties, thereby constituting a conclusive ground for divorce.
[. . .]

Chapter Four: on the consequences of divorce

297. In the case of divorce by mutual consent, neither of the parties shall be permitted to contract a new marriage until three years have elapsed from the date of the divorce.
298. In the case of divorce admitted by law on the ground of adultery, the guilty party shall never be permitted to marry his/her accomplice. The adulterous wife shall be condemned by the same judgement, and at the behest of the public prosecutor, to confinement in a house of correction for a fixed period not exceeding two years and not less than three months.
[. . .]

Book Two: on property and the various modifications to which it is subject

Title One: on the characteristics of property

Chapter Three: on property in relation to possession

537. Individuals are free to dispose of property belonging to them, subject to the modifications laid down by the law.
[. . .]

542. Communal possessions are properties, the ownership or usufruct of which, the inhabitants of one or several communes have an established title to.

Title Two: on property

544. Property is the faculty to enjoy the use of, and to dispose of, things in the most absolute manner, provided that no use of them is made which is forbidden by law or by regulations.

545. No one can be obliged to give up his property unless it be in the public interest, and only then on condition of a previous just indemnity.

546. Property in a thing, whether movable or immovable, confers entitlement to all that it produces [. . .]

Book Three: on the various ways in which property is acquired

Title Five: on marriage contracts and the respective rights of married persons

Chapter Two: on the regime of community

1421. The husband alone administers property held in community.

1422. He can sell it, dispose of it, or pledge it without the agreement of the wife.

      [. . .]

1428. The husband administers all the personal possessions of the wife [. . .] He may not dispose of real estate owned personally by the wife without her consent.

Source: Bourguignon, M. *Conférence des cinq codes* (Corby, libraire, rue St-André-des-Arts, Paris, 1823), pp. 2–3; 42–3; 45–6; 55; 94–5; 237. Translated by Peter Jones.

Further Reading

The literature on the French Revolution is enormous and expands all the time. What follows is a selection from the material available in the English language. The selection draws attention to those books and articles that have been used in the preparation of this 'Seminar Study' which are particularly accessible to sixth-form and undergraduate readers. No attempt has been made to provide a comprehensive bibliography, or one that will satisfy more advanced students.

Translated Documents

There are several such compilations, of which the following can be recommended:

Dwyer, P.G. and McPhee, P. (eds) (2002) *The French Revolution and Napoleon: a Source Book*. London and New York: Routledge.

Hall Stewart, J. (1951) *A Documentary History of the French Revolution*. New York: The Macmillan Company.

Hardman, J. (ed.) (1999) *The French Revolution Sourcebook*. London: Arnold.

Levy, D.G., Applewhite, H.B. and Johnson, M.D. (eds) (1979) *Women in Revolutionary Paris, 1789–1795*. Urbana, IL: University of Illinois Press. This is no longer in print.

Mason, L. and Rizzo, T. (1999) *The French Revolution: a Document Collection*. Boston: Haughton Mifflin.

Readers

These are volumes containing articles of seminal or historiographical importance. They can provide a quick route to material that might otherwise prove difficult to locate. The best readers also contain a 'state of play' account of the subject and commentaries on the articles chosen for inclusion. The following can be recommended:

Blanning, T.C.W. (ed.) (1996) *The Rise and Fall of the French Revolution.* Chicago, IL and London: University of Chicago Press.

Censer, J.R. (ed.) (1989) *The French Revolution and Intellectual History.* Chicago, IL: The Dorsey Press.

Jones, P.M. (ed.) (1996) *The French Revolution in Social and Political Perspective.* London: Arnold.

Introductory Accounts

For the student who has no prior familiarity with the French Revolution, the short survey is the place to begin. There are plenty to choose from, but chronological coverage varies from volume to volume. For an uncomplicated and sure-footed narrative, Goodwin, A. (1977) *The French Revolution.* London: Harper Collins, is hard to beat. However, the book has now gone out of print. The following can be recommended:

Campbell, P.R. (1988) *The Ancien Régime in France.* Oxford: Basil Blackwell.

Crook, M. (1998) *Napoleon Comes to Power: Democracy and Dictatorship in Revolutionary France, 1795–1804.* Cardiff: University of Wales Press.

Ellis, G. (1991) *The Napoleonic Empire.* London: Macmillan.

Gough, H. (1998) *The Terror in the French Revolution.* London: Macmillan.

Temple, N. (1992) *The Road to 1789: from Reform to Revolution in France.* Cardiff: University of Wales Press.

Rather longer, but highly readable nevertheless, are:

Forrest, A. (1995) *The French Revolution.* Oxford: Basil Blackwell.

Lyons, M. (1994) *Napoleon Bonaparte and the Legacy of the French Revolution.* London: Macmillan.

McPhee, P. (2002) *The French Revolution, 1789–1799.* Oxford: Oxford University Press.

Sutherland, D.M.G. (1985) *France 1789–1815: Revolution and Counterrevolution.* London: Fontana Press.

Sutherland, D.M.G. (2003) *The French Revolution and Empire: the Quest for a Civic Order.* Oxford: Blackwell Publishing.

Historiography

A minefield! Students are strongly advised to gather information before plunging into the controversies spawned by the events of 1789. That done, they should consult:

Furet, F. (1981) *Interpreting the French Revolution.* Cambridge: Cambridge University Press.

Lewis, G. (1993) *The French Revolution: Rethinking the Debate*. London and New York: Routledge.

Soboul, A. (1988) *Understanding the French Revolution*. London: The Merlin Press.

Themes

Origins:

The origins of the revolution are best tackled via:

Baker, K.M. (1990) *Inventing the French Revolution: Essays on French Political Culture in the Eighteenth Century*. Cambridge: Cambridge University Press.

Doyle, W. (1999) *Origins of the French Revolution*. Oxford: Oxford University Press.

Lefebvre, G. (1947) *The Coming of the French Revolution*. New York: Vintage Books.

Soboul, A. (1974) *French Revolution, 1787–1799: from the Storming of the Bastille to Napoleon*. London: NLB.

Stone, B. (1994) *The Genesis of the French Revolution*. Cambridge: Cambridge University Press.

Country dwellers:

Jones, P.M. (1988) *The Peasantry in the French Revolution*. Cambridge: Cambridge University Press.

Markoff, J. (1996) *The Abolition of Feudalism: Peasants, Lords and Legislators in the French Revolution*. University Park, PA: Pennsylvania University Press.

The transition of 1789:

Jones, P.M. (1995) *Reform and Revolution in France: the Politics of Transition, 1774–1791*. Cambridge: Cambridge University Press.

Price, M. (1990) 'The "Ministry of the Hundred Hours": a Reappraisal', *French History*, 317–38.

Tackett, T. (1996) *Becoming a Revolutionary*. Princeton, NJ: Princeton University Press.

Religion:

Aston, N. (2000) *Religion and Revolution in France, 1789–1804*. London: Macmillan.

The clerical oath:

Tackett, T. (1986) *Religion, Revolution and Regional Culture in Eighteenth-Century France: the Ecclesiastical Oath of 1791*. Princeton, NJ: Princeton University Press.

Rural revolution:
Jones, P.M. (2003) *Liberty and Locality in Revolutionary France: Six Villages Compared, 1760–1820.* Cambridge: Cambridge University Press.

The press:
Gough, H. (1988) *The Newspaper Press in the French Revolution.* London: Routledge.

Clubs:
Kennedy, M. (1982–88) *The Jacobin Clubs in the French Revolution* (2 vols). Princeton, NJ: Princeton University Press.

Women:
Godineau, D. (1998) *The Women of Paris and their French Revolution.* Berkeley, CA: University of California Press.
Goodman, D. (1994) *The Republic of Letters: a Cultural History of the French Enlightenment.* Ithaca and London: Cornell University Press.
Hufton, O. (1992) *Women and the Limits of Citizenship in the French Revolution.* Toronto: University of Toronto Press.

Slavery and the colonies:
Dubois, L. (2004) *A Colony of Citizens: Revolution and Slave Emancipation in the French Caribbean, 1787–1804.* Chapel Hill and London: University of North Carolina Press.
Popkin, J. (2007) *Facing Racial Revolution: Eyewitness Accounts of the Haitian Insurrection.* Chicago and London: University of Chicago Press.

Elections:
Crook, M. (1996) *Elections in the French Revolution.* Cambridge: Cambridge University Press.
Gueniffey, P. (1993) *Le Nombre et la raison: la Révolution française et les élections.* Paris: Editions E.H.E.S.S.

The king:
Hardman, J. (2000) *Louis XVI: the Silent King.* London: Arnold.

The revolutionary wars:
Blanning, T.C.W. (1986) *The Origins of the Revolutionary Wars.* London: Longman.

Counter-revolution:
Petitfrère, C. (1988) 'The Origins of the Civil War in the Vendée', *French History*, 2, pp. 187–207.

Sutherland, D.M.G. (1982) *The Chouans: the Social Origins of Popular Counter-Revolution in Upper Brittany, 1770–1796*. Oxford: Clarendon Press.

Jacobins and Girondins:

Whaley, L. (2000) *Radicals, Politics and Republicanism in the French Revolution*. Stroud: Sutton Publishing.

Federalism:

Forrest, A. (1988) 'Federalism', in C. Lucas (ed.) *The French Revolution and the Creation of Modern Political Culture*, vol. 2, *The Political Culture of the French Revolution*. Oxford: Pergamon Press, pp. 309–28.

Terror:

Baczko, B. (1994) *Ending the Terror: the French Revolution after Robespierre*. Cambridge: Cambridge University Press.

Gough, H. (1998) *The Terror in the French Revolution*. London: Macmillan.

The sans-culottes:

Lewis, G. (1964) *The Parisian Sans-Culottes and the French Revolution*. Oxford: Oxford University Press.

Rose, R.B. (1983) *The Making of the Sans-culottes*. Manchester: Manchester University Press.

Robespierre:

Hampson, N. (1974) *Life and Opinions of Maximilien Robespierre*. Oxford: Duckworth.

Haydon, C. and Doyle, W. (eds) (1999) *Robespierre*. Cambridge: Cambridge University Press.

Danton:

Hampson, N. (1978) *Danton*. Oxford: Basil Blackwell.

Dechristianisation:

Tallett, F. (1991) 'Dechristianizing France: the Year II and the Revolutionary Experience', in F. Tallett and N. Atkin (eds) *Religion, Society and Politics in France since 1789*. London: Hambledon Press, pp. 1–28.

Vovelle, M. (1991) *The Revolution against the Church*. Cambridge: Polity Press.

Thermidor:

Lyons, M. (1975) 'The 9 Thermidor, Motives and Effects', *European Studies Review*, 5, pp. 123–46.

The armies:
Bertaud, J.P. (1989) *The Army of the French Revolution*. Princeton, NJ: Princeton University Press.

The Directory:
Lyons, M. (1975) *France under the Directory*. Cambridge: Cambridge University Press.

The Babeuf conspiracy:
Rose, R.B. (1978) *Gracchus Babeuf, the First Revolutionary Communist*. Stanford, CA: University of Stanford Press.

Thomson, D. (1947) *The Babeuf Plot: the Making of a Republican Legend*. London: Kegan Paul.

Royalism:
Fryer, W.R. (1965) *Republic and Restoration in France, 1794–1797*. Manchester: Manchester University Press.

The transition of 1799:
Brown, H.G. and Miller, J.A. (2002) *Taking Liberties: Problems of a New Order from the French Revolution to Napoleon*. Manchester: Manchester University Press.

The Bonapartist regime:
Lyons, M. (1994) *Napoleon Bonaparte and the Legacy of the French Revolution*. London: Macmillan.

Woloch, I. (2001) *Napoleon and his Collaborators: the Making of a Dictatorship*. New York: Norton.

Economic impacts
Horn, J. (2006) *The Path Not Taken: French Industrialisation in the Age of Revolution, 1750–1830*. Cambridge, MA: MIT Press.

Reference Works

The key book for the period up to 1799 is Jones, C. (1988) *The Longman Companion to the French Revolution*. London: Longman. For the period after 1800 there is no comprehensive volume providing coverage of both domestic and foreign affairs, but see Emsley, C. (1993) *Napoleonic Europe*. London: Longman.

Websites

Good starting places are http://www.fordham.edu/halsall/mod/modsbook13.html and http://culturalform.wordpress.com/frlinks/

References

Andress, D. (2000) *Massacre at the Champ de Mars: Popular Dissent and Political Culture in the French Revolution*. Bury St Edmunds: The Royal Historical Society.

Aubert, R. (ed.) (1974) *Journal de Célestin Guittard de Floriban, bourgeois de Paris sous la Révolution*. Paris: Editions France-Empire.

Aulard, A. (ed.) (1903–09) *Paris sous le Consulat* (4 vols). Paris: Cerf.

Bacourt, A. de (ed.) (1851) *Correspondance entre le Comte de Mirabeau et le Comte de La Marck pendant les années 1789, 1790 et 1791* (3 vols). Paris.

Baker, K.M. (ed.) (1987) *The French Revolution and the Creation of Modern Political Culture*, vol. 1, *The Political Culture of the Old Regime*. Oxford: Pergamon Press.

Baker, K.M. (ed.) (1990) *Inventing the French Revolution: Essays on French Political Culture in the Eighteenth Century*. Cambridge: Cambridge University Press.

Baker, K.M. (ed.) (1994) *The French Revolution and the Creation of Modern Political Culture*, vol. 4, *The Terror*. Oxford: Pergamon Press.

Bodinier, B. and Teyssier, E. (2000) *L'Evénement le plus important de la Révolution: la vente des biens nationaux*. Paris: Editions du Cths.

Boudon, J.O. (1997) *Le Consulat et l'Empire*. Paris: Monchrestien.

Boutier, J., Boutry, P. and Bonin, S. (eds) (1992) *Atlas de la Révolution française*, vol. 6, *Les sociétés politiques*. Paris: Editions de l'Ecole des Hautes Etudes en Sciences Sociales.

Boyd, J.P. (ed.) (1956) *The Papers of Thomas Jefferson*, vol. 13, *March to 7 October 1788*. Princeton, NJ: Princeton University Press.

Boyd, J.P. (ed.) (1958) *The Papers of Thomas Jefferson*, vol. 14, *8 October 1788–26 March 1789*. Princeton, NJ: Princeton University Press.

Boyd, J.P. (ed.) (1958) *The Papers of Thomas Jefferson*, vol. 15, *27 March 1789–30 November 1789*. Princeton, NJ: Princeton University Press.

Brette, A. (1894–1915) *Recueil de documents relatifs à la convocation des Etats Généraux de 1789* (4 vols). Paris: Imprimerie Nationale.

Brown, H.G. and Miller, J.A. (eds) (2002) *Taking Liberties: Problems of a New Order from the French Revolution to Napoleon*. Manchester: Manchester University Press.

Browning, O. (ed.) (1909) *Despatches from Paris*, vol. 1, *1784–1787*. London: Historical Association of Great Britain.

Browning, O. (ed.) (1910) *Despatches from Paris*, vol. 2, *1788–1790*. London: Historical Association of Great Britain.

Buchez, P.-J.-B. and Roux, P.-C. (1834–38) *Histoire parlementaire de la Révolution française* (40 vols). Paris: Paulin.

Burke, E. (1790/1973) *Reflections on the Revolution in France and on the Proceedings in certain Societies in London relative to that Event* (Conor Cruise O'Brien edn). Harmondsworth: Penguin Books.

Cabanis, A. (1975) *La Presse sous le Consulat et L'Empire, 1799–1814*. Paris: Société des études robespierristes.

Campbell, P.R. (1988) *The Ancien Régime in France*. Oxford: Basil Blackwell.

Carré, H. (ed.) (1932) *Marquis de Ferrières: correspondance inédite, 1789, 1790, 1791*. Paris: A. Colin.

Cobb, R. and Jones, C. (1988) *The French Revolution: Voices from a Momentous Epoch, 1789–1795*. London: Simon and Schuster.

Crook, M. (1998) *Napoleon comes to Power: Democracy and Dictatorship in Revolutionary France, 1794–1804*. Cardiff: University of Wales Press.

Crubaugh, A. (2001) *Balancing the Scales of Justice: Local Courts and Rural Society in Southwest France, 1750–1800*. University Park, PA: Pennsylvania State University Press.

Dubois, L. (2004) *A Colony of Citizens: Revolution and Slave Emancipation in the French Caribbean, 1787–1804*. Chapel Hill and London: University of North Carolina Press.

Dunn, J. (2005) *Setting the People Free: the Story of Democracy*. London: Atlantic Books.

Dupâquier, J. (1979) *La Population française au XVIIᵉ et XVIIIᵉ siècles*. Paris: Que sais-je?

Ellis, G. (1997) 'Religion according to Napoleon: the Limitations of Pragmatism', in Aston, N. (ed.) *Religious Change in Europe, 1650–1914*. Oxford: Clarendon Press.

Félix, J. (1999) *Finances et politique au siècle des lumières: le ministère L'Averdy, 1763–1768*. Paris: Comité pour l'histoire économique et financière de la France.

Figeac, M. (1995) 'Destins de la noblesse bordelaise, 1770–1830' (Thèse de Doctorat, Université de Paris-IV Sorbonne) reviewed in *Annales du Midi*, 108 (Oct.–Dec. 1996), pp. 540–1.

Fitzmaurice, E. (ed.) (1898) *Lettres de l'abbé Morellet à Lord Shelburne, depuis Marquis de Lansdowne, 1772–1803*. Paris.

Gainot, B. (2001) *1799, un nouveau Jacobinisme? La démocratie representative, une alternative à Brumaire*. Paris: Editions du Cths.

Garrett, M.B. (1959) *The Estates General of 1789: the Problems of Composition and Organisation*. New York: American Historical Association.

Godineau, D. (1988) *Citoyennes tricoteuses: les femmes du peuple à Paris pendant la Révolution française*. Aix-en-Provence: Alinéa.

Goodman, D. (1994) *The Republic of Letters: a Cultural History of the French Enlightenment*. Ithaca and London: Cornell University Press.

Goodwin, A. (1966) *The French Revolution*. London: Hutchinson University Library.

Gueniffey, P. (1993) *Le Nombre et la raison: la Révolution française et les élections*. Paris: Editions EHESS.

Hampson, N. (1974) *The Life and Opinions of Maximilien Robespierre*. London: Duckworth.

Hardman, J. (1993) *Louis XVI*. New Haven, CT: Yale University Press.

Hesse, C.H. (1991) *Publishing and Cultural Politics in Revolutionary Paris, 1789–1810*. Berkeley, CA: University of California Press.

Hincker, F. (1971) *Les Français devant l'impôt sous l'Ancien Régime*. Paris: Flammarion.

Horn, J. (2006) *The Path Not Taken: French Industrialization in the Age of Revolution, 1750–1830*. Cambridge, MA: MIT Press.

Jainchill, A. (2008) *Reimagining Politics after Thermidor: the Republican Origins of French Liberalism*. Ithaca and London: Cornell University Press.

Jessenne, J.P. and Le May, E.H. (eds) (1998) *Député-paysan et fermière de Flandre en 1789. La correspondance des Lepoutre*. Villeneuve d'Asq: Centre d'histoire de l'Europe du Nord Ouest.

Jeyes, S.H. (1911) *The Russells of Birmingham in the French Revolution and in America, 1791–1814*. London: George Allen.

Jones, P.M. (1995) *Reform and Revolution in France: the Politics of Transition, 1774–1791*. Cambridge: Cambridge University Press.

Jones, P.M. (1988) *The Peasantry in the French Revolution*. Cambridge: Cambridge University Press.

Jones, P.M. (2003) *Liberty and Locality in Revolutionary France: Six Villages Compared, 1760–1820*. Cambridge: Cambridge University Press.

Kwass, M. (1994) 'Liberté, Egalité, Fiscalité: Taxation, Privilege, and Political Culture in Eighteenth-Century France'. PhD thesis, University of Michigan.

Lefebvre, G. (1947) *The Coming of the French Revolution*. Translated by R. R. Palmer. Princeton: Princeton University Press.

Lewis, G. (1993) *The French Revolution: Rethinking the Debate*. London and New York: Routledge.

Louchet, L. (1792–94) 'Correspondance de Louis Louchet'. MS letters in Bibliothèque Municipale, Rodez, France.

Lough, J. (1987) *France on the Eve of the Revolution: British Travellers' Observations, 1763–1788*. London: Croom Helm.

Lucas, C. (1988) 'The Crowd and Politics' in C. Lucas (ed.) *The French Revolution and the Creation of Modern Political Culture*, vol. 2, *The Political Culture of the Revolution*. Oxford: Pergamon Press.

Lyons, M. (1994) *Napoleon Bonaparte and the Legacy of the French Revolution*. London: Macmillan.

Margadant, T.W. (1992) *Urban Rivalries in the French Revolution*. Princeton, NJ: Princeton University Press.

Morris, G. (1939) *A Diary of the French Revolution*. 2 vols, London: Harrap.

Mousset, A. (1924) *Un Témoin ignoré de la Révolution: le Comte de Fernan Nuñez, ambassadeur d'Espagne à Paris, 1787–1791*. Paris: Champion.

Norberg, K. (1994) 'The French Fiscal Crisis of 1788 and the Financial Origins of the Revolution of 1789', in Hoffman, P.T. and Norberg, K. (eds), *Fiscal Crises, Liberty and Representative Government, 1450–1789*. Stanford, CA: Stanford University Press.

Phillips, R. (1981) *Family Breakdown in Late Eighteenth-Century France: Divorce in Rouen, 1792–1803*. Oxford: Clarendon Press.

Popkin, J. (2007) *Facing Racial Revolution: Eyewitness Accounts of the Haitian Insurrection*. Chicago and London: University of Chicago Press.

Price, M. (1990) 'The "Ministry of the Hundred Hours": a Reappraisal', *French History*, 317–38.

Ruault, N. (1976) *Gazette d'un Parisien sous la Révolution. Lettres à son frère, 1783–1796*. Paris: Perrin.

Soboul, A. (1974) *The French Revolution, 1787–1799: from the storming of the Bastille to Napoleon*. Translated by A. Forrest and C. Jones. London: NLB.

Soboul, A. (1988) *Understanding the French Revolution*. London: The Merlin Press.

Stone, B. (1994) *The Genesis of the French Revolution: a Global-Historical Interpretation*. Cambridge: Cambridge University Press.

Stone, B. (1986) *The French Parlements and the Crisis of the Old Regime*. Chapel Hill and London: University of North Carolina Press.

Sutherland, D.M.G. (1985) *France 1789–1815: Revolution and Counterrevolution*. London: Fontana Press.

Tocqueville, A. de (1969) *L'Ancien Régime* (Headlam edn). Oxford: Clarendon Press.

Whaley, L. (2000) *Radicals, Politics and Republicanism in the French Revolution*. Stroud: Sutton Publishing.

Woloch, I. (2001) *Napoleon and his Collaborators: the Making of a Dictatorship*. New York: Norton.

Young, A. (1794/1900) *Arthur Young's Travels in France* (Betham-Edwards edn). London: George Bell and Sons.

INDEX